Careers in Library and Information Services

Careers in Library and Information Services

First-Hand Accounts from Working Professionals

**Edited by
Priscilla K. Shontz**

BLOOMSBURY LIBRARIES UNLIMITED
NEW YORK • LONDON • OXFORD • NEW DELHI • SYDNEY

BLOOMSBURY LIBRARIES UNLIMITED
Bloomsbury Publishing Inc
1385 Broadway, New York, NY 10018, USA
50 Bedford Square, London, WC1B 3DP, UK
29 Earlsfort Terrace, Dublin 2, Ireland

BLOOMSBURY, BLOOMSBURY LIBRARIES UNLIMITED and the Diana logo are trademarks of Bloomsbury Publishing Plc

First published in the United States of America 2025

Copyright © Bloomsbury Libraries Unlimited, 2025

For legal purposes the Acknowledgments on p. xvii constitute an extension of this copyright page.

Cover image © pavan trikutam/unsplash

All rights reserved. No part of this publication may be reproduced or transmitted in any form or by any means, electronic or mechanical, including photocopying, recording, or any information storage or retrieval system, without prior permission in writing from the publishers.

Bloomsbury Publishing Inc does not have any control over, or responsibility for, any third-party websites referred to or in this book. All internet addresses given in this book were correct at the time of going to press. The author and publisher regret any inconvenience caused if addresses have changed or sites have ceased to exist, but can accept no responsibility for any such changes.

Library of Congress Cataloging-in-Publication Data
Names: Shontz, Priscilla K., 1965- editor.
Title: Careers in library and information services : first-hand accounts from working professionals / Priscilla Shontz, editor.
Description: New York : Bloomsbury Libraries Unlimited, 2025. | Includes index.
Identifiers: LCCN 2024026307 (print) | LCCN 2024026308 (ebook) | ISBN 9798216185758 (paperback) | ISBN 9798216185864 | ISBN 9798216185772 (ebook) | ISBN 9798216185765 (epub)
Subjects: LCSH: Library science–Vocational guidance–United States. | Information science–Vocational guidance–United States. | Librarians–Employment–United States. | Librarians–United States–Anecdotes. | LCGFT: Essays.
Classification: LCC Z682.35.V62 C367 2025 (print) | LCC Z682.35.V62 (ebook) | DDC 020.23/73–dc23/eng/20240724
LC record available at https://lccn.loc.gov/2024026307
LC ebook record available at https://lccn.loc.gov/2024026308

ISBN: HB: 979-8-216-18586-4
PB: 979-8-216-18575-8
ePDF: 979-8-216-18577-2
eBook: 979-8-216-18576-5

Typeset by Newgen KnowledgeWorks Pvt. Ltd., Chennai, India
Printed and bound in the United States of America

To find out more about our authors and books visit www.bloomsbury.com and sign up for our newsletters.

Contents

Preface xiii
Foreword *by G. Kim Dority* xv
Acknowledgments xvii

Introduction 1
Priscilla K. Shontz and G. Kim Dority

PART 1 PUBLIC LIBRARIES

Adult and Teen Librarian 5
Zack North

Branch Manager 8
Delaney D. Daly

Branch Services Division Manager 10
Lee Schwartz

Children's Librarian 13
Yesenia Villar

Consultant, Regional Library System 16
April Oharah Hernandez

Education and Outreach Manager 19
Ayesha Hawkins

Executive Director, Library System 22
Laura Marlane

Information Services Manager 24
Lorene Kennard

Library Director 27
Susan Fulkerson Gregory

Local History and Genealogy Manager 31
Angela O'Neal

Supervising Librarian 34
Mychal Threets

Technical Services Manager 37
Somer Newland

Technology Coordinator 40
Louise Alcorn

Teen Librarian 44
Kathleen Breitenbach

Youth Services Manager 47
Alissa Raschke-Janchenko

PART 2 SCHOOL LIBRARIES

Independent Middle School Librarian 51
Jean Myles

International K-12 School Librarian 55
Jill Egan

Lead Librarian, Public School District 58
Amy Pulliam

Librarian, School for the Deaf 61
Nell Fleming

Library Services Director, Public School System 64
Deborah Lang Froggatt

Public Elementary School Librarian 68
Michael Rawls

Public Middle School Media Specialist 72
Dale F. Harter

PART 3 ACADEMIC LIBRARIES

Access Services Librarian 77
Glen J. Benedict

Arts and Humanities Librarian 80
Sarah Elizabeth Sheridan Bull

Collection Development Librarian 83
Monica Cammack

Collections Care Coordinator 86
Shelby Strommer

Community Engagement Director 90
Morgan Brickey-Jones

Curator 92
Alba Fernández-Keys

Data Librarian 96
Michele Hayslett

Dean of Libraries 100
Linda Marie Golian-Lui

Digital Archivist 104
Andrew McDonnell

Digital Preservation and Project Management Librarian 108
Ira Revels

Digital Scholarship Librarian 111
Julia Stone

Electronic Resource Management Librarian 114
Lucy Campbell

Electronic Resources and Cataloging Librarian 118
Daniel Stevens

Games and Media Arts Librarians 121
Diane Robson, Steven Guerrero, and Emily Pojman

Human Resources Director 125
Laura Blessing

Information Literacy Librarian 129
Joy Oehlers

Instructional Technology Specialist 132
Lara Taylor

Metadata Librarian 135
Chad Deets

Music Librarian 138
Marci Cohen

Open Educational Resources Librarian 142
Kate McNally Carter

Part-Time Librarian 145
Emily Weak

Research Services Coordinator 148
Emerson M. Morris

Resident Librarian 151
Elizabeth S. Blake

Resource Sharing Librarian 154
K. Zdepski

Scholarly Communications Librarian 158
Elaine Walker

Social Sciences and Government Information Librarian 161
Amanda McLeod

Student Support and Engagement Librarian 165
Mary Kamela

Systems and Discovery Librarian 168
Emily Wros

Technical Services Director 171
Susanne Markgren

University Librarian 175
Rick Anderson

User Experience Research Librarian 178
Beth Filar Williams

PART 4 SPECIAL LIBRARIES

Adult Services Librarian, Library for the Blind and Print Disabled 183
Jami Livingston

Art Museum Library Director 185
Jon Evans

Associate State Librarian 188
Michael Golrick

Audiovisual Archivist 191
Ari Negovschi Regalado

Conservation Librarian 195
Megan Burdi

Corporate Librarian 199
Eileen Davenport

Curator and Archivist, Historical Association 202
Laura Kathryn Nicole Jones

Library Development Consultant 205
Reagen A. Thalacker

Marketing and Outreach Librarian, Library for the Blind and Print Disabled 209
Ashley M. Biggs

Media Library Specialist, Department of Public Health 211
Alicia Zuniga

Mental Health Hospital Library Director 214
Lona A. Oerther

News Librarian 217
Misty Harris

Prison Librarian 221
Margaret Lirones

Research Institution Medical Librarian 223
Kelly Stormking

Research Medical Library Director 227
Clara S. Fowler

Science Librarian, Department of Defense 232
Gloria Miller

Seminary Librarian 234
Rebecca A. Givens

State Librarian 237
Jamie Markus

PART 5 BEYOND THE LIBRARY

Archival Consultant 243
Dominique Luster

Association Director 246
Jenifer Grady

Author 249
Chrissie Anderson Peters

Community and User Research Manager 252
Jamie Lin

Competitive Intelligence Director 257
Chad Eng

Consortium Executive Director 260
Nancy S. Kirkpatrick

Consultants 263
Cindy Fesemyer and Amanda Standerfer

Content and Workflow Strategy Consultant 266
Pam Matthews

Continuing Medical Education Coordinator 269
Karen Burton

Cybersecurity Analyst 273
Tracy Z. Maleeff

Development and Alumni Relations Administrator 276
Selma Permenter

Digital Asset Manager 280
Lisa Grimm

Digital Content Librarian 283
Maria Fesz

Freelance Editor 287
Priscilla K. Shontz

Independent Information Professional 290
Kearin Reid

Independent Librarian 294
Jessamyn West

Information and Content Strategist 297
G. Kim Dority

Information Specialist and Micropreneur 301
Sue Easun

International Sales and Special Markets Manager 305
Ann Snoeyenbos

Internet Research Specialist 308
Marj Atkinson

Knowledge and Information Management Consultant 312
Elizabeth F. McLean

Learning and Training Manager 316
Shanna Hollich

MLIS Assistant Teaching Professor 319
Jason K. Alston

MLIS Program Manager 322
Dee Winn

Private Librarian and Curator 326
Christy Shannon Smirl

Program Manager for Membership and Research 330
Christina Rodrigues

Public Health Analyst 333
Melody D. Parker

Rare Book Dealer 336
Patrick Olson

Records Specialist 339
Jeannine Berroteran

Research and Prospect Management Analyst 343
Laura Semrau

About the Editor and Contributors 347
Index 369

Preface

This career guidebook is a curated collection of candid insights from more than one hundred library and information sciences (LIS) professionals in a wide variety of jobs. I hope this book offers students and potential career changers a glimpse into jobs they might pursue, with practical advice from people working in those jobs. The contributors represent diverse careers; author demographics; and workplace types, sizes, and locations. I've intentionally kept each author's unique tone so that you can hear the varied voices sharing their perspectives.

This book was inspired by a life transition, one of those forks in the road that divert us into new career paths. I recently returned to academic librarianship after a long hiatus as an at-home parent and photographer, and being around librarians and students quickly revived my enthusiasm for the profession. Going through my own job search, plus working with an eager and inquisitive master of library and information science (MLIS) student doing her practicum at our library, started me thinking about how the field has changed. Years ago, I wrote and edited—often with my dear friend Rich Murray—several LIS career books. Though the core mission of information work remains the same, the career options, the actual responsibilities, and the methods we use to find those jobs have evolved dramatically. Many jobs in this book either didn't exist or were considered "alternative" when we published *A Day in the Life: Career Options in Library and Information Science*, so this seemed an ideal time to update that information.

I could not have created this book without my network, my network's network, and the broader online network. And I'm thrilled to have connected with so many remarkable new friends. It's been truly fascinating to meet so many amazing information professionals doing exciting work in such diverse methods and places.

Many contributors thanked me for the chance to reflect on their own careers while writing their chapters. In the introduction, you'll see the questions the authors were asked. Maybe take a few minutes and think about your own answers, and if you'd like, please share your thoughts with me. If you would like to share feedback for a contributor or would like to reach out for any reason, I'd love to hear from you at priscilla.shontz.lis@gmail.com.

Foreword

G. Kim Dority

When I reviewed Priscilla Shontz and Richard Murray's previous book, *A Day in the Life: Career Options in Library and Information Science,* I wrote that it was like having fascinating conversations with friends and colleagues about their jobs. It was, in fact, a sort of "everything you ever wanted to know about this job or work environment or career path but didn't know who to ask" guide to LIS jobs across a diverse range of skill sets, employers, and types of organizations. I have considered it a primary resource for the graduate students I advise about career options.

One reason I deemed it so valuable for students, new grads, and those considering career pivots is that when it comes to specific types of work, most of us have no clue what we don't know, and even less confidence about whom to ask for answers. *A Day in the Life* helped address those issues and answer those questions by giving us a place to start exploring. However, much has changed in the world of information, information technology, and information in society, and this new guide is a most welcome—and needed—resource!

In *Careers in Library and Information Services: First-Hand Accounts from Working Professionals,* we've once again been gifted with a compendium of personal insights from practitioners who share real-world details about their specific jobs, whether in public, school, or academic libraries; special libraries; or roles outside libraries. What is especially useful—and fascinating—is that within those three categories there are myriad jobs to consider. And in fact, the 101 profiles included here are a microcosm for the information profession writ large, as the career opportunities are often limited only by your imagination.

That is the good news. The more challenging news: trying to chart a path—your best path—through all those amazing options can be daunting. So perhaps you check around, do a bit of research, talk to a few colleagues or fellow students, and that's when the overwhelm hits: there really *are* more ways to use your information skills than you had imagined!

Fortunately, the practitioners included here have volunteered to help by sharing details of their highly diverse range of jobs. Writing in their own conversational voices, they've described their work, their career paths, their job likes and dislikes, and their advice for those interested in pursuing similar career paths. Enjoy the individual perspectives, the thoughtful reflections, the surprising insights, and the opportunity to better understand facets of many jobs you may have only heard of in passing (if that!). I'm grateful that, once again, we have the chance to sit down with more than 100 friends and colleagues to have fascinating conversations with each one about their careers. Thank you, Priscilla!

Acknowledgments

I can't thank all these wonderful contributors enough for sharing their personal experiences and insights with you. My acquisitions editor, Jessica Gribble, guided me through this project with such patience and grace, and everyone I dealt with at Bloomsbury Libraries Unlimited has made the entire process seamless. Kim Dority cheered me on every step of the way, from "go for it!" to contributing to the book. When I started brainstorming the plan, Ann Snoeyenbos, Snowden Becker, Rich Murray, Melody Parker, Lynn Boyden, Susanne Markgren, Michael Golrick, Susan Scheiberg, Jessamyn West, Robert Newlen, and Louise Alcorn gave me valuable feedback and motivation. Andrew McDonnell and Chad Eng provided extremely helpful perspectives on my own writing. My colleagues at Lone Star College—Montgomery helped reignite my enthusiasm for the profession; thanks, Diane Crowe, Melanie Burke, Stefanie Anderson, Lauren Gaeth, Monica Cammack, Cole Williamson, Sarah Palacios Wilhelm, and especially Amber Gedelian, for your inquisitiveness and excitement during your practicum. And as always, my family, David, Laura, and Casey, make my life and our world a better place.

Acknowledgments

Introduction
Priscilla K. Shontz and G. Kim Dority

"I wish someone had told me this in library school." Have you ever heard this comment—or said it yourself? In a master's program, we learn theory, terminology, and fundamental skills, but when we enter the working world, we often find that the reality of a job is not at all what we expected. If you're entering the job market or considering a career shift, you may wonder what options are available. In this book, practitioners share candid insights into 101 different types of work.

Each author answered six questions:

1. What do you do?
2. What are your favorite aspects of the position?
3. What are the biggest challenges in your position?
4. How did you get where you are? What has surprised you about the job or the field?
5. What advice would you give someone interested in a job like yours?
6. Anything else (optional)?

When reading their answers, you may notice some recurring themes:

Connect. Most authors mentioned how instrumental networking has been in their career development. People are sometimes surprised to discover that librarianship is not a reserved or solitary profession. Meeting people and maintaining connections can help you learn about job or project opportunities. Sharing ideas, questions, ups and downs—that's what keeps us going some days.

Adapt. Be flexible, both in your career and in your day-to-day work. So many contributors said something like "no day is the same in my job." You're certainly not in for a boring career! Stay open to inevitable change and unexpected opportunities.

Reflect. What aptitudes have you developed through school, jobs, volunteer roles, extracurricular activities? What do you enjoy or dislike doing, and why? Many authors emphasized the importance of transferable skills—gaining them, recognizing them, marketing them to potential employers—in helping them shift into unanticipated career paths.

As you reflect, consider these four baseline questions:

What work could you do? Think about your interests, skills, and experiences. This isn't a one-and-done question; we continually grow and change as we're exposed to new concepts, challenges, technologies, and people.

For whom or where could you work? Think outside the box. Assess your transferable skills and think creatively about how and where you might use them.

What are your priorities? What attributes do you find most important in a position or workplace? How does your work life align with your personal commitments and values?

What are your deal breakers? What would make you say no to a job? Both your priorities and your deal breakers will likely change as your life circumstances fluctuate, so re-evaluate from time to time.

As you evaluate your goals and strengths, dive into these chapters to explore career options. First, read the job descriptions that interest you. Note your reactions in the margins or in a career journal. Then, read the profiles of jobs that you don't think you're interested in. You might stumble across possibilities or ideas you hadn't considered, and as you'll hear from many of these authors, serendipity can be a career supercharger.

Here are a few possible questions to consider when reading a profile:

- Does this work sound interesting to me?
- Does it seem like it would be fun to do?
- Is the requisite skill set for this job one I have or would like to grow into?
- Does a job like this fit my personality?
- Does working for this type of employer align with my values?

- Is this type of employer likely to pay the salary I'm interested in?
- Does this sound like an environment I'd enjoy and feel comfortable in?
- Does this work or employer support or further my professional development goals?
- Would this job support the scheduling preferences that I'm looking for?
- If I'm fascinated by this type of work but have a skills gap, how would I overcome that?
- Would this job provide an opportunity for me to be my best self, that is, bring my unique personal and professional strengths?

These contributors provide brief snapshots of 101 job options, but the possibilities are limitless. Where and how might you apply your information skills? Use these insights, shared so candidly by this diverse group of information professionals, to help you navigate your career path with realistic expectations and an optimistic spirit.

1 Public Libraries

Adult and Teen Librarian
Zack North

What I Do

I work in a public library as an adult and teen services librarian. In my role, I plan programs, manage the adult and young adult (YA) collections, and represent the library for library tours or outreach events. I have additional responsibilities as the serials and reference librarian. The largest portion of my day is spent assisting patrons with questions, helping them use computers, and doing readers' advisory. When not serving in those functions, I plan adult and teen programs, develop and maintain the adult and YA collections, assist with the maintenance of our library management system, and provide reference services.

My Favorite Things

I adore my patrons. They're the reason I love my job. Working alongside them on their reading journeys has been exciting, and I have seen so many of them get out of their reading shell with new authors and genres. Those patrons have pushed me to be a better librarian for them and the community. So many of the services we've modified and expanded have been because our patrons have come in with excellent ideas and are invested in the library being successful.

I've had a wonderful time building a community around our library that values services, promotes us, and cheers us on when we do new things. I'm glad my patrons are comfortable enough to approach me when they need resources during tough times. Our community is at its best when the library can serve patrons at all points of their lives.

I would recommend a position like mine for someone who is a people person, dedicated to lifelong learning, and looking to provide library services for an age group with diverse needs at every stage in life.

Challenges

When I was hired as a circulation assistant four years ago, four of the six full-time staff had been with the library for thirty or more years. Service was stagnant, and programming for older age groups was largely nonexistent. Processes were inefficient because library staff had been told not to trust the library management system. A couple years ago, staff members retired, and new dynamic leadership was brought to the library. I've worked with coworkers to address inefficiencies, modernize internal processes, and drastically expand services to meet the demands of patrons. It's been a long path because we've discovered many issues during this process.

The biggest challenge I have faced is a product of apathy in collection management. When I became the adult services librarian, adult collections had not been consistently weeded in more than five years. Shelves were at capacity, and standing orders were streaming in from vendors. I spent the better part of my first year getting control of standing orders, developing internal guidelines to weed the collection in addition to our use of the Continuous Review, Evaluation, and Weeding (CREW) method, and starting to remove material from the shelves. The process is still ongoing and improving each day.

After a staff retirement, I was asked to add teen services to my responsibilities. I was excited to take on the additional role as I saw opportunities for expanding services, but at times I feel like I'm unable to dedicate the time needed to give teens the service that they deserve. Working in a smaller library can sometimes be particularly hard when you may need to change hats suddenly to serve the needs of different groups of patrons.

My Career Path

My path started as a split path while I was a student at Northern State University in Aberdeen, South Dakota. During that time, I worked in residence life as a resident assistant and worked at the university library as a work-study student in circulation, then interlibrary loan (ILL). Leading up to my senior year, I debated between pursuing higher education administration and library science. I loved the work I was doing in both places. I was passionate about supporting staff and students with their education endeavors through the library while also building community and planning events in residence life. At the time, I knew I could thrive in either environment.

I completed a practicum in archives with the university archivist during the summer between my junior and senior years. This allowed me to flex some of the basic skills I had been learning in public history courses and apply them to an archival collection. Then, during my senior year, I began to realize how stressful working in residence life felt. After a series of harrowing events in the residence hall, I took stock of how I felt about residence life and student affairs. I still enjoyed it, but a lack of stable leadership and my concerns for my mental health soured me on the idea of working in student affairs. I pursued an MLIS at Simmons University and accepted a circulation assistant position at Mitchell Public Library. Three years ago, I was promoted to the newly created adult services librarian position and then added teen services last year.

Advice

Weirdly enough, I think that my time working in residence life has served me better than my MLIS. The skills needed to work through challenging situations and build community have been the most significant factors in my success. You need to be a people person to work in a service position. People want to talk to the librarian and tell you about their weekends and the books they found on the shelf that they had no clue existed. People also need our expertise in finding resources. Knowing the available resources for adults in your community is so important. We can't be everything for every person, but we can seek solutions to their needs. The number of times I have said "I don't have that expertise, but I think I know where we can find it" is immeasurable.

When I started my MLIS, I had goals in mind. I wanted to work at an academic library in the archives. I wish someone had told me to look harder at public librarianship. I think public libraries are where some of the most exciting librarianship is taking place. There are so many librarians who are passionate about their communities; it's intoxicating. Working in a small public library has changed my view of librarianship and my career trajectory. Work in a public library at least once. You'll grow and learn so much in so little time.

Join your state or regional library association. Being surrounded by others in our field with skills different from your own is part of your personal and professional growth. If a union is available to you, join it and get involved. We must empower each other and our coworkers in other areas of municipalities and academic institutions. Unions help us achieve that.

Lastly, protect your own mental, emotional, and physical health. As librarians, we give so much to others that taking time for ourselves can be difficult. Utilize your employee assistance programs (EAPs) and get a therapist. Even helpers need help.

Branch Manager
Delaney D. Daly

What I Do

I do a great many things, but fortunately, all are things I sincerely enjoy doing. First and foremost, I train, schedule, coach, and evaluate my staff. Outside of that, a good portion of what I do is administrative: I complete and submit paperwork such as monthly statistics and reports, approve staff time, respond to emails and requests from various departments at our administrative offices, and so forth. Additionally, I am in charge of handling any unexpected or urgent situations that may arise at my branch and ensuring I communicate these incidents through the proper channels. Some more creative activities I do include working on projects to improve the overall aesthetic and usability of the library space for patrons and staff, establishing community partnerships, working with staff to develop programming, approving ideas for bulletin boards and displays in the library, and more.

My Favorite Things

I'm extremely passionate about everything pertaining to my job but my favorite things are training my staff in order to see them grow and develop in their roles, working to ensure they have the tools and skills necessary for them to succeed, building community partnerships, and working directly with the various departments at our administrative offices to develop and implement programs and services that benefit the community we serve.

Challenges

There are challenges built into any role you take on and any stage of your career (yes, even in libraries), so it helps to observe and embrace them with an open mind as much as you can. In my current role, the primary challenges are evaluating and working to resolve any performance-related issues in staff, addressing situations or incidents involving library patrons, and working to increase program attendance and circulation statistics as this helps me measure the overall impact of the branch.

My Career Path

Oddly enough, I began working in public libraries on a whim. I often tell people that I've always adored libraries and what they do for their communities, but I did not go looking for a career in libraries—a career in libraries found me. Almost immediately after graduating from college, I was a little bit down in the dumps as I realized I still didn't know what I wanted to be when I grew up or where my postgraduate life was headed. Randomly, my mother suggested I volunteer to shelve books at the Town of Vail Public Library in Colorado. Soon after I began my volunteer shelving, I accepted a part-time position there. And quickly, I fell in love with all aspects of library service. The rest is history.

Advice

Learn from your mistakes and maintain a strong sense of self-awareness. Be coachable and embrace feedback from your leaders as well as your counterparts and your staff. Express gratitude as often as possible to everyone you work with. Be responsive and polite in your responses. View every working day as a gift and a new opportunity to learn. Understand that critical thinking is the foundation of strong decision making. Take care of your team and be clear in your expectations. Embrace any and all opportunities for creativity. Be a champion and an advocate for your community. And finally, always say hello to your patrons as they walk through your doors, and as they leave for the day, thank them for coming in.

Anything Else?

Approximately a year after earning my MLS degree, I found myself working at a library where the culture was less than supportive or professional and where community members were adamantly challenging the materials in our collection. Materials challenges are certainly nothing new in the realm of librarianship, but what I dealt with bordered on threatening and abusive. Sadly, we are seeing more and more of this aggression, primarily in school and public libraries. I've learned that it helps tremendously to work for a library or library system that shares your values. As you accept and schedule interviews with potential employers, it is also your opportunity to interview them and to get a sense of how you will be supported in your role. Listen to what your gut tells you. Supportive organizations will shine through before you are even hired, and they will recognize that first, you are a human being, and second, you are a librarian.

Branch Services Division Manager
Lee Schwartz

What I Do

Everything I do is as part of a team. My primary job is to hire, train, and support public library employees. We want every library location to be a warm, welcoming environment with a highly trained staff. We have an exceptional public library system and I help guarantee that the patrons receive outstanding library services, consistently, at every location.

There are many processes that are partly my responsibility. Finding extraordinary library employees is an important part of my job. Working with a panel of colleagues to review applications and assess potential employees is key to developing a good library team. Similarly, the onboarding and training process are integral to developing skills and culture. Evaluating and training employees is ongoing and collaborative.

We are all responsible for making the public library the best it can be, and I do my part to make it so.

My Favorite Things

It is wonderful to work in a career that makes a positive difference in the world. Being part of a collective effort that makes a noted difference in people's lives and in our community is very satisfying. The best part of this job is the people. I work with interesting, talented folks who bring encouraging, creative energy to the library each day. Together, we are an essential part of the community. Helping people and seeing the tangible impact the public library makes sparks joy in me. I have many treasured memories from working in the public library and delight in creating more. Helping colleagues be successful and develop a passion for public library service is personally gratifying. I have particularly liked my role in improving our onboarding process. It has been interesting to see new hires welcomed to the library and encouraged to become integral team members. Library people are amazing people!

Challenges

Time management and workload prioritization are the biggest challenges of my position. It is essential to prepare and communicate as much as possible. I have a hand in many ongoing responsibilities, such as budget, hiring, training, evaluation, and discipline. Staying on top of all of my duties requires me to manage my time effectively. I have learned through hard experience that consistent, scheduled effort is required. More importantly, teamwork and division of labor is essential. Although I sometimes begrudged group work in graduate school, it really did prepare me for success. I would suggest to anyone thinking about this career to embrace change and adapt to circumstances. Looking at the big picture and reminding myself of our mission and purpose helps me adjust to whatever challenges come my way.

My Career Path

A wonderful aspect of working in public libraries is that all my interests and experiences have been applicable to my career. I had about twenty years of experience working in hospitality and finance. This previous work experience helped me succeed in my library career.

When my children were infants, I reflected upon my purpose and my career. I owned a small mortgage company and, although prosperous, I did not feel fulfilled by my work. One day, when taking my son to storytime, I had an inkling that working in the public library could be rewarding. As a patron, I chatted with librarians and circulation staff to see if this might be a good fit. I applied for and was offered a circulation position but turned it down because I realized I could not afford to work at this entry-level wage.

I spent the next year working diligently to save and eventually accepted an entry-level librarian position. From the outset, I knew that public libraries were for me. It was exciting to continually learn and use my skills to help people. I was encouraged to pursue a MLIS degree, and the Friends of the Library supported the effort. I am grateful for the people that helped me find my way. The encouragement and expertise of colleagues is a great resource to anyone pursuing this career. Advice: Find people you respect and ask lots of questions!

Advice

It sounds obvious, but anyone interested in public libraries should work in them. Put yourself in a position to gain experience in a public library environment. When I was in graduate school, it was tremendously beneficial to bring my work experience to my studies and vice versa. I had many important conversations with professional colleagues that helped me apply and understand what I was learning. It was enlightening to work on school projects utilizing the data from our library system. By adding context to what I was learning in class, I was prepared to take future steps in my career. Even volunteering at a public library helps in this regard.

Anything Else?

When facing challenging situations or circumstances, I try to remember the many times we make a difference. Every experienced librarian has many rewarding stories that motivate them. Once, with a few kind words and patient assistance, I helped a patron format a resume and navigate an online job application. Over a year after this incident, I was in a retail parking lot on the other side of town when a passing car slammed on its brakes and a man jumped out of the car shouting "Hey, Library Guy!" I didn't recognize this fast-approaching person, but he knew *me*. He told me that he got the job I helped him apply for and then never saw me to thank me (I had transferred to another library location). He was still very grateful many months later, and I was happy to hear his story. Even though you are not always told you make a difference, you feel it working at the public library. What a difference you can make!

What else? Storytelling is awesome and has many applications in public libraries, from developing staff, selling library services, and connecting people to literature (and each other). My supervisor encouraged me to take a storytelling class in graduate school. One semester with Dr. Koontz at Florida State University changed me forever. Everyone should learn to deliver a proper folktale to an audience; it makes you appreciate the world and people a little more.

Children's Librarian
Yesenia Villar

What I Do

I'm an acclaimed radical librarian. I'm currently a library manager and have also held roles as a children's librarian and bilingual outreach librarian. I work for one of the oldest and largest public libraries in the country; there are approximately 1,300 employees and we serve a population of over four million people.

A major misconception about our profession is that we "read all day." While I certainly read to build my collection and to conduct programming, it's far from my major responsibility. As a children's librarian my ultimate responsibility is to entice people, especially new users, to use the library by connecting with children, their parents, and caregivers.

I connect with these communities and build relationships by going out into the community and bringing awareness of library programs, services, and resources. For example, this might mean going to a community fair, a K-12 school, a religious community, or partnering with a local nonprofit. It's vital to build these connections in order to understand what the current and anticipated community needs are.

When purchasing books, for example, I combine my knowledge gathered through outreach with pertinent statistical data to attain insights into factors such as median income, educational attainment, racial demographics, and languages spoken. These all play key roles in understanding a community's information, recreational, and educational needs.

We must also recognize library resources are limited and, when possible, partner with local nonprofits already meeting community needs. For example, during the summers I collaborate with a local food bank to provide meals in the library for children ages ten to seventeen. I've also partnered with religious organizations providing immigrant services, optometrists providing free eye examinations and glasses, dentists providing free dental examinations. Public librarianship requires advanced people skills, creativity, innovation, and a genuine passion for community service.

My Favorite Things

I recommend children's librarianship to anyone who cares about the wellbeing of children *and* their families. The experiences of children vary widely. One day I may be recommending a book to an avid reader, another day I may be the person an undocumented mother trusts enough to ask for help obtaining citizenship, and on an especially difficult day, I may be the trusted adult to whom a child discloses they are being sexually abused.

This career is far from the perception of an "easy" and "stress-free" job. Whenever we work with the public we are exposed to their joy, hardship, and everything in between. Knowing that I'm making a difference in the lives of others is deeply fulfilling; it adds to the aspects of my life that give it purpose. Knowing that I'm influencing multiple generations and creating opportunities for them to live better lives brings me an immense amount of joy.

Challenges

The biggest challenge by far is the demands that are made on children's librarians without structural or financial support. We are constantly given additional responsibilities, tasks often far exceeding those of young adult and adult librarians. As new goals and initiatives are added, we are expected to tack these on to our already-demanding position. It's easy to spread ourselves too thin and burn out. I strongly advise all librarians to work within a framework that allows them to live a balanced life. Learn to establish boundaries, say no when necessary, and advocate for yourself when you need support. Often librarians overidentify with the career and make sacrifices that go against their best interest. If we deplete ourselves, we are of service to no one. You come first.

My Career Path

At thirteen, I discovered the library and it changed the course of my life. The public library created opportunities I never knew existed. It helped provide the resources to nurture my reading, writing, and critical thinking skills that helped me excel in school. Because I excelled in school, I was able to earn the grants, scholarships, and fellowships that enabled me to attend college and pursue a career that helped me break the cycle of poverty in my life. For me, becoming a librarian required continuously overcoming adversity, but no experience could have prepared me for the cultural shock I experienced in library school.

Library school was my first introduction into the rampant racism and oppressive nature of the profession. These oppressive systems are so deeply interwoven into the foundation of libraries that many of us are unconsciously complicit in a system that excludes marginalized people from the collections we create, the programs and services we provide, and the people we hire and promote. Libraries have an excellent public-relations-created image of us as benevolent institutions for the greater good of society. I wholeheartedly believe libraries are incredible institutions that allow for the growth of humanity, but they are also deeply flawed. As government organizations we are guided by people and policies that aren't motivated by inclusion. Libraries will create catchy slogans such as "We welcome all," merely as performative statements without the action to implement real change.

I don't write these realities to dissuade you from the profession, but rather as a call for social justice minded librarians. If you also happen to be a person with a marginalized identity, we need you! The community needs you. We need people with diverse experiences and the courage to create the change to help transform libraries for the betterment of all people.

Advice

Early in my career I received the best professional advice I would ever receive, though I didn't realize at the time how powerful a statement it was. My then mentor, now lifelong friend said, "Forget all that shit you learned in library school." Library school teaches us the formula to reach a white middle-class traditional library community. It teaches us nothing about building authentic connections with people outside of normative library users. If we drop the expectation of what a librarian *should* be based on archaic and oppressive standards, we can become the librarians we are *meant* to be. There is someone—*lots* of someones—that need us just the way we are. Unhindered by expectations of what a "good" librarian is. Empowered with the knowledge that our diversity and courage to be authentic is what brings libraries to life.

Consultant, Regional Library System
April Oharah Hernandez

What I Do

I am the System Consultant for the Southeast Kansas Library System (SEKLS). Let me explain the premise behind regional library systems in Kansas: because there are so many small and rural libraries across the state that cannot afford to hire a director with an MLS, the regional systems were created to provide all libraries access to professional MLS knowledge. These systems were created under statute by the Kansas Legislature in 1966.

One of my responsibilities is organizing continuing education for public and academic library staff and public library trustees. This means planning two to four large events per year along with smaller workshops. I either find presenters outside of our organization, present training myself, or have other SEKLS staff present. Organizing these events entails contacting and securing speakers, reserving facilities and caterers, creating marketing content, and overseeing the event. If there are any issues, such as a speaker who notifies me at the last minute that they cannot attend in person, I must be flexible enough to switch gears and make other options work.

Another responsibility of my job is providing in-person trustee or one-on-one library staff training. I attend a lot of library board meetings either for specific training, for answers to specific questions, or for support. To perform this role, I need to know Kansas library statutes, attorney general opinions, library staff and administration processes, best practices for library policy, statistical compilation and analysis, and I need to keep up to date on changes in all aspects of librarianship.

Other responsibilities include soliciting, compiling, and editing articles for the system's bimonthly newsletter; managing the SEKLS Niche Academy; creating learning and information documents as well as web-based tutorials; visiting all public and academic libraries in the system at least annually; consulting with and training library directors and boards; managing social media and web pages; managing the professional collection; training new library directors statewide through our yearly APplied Public Library Education (APPLE) program; and branding and marketing the library system.

The APPLE program was created to educate and support library directors in Kansas. The program begins in April of each year and runs through March of the next year. Because many small communities cannot afford to hire a director with an MLS, this program is greatly needed. Even with an MLS, becoming a new library director is challenging. An MLS gives you foundational principles and ethics of the profession but cannot focus on day-to-day operations. APPLE covers the basics such as budget, facilities management, community engagement and demographics, planning, and human resources. I invite new directors in my region to take part in the program, support and encourage them throughout, and present at the in-person kickoff event and one other virtual training.

My Favorite Things

I love being able to impact and support so many libraries. It is nice to have a position that gives me an opportunity to support libraries across the region, and that has varied job duties to keep me engaged. A recent example was when a library suddenly lost its director, and the library board realized how much they needed to learn in a short amount of time. Being able to visit the library and answer their questions knowledgeably was a great feeling. In a way, I am helping to lay the foundation for change and growth within that library and its community.

I also enjoy getting to meet other professionals in the field, networking to create educational opportunities, and collaborating with other system staff across the state to bring bigger programming and training to the area.

Challenges

The biggest challenge of this position is the need for an event coordinator who can take care of the entertainment parts of events, such as breakfast and lunch. Having someone handle these tasks would give me more time to focus on the presenters, attendees, and my own presentations.

Also, the amount of responsibility makes it difficult to complete projects in a timely manner. Lastly, waiting for others to get back to me about presentations, venues, and other details can be frustrating and add stress.

My Career Path

I grew up loving books and libraries. My summers were filled with stacks of books to share my days with. I never considered being a librarian when I was younger because I was the one always getting shushed. Libraries changed, and after getting my first job as a library assistant in an academic library, I was hooked. I began the MLS program five months later.

I made the change to public libraries, as a library technician in Idaho, a year and a half after starting my first library position. I then took a community librarian position in Washington, and finally, a library director position back in Kansas. Because I began my career much later than many people, I have changed jobs often, but always to a more responsible position.

My goal when I started my graduate program was to become a library director. I graduated with my MLS in August and started as a public library director five months later. I was thrilled. I also didn't know what I was getting myself into. I spent seven years as a public library director at two very underutilized libraries. At both, I developed great teams that reached out to the communities and provided the services and programs that were needed. Using outreach and community engagement, we turned both libraries into thriving spaces. My team and I worked so hard to stay connected to our community during the Covid-19 pandemic that we surpassed our previous circulation statistics while the pandemic was still going strong. Not a small feat and something I am very proud of.

Advice

To succeed in a job like mine, get a broad background in libraries. Working as a public library director is probably the most helpful position that informs this job. Inevitably, I work mostly with public libraries, and my background as a director definitely gives me the knowledge I need to do this job. Also, always be willing to learn. To be able to support the growth of libraries, you need to constantly keep learning and growing. Lastly, be ready to move; not all states have regional library systems.

Anything Else?

Remember that libraries are all about connections, relationships, and communities. The partnerships you build with community businesses and organizations help your library reach its vision and grow. To have a thriving library, it must be an integral part of its community. A library can be anything its community needs it to be, so go out and make those connections, build those relationships, grow your library, and thrive.

Education and Outreach Manager
Ayesha Hawkins

What I Do

I am the manager of the education and outreach unit at the Fort Worth (Texas) Public Library (FWPL). I oversee the partnership development and community engagement for my library system. In the library world, many people refer to this job as a community librarian. In the FWPL system, I am classified as a regional librarian and report directly to an assistant director. I supervise two senior librarians, who oversee a library assistant, a public education specialist, and an office assistant. I manage everything that happens outside the library locations and in the community. I spend a lot of time in partnership meetings or at large community events. Partners can be both internal to the city, and external. I work closely with city leadership and library communication to help create library advocates, which in turn help with fundraising, program attendance, and circulation.

My Favorite Things

I love the variety of my job. There are days when I am in meetings all day. There are days when I am at a table promoting the library and library cards to the community. There are other days when I am in a classroom speaking about how to work at the library. Then there are days when I am conducting training for educators or community partners. There are also days when I am strategy planning for the fiscal year.

Challenges

The biggest challenge of this job is partnership management. You are dealing with organizations or internal city departments that have their own wants and needs, and often those do not align with what the library is capable of providing.

Another challenge at this level is spending a lot of time in meetings. Sometimes the day starts at 7 a.m. and ends late in the evening. In this type of job, you work a lot of weekends and tend to be out of the office quite a bit, so trying to keep within a forty-hour work week can be a struggle.

The last challenge is contract management. You must understand how your city handles a memorandum of understanding (MOU). You will need everything in partnership spelled out in these types of signed agreements, which could take months to be signed off on, depending on how your city works and how big the partner is regarding legal agreements.

My Career Path

I ended up in the library field after a twenty-year career in higher education. I was looking to transition out of higher education, and my home library system was creating a new position in marketing. I spent three years in that medium-sized suburban public library system. I was asked to apply for my current position after a former coworker began working here. The library was having a hard time finding the right person for a newly created unit. They needed someone who had a background in education, marketing, libraries, and community outreach. They also needed someone who was comfortable with speaking to the public and connecting with city officials and citizens alike. I think what helps is that I am open to new things, and I am a builder at heart. Newly created or never-previously-existing positions invigorate me. They encourage me to challenge my skill set and grow to meet the needs of the position.

Advice

The role of a community librarian or someone in a division that is focused on community relationships is for a person who is an extrovert or a non-shy introvert. You are always with people. Also, time management is important. In this position, it would be easy to work over forty hours and create burnout. This position is also ideal for a person who understands the return on the investment of partnering with the library or having a connection with the library. As a person in management, you should also understand your leadership style and philosophy. It is also important to understand how budgets are managed. In this job, flexibility is a major key to success.

Anything Else?

Public libraries are part of municipal government. While we are not elected officials, we are paid by the citizens, so understanding how funding, bonds, and other city policies work is very important. If you move into upper-level management for a city, it is also important to understand economic development. Understanding economic development and how libraries play into creating a high-value city for companies is vital to the survival of local libraries.

Often when I am speaking to partners, I talk about shifting minds from book repositories to knowledge access centers. We help create equity in knowledge access for the public no matter who they are and what they do. This is helping to shape the strategic plan for the library going forward.

Executive Director, Library System

Laura Marlane

What I Do

I'm the executive director of the Omaha Public Library (OPL), a large system with thirteen branches and approximately 258 staff. We serve the population of Omaha and Douglas County (approximately 585,008) and have approximately 273,000 library card holders.

My first job as a library director was at my hometown library, a small building in a community of about 20,000 people. You learn a lot in a small library because, no matter what your role, you do a little bit of everything. I cataloged, helped troubleshoot technology questions, developed and implemented the budget, covered the front desk, and maintained the facility (which mostly means fixing the copier and making sure the plumbing is working). I also wrote grants and policies and did a bit of fundraising.

Now, as the director of a large library system, I'm further removed from those roles, but I understand how they work, and that helps me connect with the staff and the patrons. My job involves relationships—working with the library board (a governing board) on policy, facilities, and budgeting. And, since OPL is a city department, I develop and maintain relationships with local legislators, the mayor, and other city departments. It's also important to know what other organizations in your city or town serve the community. This will give you a sense of what your community needs and also show you who could be potential partners.

My Favorite Things

My favorite thing about being a librarian has always been connecting people with the information and resources they need—whether it's recommending a new author I know they'd like, helping them find the materials they need to complete a homework assignment, or helping them access technology they need but can't afford on their own. Being a library director shifts your focus from the individual to the community, and the bigger picture issues that affect every segment of the community you serve. At the end of the day, it's always about helping people, and that's the part I enjoy the most.

Challenges

The biggest challenge I've encountered in every community I served was politics. They don't prepare you for this in library school. Being a library director is a political job, and it's important to navigate that while keeping the library nonpolitical. The politics in a small town are very different from those in a large city, and they can be more intense. In one of my previous positions, the mayor told me I'd be hiring a retired police officer as my new assistant director so he could be rewarded for his work on the mayor's most recent campaign. Fortunately, my library had to comply with state minimum standards to receive state funding, and an assistant director had to have a library degree, so I was able to avoid that situation.

There are also the politics of library boards. I used to work with a board of twenty-five people, all with different ideas about what the library should do and how we would do it. As a board, they couldn't accomplish much because they could rarely get together around big picture ideas or projects.

My Career Path

I've been an official librarian for about twenty-five years, but I've been working in libraries since the 1980s, right out of high school. My first director job was the best training ground because that small library was not departmentalized, so we all did a little of everything. Before that job, I was the associate director and head of technical services at a historical society library. That was in the late 1990s and, because computer networking was still new, it was not something they prepared you for in library school. The historical society's budget was tight, so to save money they decided they would ditch the tech consultant who came in a couple of times a month to troubleshoot our network. They decided that because I was head of technical services, and tech coordination was "technical," I would handle technology troubleshooting now, too. I didn't mind—it was a new challenge, and I was eager to learn. Developing that skill set led me to my next job as the technology coordinator for a public library. There I discovered that I really liked being in a public library and that's where I wanted to stay.

Advice

Getting my master's was necessary to move forward in my chosen profession, but by the time I went to library school, I had already worked eleven years in libraries and learned a lot. Library school gave me the opportunity to see how my work experience complemented my learning experience and made me a better librarian.

One essential strategy for new library directors advocating for your library is to know your audience. If it's support from the city council that you need, learn what is important to them. If they're analytical, give them the data. Know your circulation and usage numbers, know what the per capita cost is for other libraries in your area and how your city/town measures up. If their approach is more emotionally based, share stories of how your library has impacted the community, how your literacy program gave someone the skills to get a job and provide for their family. Whomever you're appealing to, take a moment to stand in their shoes and think about what's important to them—what is the argument that will win their support—and go with that.

Information Services Manager
Lorene Kennard

What I Do

I manage the reference department; interview, hire, train, and supervise the reference staff; create the desk schedule and approve time off; and manage a budget. We assist patrons working on our computers as well as answer reference questions and local history questions. We also provide readers' advisory and plan events and programs. I spend most of my time working with my staff to make sure they have what they need to do their jobs effectively. We have a lot of discussions about planning for the department. How can we improve our service? What could we add that would give our patrons a better library experience? I also represent the reference department in management meetings and at community events.

My Favorite Things

I love working with my staff. We have great conversations when we discuss processes and new ideas. There are some new librarians on our staff, so I am excited to keep them engaged in their jobs and in our profession. I would recommend my role to someone else if they like having responsibility for a public services department, including staff and strategy. It's a great combination that makes me feel like I am making a valuable contribution.

Challenges

The biggest challenge of managing people in a public library is not having enough staff, which makes creating the desk schedule difficult. Managing staff can be very rewarding, but it's also a lot of work to handle all of the day-to-day interests and needs of a group of people. The desk schedule can be a bear when people are on vacation or someone calls in. Obviously, staff need to take their time off, but creating and maintaining the schedule is very challenging.

I am in middle management, but I have been at the director level. It can be challenging to stop and think which decisions I can make and which decisions need approval. During conversations with my staff, I have to remember that I cannot automatically approve everything myself. A librarian who is new to leadership might face the learning curve of getting used to making decisions without always asking their manager. There is freedom in being able to make decisions, but it can take some getting used to.

My Career Path

I am the classic case of a person wanting to be a librarian when I grew up. I finally went to library school ten years after I graduated from college. I wanted to be a public library reference librarian and grow to be a director until I worked an internship at the Advertising and Marketing Resource Center at Walt Disney World. That opened my eyes up to corporate libraries. When I was job hunting, I had job offers from a corporation in a big city and from a public library in a small suburb. I accepted the job offer from the corporation because it paid more. After eight years as a solo in a corporate library, I left to start a freelance research business. Not too long after I started my business, the economy took a turn and business became very slow. I was working part time in a public library for a steady income and decided to pursue a public library director position. I ended up holding three public library director roles, but two of them were incredibly difficult to get. I loved the work, and it fit well with my strengths and goals. Unfortunately, the boards I worked for continuously overstepped their boundaries and interfered with the operation of the library.

So, I moved into a university archivist/technical services manager role. I was there for almost five years when my position was eliminated due to a restructuring. It took me almost a year to find my current role. None of my roles have been easy to get, but I am proud of my contributions to my field. I love being able to use my expertise gained through my various experiences in the information services manager role.

I am continually surprised at how much the general public does not understand about how libraries operate. The perception is "everything is free at the library." But the library pays for everything, often paying more than a single user would pay. It's more accurate to say "everything is free to use at the library." Also, I'm often surprised that people don't understand the differences between types of libraries; for instance, academic libraries are not going to have the same collections and materials as public libraries.

Advice

I would not be equipped to do this job if I had not been a reference librarian for several years. I understand the responsibilities and the struggles of the role that my employees have. Managing nine people is a lot to juggle. It's not for the faint of heart! But it's so worthwhile to be able to help staff work to the best of their abilities to serve our patrons.

You need to be very professional and have a thick skin to work in a management role in a public library. I wish someone had told me that patrons are often very disrespectful to library staff. It's still surprising to me when I have to deal with an angry patron who is giving one of my employees a rough time.

Anything Else?

I produce and host The Librarian Linkover podcast, where I interview librarians who use skills they gained through library education and experience to work in industry and in non-library leadership roles. I also write a Substack newsletter called "Pondering Leadership," which offers practical ideas aimed at managers in any field. The Library Linkover interviews repeatedly demonstrate that we have transferable skills that can be used in any industry. We do not have *library* skills; we have *skills* we use in libraries. Listener feedback to The Library Linkover has been phenomenal; the content is helping librarians reframe and market their skills to be promoted or to move into similar roles in industry. We have the skills, and we can use them anywhere.

Library Director
Susan Fulkerson Gregory

What I Do

I am the director of the Bozeman Public Library in Bozeman, Montana. The Bozeman-Yellowstone Airport is the busiest hub in the state due to tourism for both the Big Sky ski and recreation area and the Yellowstone National Park. We see thousands of out-of-state visitors come through our library doors annually, especially in the tourist season; we have an average of 40,000 visitors per month during the summer.

As the library director, I spend much of my time in meetings with city management, the public, the Bozeman Public Library board chair, library patrons, and library staff. I spend a lot of time answering approximately 200 emails a day and several hours a day in phone conversations. I am one of sixteen city directors; we meet weekly with the city manager and have biannual management retreats.

What's interesting about my position within the city is that I am supervised by the five-member library board of trustees, not the city manager. According to Montana state law, the director of a public library is hired and supervised by the library board of trustees. The trustees told me when I was hired that one of their priorities was strengthening the relationship between the library and the city administration. This has been a key goal of mine in the twelve years that I have held this position. I've invested time into getting to know the different city administrators, directors, department supervisors and staff, and it's paid off beautifully. Putting the effort out to be friendly, available, and cheerful has resulted in work friendships with my colleagues and mutual respect for the work that we all do. Our library staff enjoys great relationships with their city colleagues that result in excellent communication and support for the library. We have a lot of fun together!

Being a library director means having the experience to know how all the pieces of the library puzzle fit together and being willing to build relationships within the community daily so that people understand the library as a whole. It's a people job. If you enjoy people, respect diversity, and have a keen sense of humor, this could be the job for you.

My Favorite Things

I love the fact that a public library brings an incredibly diverse group of people through the doors daily and that each person has their own story. Some people want a book, some want to use a laptop, and some just want a beautiful place to study. Some people are here to take a class in our creative labs and some people are just looking for a warm spot to rest. Every single day is different. Every single person is different.

If you truly enjoy working with people of all types and value a dynamic work environment, this job could be a good fit for you. One thing that I value above all else is that being a public library director means having the chance to serve others. It means being able to model being a public servant to library staff so that they realize the satisfaction in being a public servant.

Challenges

There are two current challenges that impact my work: serving our unhoused and mentally unstable patrons in a meaningful way and dealing with a conservative state library commission that has brought politics into Montana libraries.

Montana winters are harsh and we know that some of our patrons sleep outdoors. They either don't like the warming center or they have been kicked out for misbehavior. We work very closely with social services and the police department in trying to get these folks sheltered for the night.

Our state library commission is currently made up of a majority of extremely conservative people who want local control of public libraries and their collections. They are in favor of dismissing the public standard of a library director having a MLIS degree.

My Career Path

My first library job was as an undergraduate in the University of Oklahoma (OU) main library, where I shelved and worked in circulation. I was surprised by how much fun it was and worked in different library departments for several years. After graduation, I earned my MLIS from OU. My first professional job was as the reference and adult programming librarian in a five-county library system in southern Oklahoma. From there, I moved to a three-county public library system based in Norman, Oklahoma, and was the manager of a branch library. I moved up to supervise three branches, then six branch libraries as a small branch coordinator. Next was a move to the branch manager of the headquarters library in Norman, a job I held for eleven years. I realized that I wanted a library director's position, so I worked with both an out-of-state recruiter and the ALA Jobline to get interviews. I applied for the Bozeman job through the Jobline. It was my dream job, so I did a lot of research for several months on the community and library, including reading the local paper online. My years of being active in the American Library Association, numerous committee appointments, and two terms on ALA Council helped get me the interview; my research got me the job.

Advice

Work in as many different library departments as possible so that you understand how the parts form the whole. Decide if you want a people job and can deal with occasional controlled chaos. A good sense of humor is mandatory. You need to be visionary, proactive, and nimble as events require. Be a good listener. Practice public speaking. Use practical compassion with disruptive patrons; be compassionate but clear about expectations and consequences. Say yes to the new, cherish the traditional, and be sure to laugh.

Anything Else?

The world of the public librarian involves a lot of social work. Many people come to the library when they're exhausted, hungry, broke, sick, cold, scared, and lonely. Because they don't know where else to go or where to send their children until they get off work.

When I was a branch manager seventeen years ago, I met a young family in the library. The single mom worked twenty miles away in Oklahoma City, so she sent her six small children to the library until she could collect them after her commute. The youngest was six. Despite the uncertainty of their lives and obvious poverty, the children were all cheerful and loving. The middle child had a hard time controlling her temper, so she spent a lot of time in my office coloring pictures and talking with me about life. I fell in love with this family. Their mom did her best to take care of them and spent Sundays braiding everyone's hair for the week. She broke down in tears in my office one night, and I listened to her problems and assured her that she was doing a good job.

They moved after being in town for seven months. The mom was going through a manic phase; the kids told me that they moved at least once a year, if not more. The mom and I stayed in touch for fifteen years, even after we both had moved, until she died two years ago. She asked me to write her a letter of reference for culinary school, which I was delighted to do, and she then worked as a chef in the Bahamas. I met one of the daughters for dinner in Washington, DC, last year. She, against all odds, got a master's degree in international studies at an Ivy League university and worked in Jordan for five years. The middle child who spent hours in my office still struggles with the bipolar disorder that plagued her mom; she and I text several times a week and I try to encourage her. She misses her mom and has told me that I'm a role model. I am humbled by the fact that the few months we all interacted in the library all those years ago had some impact and that we are all in touch.

My life has been so enriched by my friendship with this family. I am overwhelmed with gratitude that my profession as a library director has allowed me to build relationships like these that endure over the years. I am proud when I see my staff members working with some of our patrons patiently and with practical compassion. We never know how our actions in the library will affect someone's life, and that's meaningful.

Local History and Genealogy Manager
Angela O'Neal

What I Do

Managing a local history and genealogy (LHG) division in a public library is all about helping people make connections to the past. My first priority is ensuring that library customers get answers to their questions, whether they are in-person, on the phone, or virtual. At the Columbus Metropolitan Library (CML), we have a "customer first" philosophy that prioritizes helping people above other tasks and includes defined service expectations for creating positive customer experiences. The core of customer first is making sure that people who interact with us feel seen, heard, and helped.

In addition, my role includes developing programs, managing archival collections, overseeing digital collections, and creating exhibits. While this may seem like a laundry list of responsibilities, they are all connected to helping people learn from history. Developing a collection that serves the needs of the community and tells the stories of all people, for example, is critical to being able to support quality programs and exhibits. When people see themselves represented in the collection, they want to get involved. At CML, we work with customers who want to share their historical materials related to central Ohio by encouraging them to loan items for digitization and occasionally to donate them for the physical collection. This approach builds community and encourages people to get involved by attending programs, sharing their stories through oral histories, or engaging with us in other ways.

As manager, much of my time is spent working with staff and overseeing projects. While it is important that the manager knows how to do most aspects of the positions in the division, I do not get a lot of time to work with the collection or other behind-the-scenes tasks. Instead, I focus on creating a positive culture, responding to staff questions, and promoting our work to external partners. Outreach is especially important in this role, as sometimes people do not realize the services that are offered by the library. I often work with historical societies, museums, neighborhood groups, churches, or organizations that are celebrating anniversaries. Building these relationships helps to get the word out about the services we provide, but also can lead to programs, exhibits, digital collections, or other partnerships.

My Favorite Things

The serendipitous moments when we help a customer find exactly what they are looking for or when we uncover a hidden piece of history are especially rewarding. I enjoy the variety of work that happens on any given day. There are many days where we respond to questions for most of the day. Other days, there is more time to focus on creating metadata for digital collections, processing archival collections, or preparing for programs. Flexibility is a key aspect of working in a public library. It can be stressful for people who prefer a more regimented schedule, but if you prefer to do something different each day it can be very fulfilling. Finally, curiosity is the most important aspect of this work. If you are a problem solver who will not let a question go until it is answered, this may be the field for you.

Challenges

The biggest challenge in managing an LHG division is balancing the sometimes-conflicting interests of library customers, staff, administrators, and external partners. Changes in policy, workflow, technology, equipment, and staffing all need to be communicated and managed. Prioritization is also hard. As a public library, we always want to say yes to projects and programs, but this can be difficult when we reach our capacity, and we have to turn down an opportunity. Overall, managing a local history and genealogy team is incredibly rewarding. I see the impact of our work every day when library customers make a connection to an ancestor, learn a new fact about their neighborhood, or attend a program.

My Career Path

My career path to librarianship began with a love of history and a plan to be a history professor. During college, I focused on public history and did several internships at archives, historical societies, and museums. Then I started working on Ohio Memory, an early digitization project led by the Ohio History Connection (OHC). I loved the community outreach component of the project and the behind-the-scenes work to build the digital collection. I was offered opportunities to progress through the organization, eventually serving as director of collections and overseeing digital collections, reference, manuscripts, and state archives. My time at OHC and all of my internships prepared me with an understanding of a variety of fields within archives and special collections. It was also helpful in understanding the convergence between libraries, archives, and museums.

About ten years ago, I became manager of local history and genealogy at the Columbus Metropolitan Library. While I had worked with public libraries before and was even a shelver during high school, the transition from an archives/museum environment to a public library was a big change. My current position emphasizes community engagement and access. I use skills from my archives background in my current position. I also have the opportunity to push the boundaries of access and be part of a community that is invested in the history of our city.

Advice

Always take advantage of opportunities for internships or tours of archives and libraries. Show up for programs and get to know people. This gives you an understanding of the real day-to-day work and can help you to choose an area of focus. You also make connections with people who may be future colleagues or even on your hiring committee. If you do participate in an internship or volunteer opportunity, be sure to give your best work so that you can get a positive recommendation at the end.

Also, stay up to date with what is happening in the field more broadly. You may have a particular focus that connects you to one professional organization, but read newsletters and email lists from others as well. In my work, I encourage staff to be aware of what is happening with the American Association of State and Local History and multiple genealogical organizations in addition to the standard groups such as the American Library Association (ALA), Society of American Archivists (SAA), and the Public Library Association (PLA). Many conferences offer scholarships for students to attend conferences.

Anything Else?

In archives and special collections, there is always a tension between preservation and access. Both are important for the sustainability of your library. Balancing the care of the materials with the public's need to use them is a daily conversation.

Supervising Librarian
Mychal Threets

What I Do

As a supervising librarian, my primary responsibilities include schedules, timecards, and meetings with library workers. Some days I'm in meetings all day, some days I'm working mostly with library staff, and some days I'm walking amongst the library users, bothering them.

Honestly, though? My job is to advocate for my library. I am my library's chief supporter. That's how I see my role.

My Favorite Things

I love that the public library can offer something for every person who walks through the library doors. Having diverse books on the shelves is important to me because there are all sorts of people who come into the library, and they should feel seen when they come to the library. There should be a book that represents every single person, not just one race, one background; everybody should be able to see themselves and fall in love with characters who are like them in books. I want to show kids of color that the library is a place where they can belong. I love it when a kid comes up to me and says, "I didn't realize that people of color could work in the library." That's not something they see every day, even in Solano County, one of the most diverse places in America. I think that's the most crucial aspect: there's me who's covered in tattoos and usually has giant hair, there's the unhoused, there are elderly grandmas and their grandkids, and everyone's just doing their own thing, but they're all in one safe, welcoming place.

You can make a job anything you want it to be. I appreciate the ability to use social media to make connections, to tell library stories, to emphasize the importance of the library. I love being a librarian so much. Being a library worker isn't perfect but hearing children's funny stories, their unhinged truths can see you through the day. That's why I started sharing their stories online. There are positive, funny, wholesome library stories happening every day. I enjoy observing them and being lucky enough to tell those stories to a wider audience on my social media to highlight the joy of libraries.

Challenges

Being a supervisor is definitely the hardest library job I've ever had. You deal with everything—the good, the bad, the monotony. The most difficult thing about my role as a supervisor is all the hats I have to wear. Tasks like approving timecards, managing schedules, and cleaning the restrooms may be part of my day-to-day tasks.

And of course, one challenging thing most public library workers face is the negativity and backlash from some community members, because we know that banning books discourages kids from wanting to read.

Taking care of our own mental health can be another challenge, but we can support each other. One time I was really struggling with my own mental health, and this library kid came to me and said, "I'm so happy you're here." That filled my heart with joy. Another time, a library grown-up came into the library after seeing a mental health video I shared online, and said it prompted him to come into the library. And that is the power of the library universe. People sometimes tell me, "I have anxiety and depression, too. Thank you for being real. Thank you for talking about it." I think being honest just opens up the door for people to have conversations that need to be had, so that we can all keep on surviving and persevering together. We all need that message sometimes saying it's OK to not be okay; you are doing your best. I have plenty of those days, but I keep on going because I know there are people who care.

My Career Path

Libraries have been part of my life as long as I can remember. I am a true library kid who was lucky enough to have grown up with my library grown-ups being my mom and dad. My dad always encouraged me and my siblings to have respect and appreciation for our privilege to be able to read and to have access to books. My mom was the one who homeschooled us, took us to the library, got us a library card at a very early age, brought us to all the programs, encouraged us to fall in love with books. She would read to us at home, and she would do all the voices.

Being homeschooled, I was at the library weekly. It was a place where I sought refuge. Books have always been my joy. I struggled throughout my life, and when my future was looking particularly sad, I returned to my local library and asked how you get a library job. I was hired, got my bachelor's and master's degrees, and worked myself to this point in my life. I have been a shelver, library aide, library assistant, library associate, children's librarian, and marketing librarian before taking on this supervising library role.

Then I started writing down all these observations that I started sharing on social media, taking note of the funny things the little humans enjoyed telling me. I would jot them down, thinking, "This is fun. Remember this is what got me through today."

Advice

Prepare to always be surprised. Expect the unexpected; abnormal is the new normal! But you'll have so much fun. Enjoy it! Applaud your coworkers. Support your community. Promote the library. I said you never know what will happen in the library? It's true, because you never know who you'll impact. You never know which story is going to find you in the library. Stay ready! Stay excited! There are always going to be library stories that'll keep you going.

Technical Services Manager
Somer Newland

What I Do

The responsibilities of the technical services manager (aka collection services manager, library materials services manager, and other variations) really depend on the size of the library. In larger libraries, the role often involves a lot of decision-making and committee work and not as much hands-on work, while in smaller libraries, the "manager" may do everything from book selection to paying invoices. In my library, I manage staff who are responsible for selecting the items we purchase, ordering and paying for all incoming materials (physical or digital), receiving and processing the physical items, and cataloging. I am intimately involved in all levels of decision-making regarding the library collection. While I have staff who are the point of contact for everyday questions from our vendors, if there are issues that need to be escalated or significant decisions that need to be made, I am the one to lead those conversations. I am also responsible for running regular statistical reports on circulation and collection data, which are reported to the library board and the state library for annual accreditation.

Another hat I wear is that of system administrator for our integrated library system (ILS). We participate in a larger consortium, and most of the administration is the responsibility of the larger system that hosts us. However, I take care of tasks specific to my library, such as creating new user profiles, modifying circulation policies, and troubleshooting problems affecting my library. In libraries that do not share an ILS, maintaining the system is often included in the technical service manager's duties. In addition to the above-mentioned tasks, this may involve performing software upgrades, implementing new services, running maintenance reports, and communicating with the ILS vendor.

My Favorite Things

I love making the larger-scale decisions that come with working in technical services. My team's ultimate goal is to get library materials into the hands of the user, and along with that comes findability. I enjoy looking at the big picture and figuring out what we can change to help increase our collection's visibility and circulation. I enjoy running reports and trying to tell a story based on the data.

I also like the flexibility that comes with working in technical services. Because my position is not a frontline position, my daily schedule isn't determined by the hours the library is open to the public. This allows me to work hours that better accommodate my life outside work, helping create a better work-life balance. This flexibility, of course, varies from library to library.

I would recommend this position to someone who loves working in libraries but perhaps doesn't enjoy working in a frontline position so much. It is also a great job for someone who enjoys the tasks that some people find tedious and detailed.

Challenges

Along with big decisions come big responsibilities. In many libraries, technical services has one of the largest budgets in the library other than salaries, and it is important to spend that money in a way that best serves your community. This means that my selectors and I often have to make purchase decisions that may not represent our personal beliefs. We also live in a time when book challenges are rising. If my library is subject to a challenge, as technical services manager, it is largely my responsibility to defend our collection development policy.

Another challenge, in a smaller library, is establishing and enforcing job expectations for technical services staff. In my library, technical services staff is not expected to cover public desks regularly, but when the public services department is short-staffed, we can be asked to help out. I try to be a team player and offer assistance when possible, but sometimes, such as when we receive a large shipment of books, I need all hands on deck to keep things running smoothly in my own department. Because technical services tasks are somewhat invisible to the rest of the library, unless something goes wrong, other staff members may not understand why we aren't always able to step in.

My Career Path

I took the long road to technical services. I had a keen interest in technical services in library school, but job availability upon graduation led me down a different path. However, my interest in technology in libraries led me a step closer with every new position I took. I have worked as a children's librarian, medical librarian, reference librarian, web services librarian, systems librarian, and, ultimately, technical services manager. Believe it or not, my reference skills probably have helped me the most! My ability to research a problem has helped me in every job I have had, whether answering questions for library patrons or figuring out how to troubleshoot a problem in the library catalog.

Advice

Think about what you enjoy most about working in libraries. If you enjoy patron interaction and helping people one-on-one, technical services may not be the best fit for you. However, if you enjoy working directly with the library collection, whether selecting books, working with a budget, or cataloging, you would probably do well in technical services. One of the most critical skills for my position is working well with staff in all departments across the library. The public services staff works directly with the public on a daily basis, and it's essential to listen to their feedback and make adjustments to processes and policies when necessary.

Take advantage of networking opportunities. In my career, I have benefited most from my colleagues. Almost every position I have had opened up to me because of the people I knew, whether they were in a hiring position or who just passed on information about positions for which I was qualified. When you engage with the library community around you, people get to know you and what your skills are. Then, when opportunities become available that are a good fit, they will remember you.

Anything Else?

Don't be afraid to switch gears. Take advantage of conferences to learn more about different aspects of the library field. Not only might your interests change over time, but also the library field is evolving. You may discover that there are things you can do with your degree that you may not have been aware of when you started your career or may not have even existed when you started!

Technology Coordinator
Louise Alcorn

What I Do

My position was originally created when such jobs were new to libraries—someone to oversee the library's web presence and think broadly about providing access to technology in a public library. Originally it could have been described as webmistress plus web services manager. Obviously, this has grown and morphed over time, as tech and needs changed, and other staff took charge of our day-to-day web and social media communication, while I retain overall responsibility. My job includes:

- Database and web service management (manage budget, review usage statistics, recommend additions/deletions from offerings, negotiate with vendors)
- Liaison for information technology (IT) support (overseeing staff and public tech and working with city IT and vendors to keep things running). This is a lot of relationship-building, gentle nudging, and project/problem tracking
- Training staff on new or changing resources and technologies
- Creating patron training materials on the same
- Collection development for tech-related nonfiction

A large part of this position is relationships with vendors, other city departments, all library divisions, regional and state library entities who provide services to us, and so forth.

My Favorite Things

Variety. My inner nerd likes to keep current with emerging technologies, examining them for library use in general, and figuring out how they might fit my library's mission. Equally, I like to keep our existing infrastructure running, working with vendors and city IT to keep our tech updated, useful, safe, and accessible. It's also satisfying to be the go-to person when there are technology-related questions: I may not know the answers, but I like looking, then bringing back solutions to my organization. This also gives me an opportunity to reach out to other librarians with technology responsibilities—my "friends inside the computer"—to share tips and tricks and new nerdy options.

I'm also delighted to still work the adult reference desk. It's valuable for me to know what questions staff are being asked every day, firsthand. And really, that's why I became a librarian. That said, I was pleased when we were able to reevaluate my position's responsibilities and give me more time for project management off-desk. Variety is great, but balance is also important.

Speaking of balance, it took me many years to learn to ask for what I need to stay happy in my job. I currently select the science fiction for the library; it's not a task that's tied to my position, but I quickly volunteered when the previous selector lost interest. Why is this important? Because when other parts of my job are annoying me, I can go buy great books. Be sure you feed the passions you have inside the profession whenever you can: this is how you avoid becoming a burned-out librarian.

Challenges

Ironically, the same answer: Variety. This is not a job for someone who cannot jump from one thing to another and back again with ease. This job includes assisting the public and staff with technology needs, technology planning and evaluation, managing budgets and analyzing statistics, and explaining all of the above to upper-level management and boards. A broken copier or a printer glitch can derail the day's work plans, and you have to be okay with that, then quickly regroup and reprioritize.

Technology stresses people out, and you become the focus for that stress. Key strategies include explaining—when you can—any change in projects in advance, making everyone aware of *what* will be changing, *why* it's changing, and *how* it will all get done. Also learning to give people grace when you know they're angry at the tech, not at you.

I will admit that I wish hardware was not any part of my position. Even though it's mostly "This copier isn't working? Try all your regular tricks, then call the maintenance contract vendor," dealing with hardware is still stressful and annoying, if necessary.

My Career Path

My job path is both unusual and (to an outsider) slightly boring, as I've been with the same employer since graduate school. About five minutes before I finished my master's, my best friend from high school called and asked, "Isn't this job listing exactly what you wanted when you got your degree?" A new hybrid position where I could create a brand new web presence, choose technology, and build a tech plan for a growing, well-funded public library in a community that was forward-looking, while also working as a reference librarian. Perfect! Over time, I found a gift for explaining technology topics to library staff and the general public, ultimately conducted training for our state and regional library systems, and even briefly becoming "famous in Canada!"

Over time, my original job morphed into a nonsupervisory management position, where I oversee aspects of the library that touch everyone—technology, web presence, future proofing, and technical support. This has been a balancing act, as technology is both essential and frequently frustrating or frightening to introduce. I work with nearly everyone in my organization at some point—planning, implementing, training—but have no clear authority in the organization, such as a department supervisor has. This could be challenging, especially when I was younger than all my colleagues.

My greatest professional development has been in project management, which includes potentially tricky resource management and people management. However, I will note that as I've had no official supervisory responsibilities, my professional options have been limited. When a professional opportunity "requires X years of direct supervision" I've been able to make a good case that project management has provided me with these skills, but that's not an obvious connection for everyone. This is a trade-off I have accepted, but I mention it to those new in the field: my usual advice is "don't do what I did" and instead get experience with every aspect of management if you plan to rise in it. For me, a more sideways approach has been fulfilling and fruitful.

I have been deeply lucky and am grateful daily for where I ended up.

Advice

Absolutely key attributes for this position: Flexibility in thought and scheduling; ability to jump from one thing to another, then back again, without losing track of project goals; openness to new ideas; ability to keep on mission (this one is hard when new toys are presented); ability to explain technology concepts to others without condescension; ability to manage change for oneself and others.

As time has gone on, I have also learned to be forthright and honest with vendors, while being wary of sales pitches. I tell them what we need, what we can/cannot afford, then question any vendor who tells me they have a single answer to a technology problem. Always get a demonstration, always get several quotes for products, always ask for a discount for being a loyal customer. These are not things anyone taught me in library school.

Anything Else?

Libraries and the library profession are full of smart, dedicated people. This is a great strength but can also be a challenge. Smart, dedicated people have opinions, but may or may not have experience with making projects come to life, budgeting, people management, or other challenges. If you can learn to express these skills—if you're the person who can "get it done" with clarity, respect, and calm—you will be invaluable to any organization that's open and willing to let you share your skills.

Be willing to learn from those who've come before. Most of my best learning moments came when I shut up and listened to someone who had failed. As long as they learned from the failure, they can save you a lot of heartache if you listen.

Teen Librarian
Kathleen Breitenbach

What I Do

I work in a public library, and I'm responsible for the teen/young adult (YA) collection. I create and manage all the programs and activities for children in middle school and high school, I represent the library at any middle school and high school outreach events, and I lead library tours for middle school and high school classes. In addition to that, I'm part of the adult reference department, so I work at a public service desk answering questions, helping people use the computers, finding materials, and ordering requested items that the library doesn't own. Despite my title, most of my day isn't spent on teens, programs, or the YA collection.

Because I work at a public service desk, every day is different. There are some predictable duties that occur on a regular schedule, like ordering books from the *New York Times* YA hardcover bestseller list (posted online by 8:00 p.m. Wednesday evening, so I check it and order from it on Thursday mornings), but most days I don't even know what hours I'll be on the reference desk until

I get in to work. A ten-minute section of a desk shift can include directing someone to the restroom, explaining our automatic renewal service, troubleshooting an application online, figuring out how to print a website when a pop-up shows on the print preview but not on a normal view, reserving private study rooms, pulling an older edition of a local newspaper, and working with someone to find a resource that we don't have but can't request because they aren't a patron of our library.

My Favorite Things

I love being able to try new things, whether that's developing new program ideas, planning new crafts, moving parts of the collection around, or even learning something new that I can use later. I love the ability to help people and connect people, especially teens, with books.

Challenges

Changes in administration (director, library board, strategic plan) can drastically impact not only one's job duties but also budgets and funding. Any funding for programs or supplies in my current position requires me to submit a wish list to our Friends of the Library group once a year; they can approve, reject, or approve only part of the requests, and they may put stipulations on what the money can be used for. If they reject a request, I either can't do the program or I need to find another funding source. Some administrations are more supportive of having teens in the library than others. It's a struggle to bounce back on teen services after that resistance, even if the next administration is more supportive. Public libraries attract little kids for storytime, picture books, and cute crafts, but if we lose teens, we've lost them until they're parents or older adults.

As a teen librarian, there can be fewer chances for job promotions or title bumps. Sometimes teen services are bundled into youth services, with either a specialist in the department, or with all staff doing some teen services along with serving younger patrons. Sometimes teen services are bundled into adult services. In my experience, teen services are only really separated into their own department in large libraries, or in systems with quite a few branches, and there are far fewer teen-specific positions than more general adult services, youth services, or reference positions. I've done teen services as part of being the Children's Librarian at a small library, and in my current position I'm the only staff member doing any teen services, but I'm also an adult reference librarian. To be a teen librarian, you need to be both very specialized (knowledge of adolescent development, Young Adult Library Services Association [YALSA]'s core competencies), and very generalized (teen services, plus at least children's, adult, or reference, if not all).

And then there are issues surrounding book bans or challenges to materials or programs. The top challenged titles from ALA's Office for Intellectual Freedom are typically either teen or YA titles or are frequently split between teen and adult collections. So far, book bans haven't hit my library, but I've worked closely with other librarians and community members on challenges at our local school districts and public libraries around the state.

Location is important for a number of reasons. On the municipal or county level, location and population inform the size of the library, its funding, where the function of serving teens in the library is housed, how the library board of trustees is formed (appointed vs. elected), and local attitudes on matters of importance of library services, privacy, and intellectual freedom. On the state level, there may be laws that impact requirements for librarians or restrict material selection. Both can impact cost of living and wages. Although the New Jersey Library Association has recommended minimum starting salaries for librarians, these salaries are not required, there's not a recommendation based on years of experience, and the cost of living in New Jersey is fairly high.

My Career Path

I feel like I'm in a weird spot right now. Like many librarians and library workers, I was a voracious reader as a child. I learned to read at an extremely young age and never stopped. I went to college to get a degree in English literature (because: reading) and had a work-study job in the Dean's Office for the Graduate School of Library and Information Science. I got my master of science in library and information science degree with a concentration in library services for children and teens. I've worked in circulation at a college library as well as a public library, and I was the children's librarian at my previous library. I've seen so many different parts of librarianship, and every library is different. You go in thinking that you're going to be *Buffy the*

Vampire Slayer's Rupert Giles—minus the vampires and demons—but end up as Wendy Yarmouth from *Shelved*.

Advice

One of the great things about being a public librarian is that you never know what obscure bit of information could be useful, so basically anything you see, read, try, hear, or experience is professional learning. Someone outside of librarianship might not realize just how valuable customer service skills or retail experience would be for public-facing library staff. I wish that when I was in school, someone had told me that even though people will assume teens are going to be the biggest problem in a library, kids and teens are great, and the problems tend to be their parents.

Youth Services Manager
Alissa Raschke-Janchenko

What I Do

Most of my responsibilities center on the day-to-day operations of a bustling, suburban library. I manage a staff of ten, and we serve children (birth through eighth grade) and their families and caregivers. Every day consists of a wide variety of tasks. In addition to working at a reference desk, I do collection development, programming, and outreach, and I sit on the library's management team, where we have biweekly meetings to discuss issues pertaining to operations. I also tackle special projects like our seasonal storybook walk and collaborate with other departments on library-wide initiatives. My management responsibilities include scheduling, hiring, training, and meeting regularly with staff to make sure organizational needs are being met. I get to provide coaching, offer continuing education opportunities, and find ways that my staff can bring needed resources to our patrons. I've also been able to sit on some state-wide committees and networking groups, present at conferences, and collaborate with local businesses and organizations.

My Favorite Things

My favorite aspects of my position change on an almost daily basis. The core reason I went into libraries, and have stayed for more than twenty-five years, is my passion for promoting information access and literacy. At my library, we are a bit of a community hub, and as such, we offer a wide array of resources. A print collection is important, but we also offer our patrons a safe, free place to gather, great programs for kids and families, and classes and tech resources that everyone can use. I've been in my current position for almost a decade, and watching the community change and grow is consistently rewarding. I also love the opportunity to offer my staff a fun place to work, and I encourage my team to take on projects and programs they feel are both challenging and interesting. I also love the collection management portion of my job; watching trends in publishing and getting my hands on new books never get old.

Challenges

For me, the biggest challenges come from the management portion of the position. Not a lot of MLIS coursework focuses on leadership or management training, so it is frequently a "learn as you go" method. Trying to navigate different personalities, communication styles, and job descriptions requires a great deal of finesse and is something that I think is glossed over in most degree programs.

No one was prepared for the Covid-19 pandemic and its impact on library work. My library closed briefly, but quickly started offering online programs and videos, as well as curbside pickup services. Our buzzword that year was "pivot," and it taught us a lot about flexibility, the basics of what we need to provide, and how access can be made easier for all our patrons.

And, of course, we all face extra scrutiny in libraries as a result of our political climate. I'm fortunate to work for a library that has an incredibly informed and supportive board of trustees, but I'm also keenly aware that book challenges are becoming more frequent.

My Career Path

I started volunteering at my local library in when I was in the fifth grade and loved it so much that I applied for a page position as soon as I was able to get a work permit. I worked in several libraries throughout high school and college, where I earned my undergraduate degree in English. After a short stint in the newspaper industry, I returned to libraries and completed my MLIS. I worked as a children's librarian, as well as specifically in children's outreach for about seven years, when I accepted a position managing the youth services department in New Lenox.

The adaptability and creativity shown by librarians, specifically public librarians, continues to surprise me. When I first entered the field, it was a profession that needed some fresh energy. As more and more young people are coming to libraries, bringing diversity and a sense of social justice, the field has become more dynamic. We still battle the stereotype of being "shushers" who enjoy getting to sit around and read all day (if only!), but in the current climate of information overload and book banning, librarians are on the front lines of the war on literacy and are anything but quiet about it.

Advice

In the more than twenty-five years that I have been working in libraries, I've found that a sense of humor and the ability to be flexible are the strongest tools I have. When working with the public, specifically children, every day can and will bring a new set of challenges and opportunities. I had already been working in the field for several years before getting my MLIS, and though I valued the knowledge gained through coursework, none of it prepared me as well as my background in working with children through volunteer opportunities and summer camp counseling.

I'd also recommend that anyone interested in a similar position network as much as they can. Even as a student in an MLIS program, reach out to local networking industry groups. I sit on the Illinois Youth Services Forum, and we table at various conferences throughout the year, hoping to connect librarians with a children's focus. There are many wonderful professional organizations out there, all with varying levels of time commitment, and I have been very grateful for those connections.

Anything Else?

People tend to think of libraries as quiet places, but thriving public libraries are anything but. In my spare time, I founded and run a nonprofit community theater, and my theater experience, particularly my improvisation training, has played greatly into my professional life. Being able to "yes, and" my way through the challenges we librarians face has taken many high-stress situations and made them a little less daunting.

2 School Libraries

Independent Middle School Librarian
Jean Myles

What I Do

My job has three main components: teaching library classes to fifth and sixth grades, maintaining the middle school collection and promoting a love of literacy, and collaborating with teachers to design units and teach students research skills.

There were no middle school library classes before I started working at the school, so I have spent the last six years developing a curriculum based on student and teacher needs, peer collaboration through library organizations and memberships, and professional development. I see every fifth- and sixth-grade student once a week. The first ten minutes of every library class are spent finding books and sustained reading, and during those ten minutes, I do readers' advisory and talk books with each student at some point once a month. Even though I do not see my seventh- and eighth-grade students on a regular rotation, I promote the love of literacy through book talks, reviews on our library website, and other fun initiatives, like first-chapter days and book trailers.

Collaborating with teachers, co-teaching, and visiting classrooms are what teachers find most valuable about what I do. Teachers come to me with a thought, a unit, or a project they have in mind, and we work together to see where I can help. Sometimes, that means meeting with the English department to give inputs on book choices for their curriculum or summer reading. Sometimes collaboration means planning a unit or a lesson together, which involves gathering resources for the class in the form of a document or a library guide. Other times, I visit the classes and explain the concept, whether it is researching a particular topic, using a specific type of database or primary source, or creating a certain kind of citation. Teachers love teaming up, having another voice in the room, and having someone who specializes in research circulate the room and help students.

Maintaining the collection, including cataloging, processing, and weeding, consumes the second largest amount of my time. There are many other responsibilities a school librarian may have. For example, at my last school, I was also responsible for the technology needs and maker space activities. Currently, I only focus on the library. The upper school librarian and I do all the collection maintenance, but parents help with processing and shelving. We also manage the budget, including purchasing materials and supplies and producing a monthly receipt reconciliation of all purchases.

My Favorite Things

All the different facets of being an independent school librarian make the job enjoyable. In other library jobs, I've focused more on one or two areas, but I do many different things here. I love going in each day, not knowing exactly what may happen.

Teaching library classes is my favorite aspect of my job because I love working with students and teaching them library and research skills. While working in a public library, I missed the school setting and realized that it was my forte and passion. I get value every day from the relationships I have with my students.

Other responsibilities I have are being an advisor to a group of eighth graders, coaching after-school sports, and running a professional learning community., I was also hired as the equity and inclusion coordinator for the school, which is a stipend position.

Challenges

The single biggest challenge in my job is time. As I mentioned, a part of the job I enjoy is being active in many different facets; still, I struggle to prioritize managing the collection and other library work. It is hard to find solid blocks of time to focus on writing lesson plans, making library guides for teachers, or responding thoughtfully to emails. Unscheduled activities push aside writing positive feedback to students, posting something on social media, or changing a display.

Unfortunately, one cause of the consistent interruptions is the lack of understanding of what a librarian actually does. People comment that we just check in and out of books (which we don't even do, because we have self-checkout and parent volunteers checking in). Some people also think it should be our job to supervise the physical space all day, every day, which would leave us with no time to plan, collaborate, create library guides, read reviews, catalog, and meet with students. Even though we go to our respective division meetings, full faculty/staff meetings, send emails, and make infographics, some people still don't grasp the bulk of what we do. The irony is that if we had more time, we'd be able to push that message out more.

Managing the budget is not my favorite aspect of the job, and I don't feel my MLIS program prepared me in that area. Still, after years of doing it, I feel empowered in this aspect of my job.

My Career Path

I was a public elementary school teacher for six years; after a four-year hiatus to raise my sons, I returned to work as a part-time public library staff member. Five years into that position, I realized how much I missed the school setting after attending school events with my sons, and I became a school librarian in a system that did not require an MLS. During my five years there and my first year at my current school, I earned my MLIS.

My current job almost fell into my lap: I was helping a peer with our online MLIS courses, and when I explained the lack of value put on libraries in the city where I was working, she mentioned the opening at St. Luke's. She reached out to a contact, and I interviewed and got my current job, where I see myself working until retirement.

I was still determining my role when I first arrived at my current school. I had been teaching a fixed schedule of six classes a day with one free period to manage my collection and do lesson plans. At St. Luke's, I have only one to three classes per day, and the rest of my time is dedicated to all the responsibilities I listed above. The first year, I had to figure out how to prioritize. At the time, the head of middle school was essential in helping me define my role. She saw the value in what I did with students and teachers, and motivated and guided me on how best to spend my time and energy. The role evolved into what it is now, mostly student-facing and teacher support. In a position where I was the first to hold the title, I had control of my direction, which was very different from the public school I had previously worked in.

Advice

As I mentioned, an independent school librarian's role differs based on the school and the community's needs. I found joining organizations and listservs of other independent school librarians incredibly helpful to learn, adapt, network, and add value to the role. I consistently attend professional development, such as conferences or online webinars. Developing a relationship with students and middle school teachers has been the most significant factor in enhancing how people see my value and in bringing me joy in what I do. My upper school counterpart finds it important to provide research materials and assistance in classes and one-on-ones. When starting as an independent school librarian, find what makes you valuable, determine what will give your students, teachers, and administration the most support, and focus there. Ask each constituent group how you can help and share your ideas on how best to support them.

Anything Else?

An independent school librarian often takes on other responsibilities typical of all faculty in independent schools. I was the yearbook advisor for three years, which I've learned through networking is an extra duty independent school librarians often take on. That may have something to do with the archival nature of yearbooks. Early in my library work, I found that equity, inclusion, and belonging go hand in hand with librarianship. Building a collection that includes windows and mirrors, doing readers' advisory, and teaching students about media literacy is rooted in equity work. My involvement in the equity and inclusion office at my school evolved naturally; I was doing many things I now do as the coordinator before even having the role. Something as simple as reading picture books with equity and inclusion or social-emotional learning themes led me into diversity work. It has opened the door for students and staff to come to me as someone safe to speak to and open difficult discussions with.

International K-12 School Librarian
Jill Egan

What I Do

I am a certified kindergarten through twelfth grade (K-12) school library media specialist, and I've spent most of my thirty-year career working abroad in international schools. There are over 13,000 international schools in the world where the primary language of instruction is English. International schools typically serve communities of expatriates who work in sectors like business, the military, or government. Local students are often enrolled at the school as well. The environment can be a true multicultural mix, with people from diverse backgrounds speaking multiple languages and intermingling in the classroom, the playground, and the library.

The work of teaching information literacy, promoting books and reading, managing a facility, and helping children is common to every school library position. But working in an international school, even one with an American curriculum, is different than being in a typical public school. For a librarian it can mean maintaining a bilingual collection or an extensive selection of materials in other languages. It absolutely means offering an inclusive, diverse representation of topics and voices in the general collection, while paying attention to worldwide publishing trends, not just those of North America. International schools are often the social center for the families of their communities, so the library may provide materials and spaces for parents and preschoolers as well as for students. And the library may support different curriculum frameworks: schools might follow American standards, the British national curriculum, the international baccalaureate (IB) program, local host country requirements, or a mix of these.

Schools range in size, but it is not uncommon for one campus to serve students in pre-kindergarten to twelfth grade, sometimes with just one librarian. This is great for those of us who love all ages of kids and all the literature, but it can be tricky as you bounce from playing with finger puppets to assisting with college application essays! In smaller schools, the librarian may also be required to teach a core subject, so any extra certification is a plus. In my experience, I was usually the sole librarian with assistants.

International schools typically have high expectations of their staff members; even nonprofit schools are very competitive and ambitious, promising parents world-class educational opportunities for their children. Beyond the school day, faculty are required to do extracurricular activities, attend school events, chaperone trips, participate in conferences and professional development meetings, and generally be a very visible part of the school community. There are also high expectations for the library: long hours of availability, frequent program offerings including author visits, and maintaining a showpiece facility.

My Favorite Things

Working at an international school in another country is a great way to be immersed in another culture, while having a ready-made circle of acquaintances and social support. Our family met people from all over the world, and we got to travel to unusual places. There are also great benefits: schools typically subsidize housing, provide free tuition for teachers' children, and assist with visas and moving. While situations vary, the schools I worked at had excellent facilities and offerings; they paid very well; and they had generous budgets for materials, programming, and professional development.

Challenges

Living in a foreign country is not the same as visiting on vacation, and it's always a challenge to settle in anywhere new. Not to stereotype, but if you are a librarian who thrives on orderliness, you may find some discomfort with the differences (or chaos!) you encounter.

For example, housing may be provided or subsidized by the school, but it is usually something quite different than what you may be accustomed to. In addition to missing your favorite American foods or products, access to books can be limited in some places—they may be locally unavailable and expensive to order. Cultural differences can be awkward and occasionally irksome. Blunders are to be expected as you attempt another language. But learning to adapt and find workarounds is part of the experience!

Another challenge to working in these positions is the impact on your entire family's lifestyle. Schools commonly hire either "teaching couples" or single teachers. If your spouse does not have a work visa in the country, they may have a hard time finding a job. Schools will also want to know about your own children, as in how many you have. Typically, tuition is provided for only one child per staff member. If you have more children than teachers in your family, it's not impossible to teach overseas, but you may have fewer options. Another consideration is special needs and health conditions in your family; some schools do not provide extensive services, and local health care can vary greatly. Finally, you must think of your extended family as well; it can be difficult to return to the United States to attend family gatherings, even in urgent situations.

My Career Path

I wanted to be a school librarian very early on, and I obtained my MLS from the University of Michigan directly after completing my undergraduate studies in English and education. What led me to a life overseas was my first job opportunity in Maui, Hawaii. Their schools were experiencing a teaching shortage at the time, and they recruited me straight from university. Taking that step showed me that there was a world to discover. Fortunately, I found a partner who felt the same way, and we just decided to keep going. After Hawaii, we got jobs at schools in Saudi Arabia, Norway, Dubai, Ecuador, and Jordan. We loved them all, and our daughters did, too.

Advice

Having teaching certification and a master's degree from an ALA accredited program are the keys to placement in most school library jobs.

The best way to land a job is to enlist with a recruiting agency. The top ones for overseas educators have been Search Associates, International Schools Services, and The International Educator. International schools recruit earlier than in the United States; ideally you should compile all resumé materials a full year in advance of the school year you intend to move abroad. International schools located in the United States use private school recruiters like Carney, Sandoe and Associates. There are recruiting fairs at which you may engage with multiple schools over a few days, or individual interviews conducted through video conferencing. Librarians and teachers with prior experience are most highly sought.

International schools range greatly in terms of size, curriculum, clientele, salary, and benefits, and to be frank, competency. Unfortunately, there are many institutions that go unregulated and unaccredited, and I've heard horror stories from teachers who've had bad experiences. I recommend doing a lot of research, as a good librarian naturally would! Find schools' websites, follow international school librarians on social media, register with a recruiter, and plan to do fall and winter interviews with the intention to start working in the following school year. Being familiar with another culture or knowing another language is helpful, but more important is having a willingness to learn, and an open mindset.

It's a great privilege to have an occupation that allows one to continue to learn, and that is a wonderful reward of a career in librarianship. Living in a foreign country is also a privilege and a continuous learning experience. Your library degree and teaching certification can be a passport to adventure; why not explore?

Lead Librarian, Public School District

Amy Pulliam

What I Do

As the lead librarian for a mid-sized public school district, my day to day is full of variety. I oversee ten libraries in the district as well as serve as the librarian for the high school. Some days I am teaching research methods to English language arts (ELA) classes and helping my high school students with readers' advisory, some days I am at another district school helping shelve books or showing a new librarian how to use our online catalog, and other days I am glued to my desk while I talk to vendors and put in purchase orders for the books/supplies/furniture/shelving that are needed to keep the district libraries in the twenty-first century. Of course, as with most librarians, the "other duties as assigned" job description gets used often in various forms such as planning and hosting an honor roll celebration for high school students, helping set up our new e-sports room, or assisting students and staff with technology.

My Favorite Things

I absolutely love my job for several reasons, but it's all rooted in the fact that my district is committed to having well-funded libraries and qualified staff to run them. So many neighboring districts have left their libraries behind the times or do not employ librarians to run the libraries and maintain collections. East St. Louis School District has routinely surprised me in their dedication to students being able to access twenty-first century libraries. Like a lot of people in the profession, I enjoy being helpful and solving problems, so the day-to-day issues I help with (some big, some small) are usually very satisfying. One of my favorite things to do is readers' advisory, or helping students find a book they will like. When I have a day booked full of English classes coming in to find books for a sustained silent reading (SSR) unit, it's always a fun day that flies by as I get to know students by their reading tastes. Helping one-on-one with research is another favorite, because research skills haven't really been emphasized in years past and I'm excited to get students acquainted with the research process.

Challenges

One of my biggest struggles is splitting my attention between my library and the rest of the district libraries. I have a media specialist (my district's title for a noncertified library worker) to help with the day-to-day tasks, but I am the point person for most things involving the library. I want to be available to all the other librarians and media specialists in my district, but also do not want my library to be neglected in the process. Another big hurdle has been trying to find the sweet spot between getting students to come to the library and getting them to be here for the right reasons. Sometimes it's dead all day, sometimes we have a moderate number of students, sometimes we have far more students than we can handle at one time. When we have the huge influxes, it can devolve into a social hour instead of students checking out books, getting research help, or working on an assignment on their own. Socializing isn't necessarily a bad thing, but when there are more than fifty students in the library at one time, the students can get a little too loud and out of hand.

My Career Path

My career has always been oriented toward education. Immediately after completing my undergrad in history and secondary education, I served in the Peace Corps in Turkmenistan as a volunteer for teaching English as a foreign language (TEFL). I continued my teaching career in Azerbaijan after my Peace Corps service ended. After a two-year gap back in the United States to go to library school, I got my first school library job in Istanbul, Turkey. Living overseas, especially as the only foreigner for fifty miles in Turkmenistan, gave me skills that have greatly aided me in my career and life in general. You have to be very flexible, learn to think outside the box when problem solving, and think quickly when things don't go the way you planned. These are all very useful skills to have in a school setting.

I started working for the East St. Louis School District after I moved back home. I worked as an elementary librarian for five years before transferring over to the high school to take over the lead librarian position. Switching from elementary to high school was an adjustment, along with all the new elements that came with the lead librarian role, but it's been an exciting experience and a position that offers me a lot more flexibility and freedom than my elementary position.

Advice

Attending the iSchool at University of Illinois Urbana-Champaign was the best decision I could have made for my career as a school librarian. I already had a teaching license in the state of Illinois when I started the program, so I got to choose from well-rounded, diverse class offerings and had a pre-professional assistantship appointment that gave me a great foundation for my first librarian job. When I first started my MLIS program with almost no library experience, it took at least a full semester to get a grip on some of the basics of the profession. Some of the most comforting advice instructors gave me was that it takes around six months to start to figure out what's going on. In my experience, they were right.

School libraries require someone willing to dive into the curriculum and find ways the library can complement it. And this seems obvious, but you will be miserable in a school library if you don't like working with kids of all ages. They are curious, moody, sweet, dramatic, kind, and rude all within five minutes. It is extremely frustrating and extremely rewarding to work with K-12 students.

In today's school library world, you need to stay as up to date on best practices as you can and be ready to advertise and defend what you provide to the school. Over the course of my career, I have had colleagues who fully supported me and the library, and I have had some who didn't think I had a real job. You need to be confident about what you add to the school and let people see what you're bringing to the table.

Librarian, School for the Deaf
Nell Fleming

What I Do

No doubt my job is unique. As a teacher librarian at a residential school for the Deaf, serving students ages three to twenty-one, it is necessary for me to be proficient in a variety of areas outside the scope of a public school librarian. However, it is also true that they do things that I don't; some school librarians teach keyboarding or English language arts (ELA) or technology courses, assign grades, and have bus duty. I serve our entire community, parents, alumni, retired folk, staff, and students. I also act as liaison between public library services and residential students.

I need to be aware of the pace of instruction for each group of students, which often takes longer due to the visual nature of American Sign Language (ASL). I must differentiate for a very large scope of ability levels in each class. I quite often have both pre-literate students and above-grade level students at the same time.

I also do all the policy writing, infrastructure maintenance or planning, collection development, and cataloging. My days are busy but usually not hectic.

On a typical day I would arrive at 7:30 a.m. and set up circulation, turn on the lights, and be ready for students. I teach most of my classes during first and second period this year. Because all of our students have individualized educational programing (IEPs), planning takes some time. As deaf children cannot hear the beep of the scanner and are not always skilled at visual attention, I point out if they missed a scan and encourage them to look at the screen.

I'm almost always being observed. I am used to it now, but my first year I felt a bit awkward, because I don't go into teachers' classrooms to observe their lessons! But the teachers also use the library, gather their books, plan their lessons, read magazines, model reading, handle a behavior if a student has a behavioral intervention plan (BIP), and so forth. We work together based on the style of the teacher. Some teachers are equal partners; we plan all our lessons together and co-teach. We can then do much more in-depth projects, which is ideal, incorporating library skills, English language arts (ELA) skills, and life skills into the projects. Other teachers, who have experience in public schools, take a preparation period, which is totally fine with me. I have a planning period, a shelving period, and a cataloging period. I cannot use parent volunteers easily due to the state's background check requirements and the fact that most live far away.

I have intermittent patrons, both staff and students, throughout the day. I answer emails and attend meetings. I write a weekly newsletter. I work with the technology department. This week I created a spreadsheet for specifications on interactive whiteboards and am setting up demonstrations for the teachers so we can choose new boards for our staff. Yesterday I took a high school student to the basement archival storage to get old yearbooks for a class project.

Working in a bilingual environment where spoken English is only used in private means that I can go whole days using my first language only in writing. Access to incidental language for our students and respect for our deaf colleagues is one of our highest priorities. We are an "ASL at all times" school for this reason and English used is mainly written.

Our administration is perhaps busier than most; positions have been combined so that they do the regular duties plus much more, such as IEP meetings *daily*. Our director is Deaf and many alumni work here. Our staff are 60 percent d/Deaf and we have many Deaf parents and grandparents as well. Many of our families settle nearby, as the proximity helps them access services that most of our community are accustomed to providing regularly.

My Favorite Things

I love that I'm constantly doing something different. A different grade, a different level, a different task—it keeps the job from getting stale. I always look forward to what flavor the new year will bring to the soup.

Challenges

Unfortunately, administrators over the years have all had different understandings of my position. Some do not see me as a teacher, even though in fact I am a teacher plus more. My current administrator is a good one, and we've made progress, so I hope in time we will get on the same page.

My Career Path

When I began library school at University of Illinois, I assumed I would work in the public sector. However, by the time I was in the job market I saw the advertisement at Wisconsin School for the Deaf (WSD), one of the only places I had ever considered working in deaf education again because of their high professional standards and easy-going staff culture in a bilingual/bicultural environment. I wanted very much to work here as a teacher, but at the time we were unable to move. The unexpected opening required exactly the two degrees I held, which was quite a surprise.

Advice

Every state has different requirements for a job like this one, but becoming fluent in ASL is the most important aspect. You may need a degree in deaf education, depending on your state's requirements.

It's essential to educate yourself about d/Deaf culture and be sensitive to their perspectives and experiences. Be aware that the term "hearing impaired" is derogatory to culturally Deaf people. Familiarize yourself with the controversial issues. Topics related to communication are especially hot topics. For example:

- whether to use sign language or not, and if so, what sign language to use
- whether to send a child to a residential school with access to Deaf Culture or to a local mainstream school
- whether to use auditory devices, and if so, when to start using them and which devices to use
- whether a baby should be altered with cochlear implants, since they cannot give informed consent

The ethics of these choices are complex, and opposing viewpoints can create animosity or isolation among deaf people. Unfortunately, physical and psychological abuse and neglect, whether intentional or not, was fairly common in the past. Some d/Deaf people may be triggered by these controversial topics, and some may make decisions for their children based on their own childhood trauma. It is vital to have a solid grasp on these issues along with empathy for diverse viewpoints.

Library Services Director, Public School System

Deborah Lang Froggatt

What I Do

When the daunting offer to become the director of library services for Boston Public Schools (BPS) came, I wondered, "How in the world will I be able to keep track of what is going on in 125 schools?" Then I realized that when I had been a given school's sole library teacher, I kept track of hundreds of students, multiple teaching teams, large school faculties, and much more. This analogy made me confident that I could support the BPS library team of librarians and library paraprofessionals and their programs.

Supporting an individual school library is akin to supporting a student. The crux of my work was to provide effective library services to all students in the schools. The compass that steered my work with the BPS library team was the American Association of School Librarians National School Library Standards for Learners, Librarians and Libraries (https://standards.aasl.org/). I navigated the pitfalls, politics, and personalities for BPS students to access holistic library learning, professional staffing, and robust programming.

My days varied widely, but they were filled and fulfilling. I typically visited five or so schools per week, meeting with library staff, teachers, and principals. Getting to know a school, from the administration support team to the custodians to the teachers to the students, was a privilege. Most of the time it was joyful, but there were also difficult situations, at times. To serve *learners*, the library team and I shared best practices to enhance student access to culturally relevant collections. Some schools depended on book fair profits and parent donations as their only avenue for new materials, but by the end of my tenure, all current libraries received a per capita amount for collections. New school libraries received an investment of an "opening day collection."

Meeting the individual needs of the *librarians* included one-on-one training, which included modeling read-alouds, reviewing lesson plans, sharing collection management tips, and troubleshooting integrated library systems. Professional development for library teachers and paraprofessionals depended on the issue at hand. For licensed school librarians, the AASL standards were integrated into inquiry-based research unit strategies and implementation. Some paraprofessionals took advantage of this opportunity and others participated in the Southern Utah University's online Library Aide Basics program. In all cases, we worked together to build students' independent learning muscles.

To support *libraries*, I regularly planned with district leaders, academic department heads, technology folks, library vendor representatives, parent council members, and nonprofit players within a school district context. I attended school board meetings and, when asked, presented library program elements including strategic plans.

My Favorite Things

Collaborating with people in a myriad of ways was a favorite part of my work. Ensuring that library programs offered students adequate resources required collaborations with many departments, from academics to human capital to facilities. I wormed my way on to many district-wide initiatives to keep up with the pulse of district needs and funding streams as they applied to school library programming. I always looked for ways to offer help with initiatives in order to benefit library programs.

A few examples: At the beginning of the school year, I supported the transportation department by answering phones to let schools know the status of late buses. This good deed was reciprocated when high school seniors needed a midday ride to and from an elementary school for a picture-book sharing event. Serving as a mentor and a university liaison for provisional *librarians* for their licensure was a way to give back to our profession. Brainstorming with a community health agency about its book contributions to the neighborhood school's *library* program educated these professionals in using AASL standards to create a diverse reading collection that met the range of developmental stages and needs of the community.

The opportunities to work with nonprofits and city agencies to serve the diverse BPS student population brought great satisfaction. For instance, the director of youth services for the Boston Public Library and I planned and facilitated two literacy summits. In order to see which students might not have access to rich literacy experiences, we brought together representatives from tutoring, writing, art, after-school, and community health agency programs, as well as library and administrative folks from charter and parochial schools. Conversations focused on agency program plans about where services may overlap or which children might not receive services at all. We used collective impact theory to ground our work and presented the planning and program outcomes at an American Library Association annual meeting.

Challenges

Sometimes working with this great team was a challenge because of difficulties within the school or personal upsets. My counseling courses from my seminary degree were put to good use. A supervisor must be a good listener and, even more importantly, must strive to follow through with whatever the library teacher or paraprofessional needs.

My district colleagues and I sometimes competed for the same funding. Strategic partnerships and reaching across the table were key for keeping the library services program on a given department's radar to possibly receive funds. I learned how to leverage my inputs at meetings at the right time and put myself "out there" toward a meetings' end if my program was not discussed. I was transparent about the "broken record" message and constantly repeated how lack of access to a school library program is a social justice issue. There were times I felt like giving up, but seeing students when visiting schools kept me inspired to keep going. It paid off as every student in Boston Public Schools now has equitable access to an effective school library program and a licensed school library teacher.

My Career Path

At each point in my career, when considering what next steps were available for me, I tried to take advantage of courses in order to acquire other certifications and pedagogical experiences, thus enlarging possible employment choices. As a public librarian, I took advantage of my state's LIS program and received my school library certification. Many states offer school library licensure pathways for those with a LIS or academic content master's degree. I was a middle school librarian in one district that partnered with a local college. I enrolled in numerous courses that broadened my skill set, including a course to acquire director licensure for becoming a department head. These courses for credit also increased my salary. I participated in school district committees including curriculum development, technology implementation, and literacy initiatives. These experiences allowed for a robust resume, which led to a culminating career position.

Advice

Sometimes it may appear that district level administrators are interested in their own careers, but one must keep a continual reminder that we all have our own agendas. Honoring the work that administrators are doing and placing aside a tough personality helped me keep my patience and allowed me to strategize how to take advantage of departmental personality strength for library services program growth. Put people aside, focus on student needs through problem solving. Strengthening communication and partnerships with district schools, departments, and community agency partnerships are key.

Anything Else?

Ending my school library career in this position was a gift. The mentoring of new librarians and recruiting those interested in this career was a great reward. Collaborating with a variety of individuals gave me enormous insights into my own practice. This in turn strengthened my ability to support the school system and the library professionals with whom I worked..

Public Elementary School Librarian
Michael Rawls

What I Do

Welcome to my world as a school librarian! In our district, the role of a school librarian isn't set in stone. Each school has its own unique flavor, and I'm fortunate to be in a place where I have the autonomy to shape our library program according to the needs of our students.

Unlike some schools where library visits are part of the usual "specials" rotation, such as art or gym, our scheduling is a bit more flexible. At the start of the school year, teachers get to pick a day and time that works best for their class, and that becomes their designated library slot for the entire year. This allows teachers to tailor their library time to what suits their schedule and the needs of their students.

This schedule also provides me with a sweet spot of flexibility and balance, making my job not only manageable but thoroughly enjoyable. It affords me ample time with students as a whole class, where I get to channel my inner teacher. Additionally, it allows for one-on-one or small group interactions with students who choose to visit the library independently. With the support of a dedicated library assistant and a self-checkout system for older students, the library remains accessible even during class time. While I'm engaged with a class, students can still utilize the library because there's another adult to assist and manage independent visitors. During those unstructured times, I often find myself helping students find books they're seeking or matching them with resources for research projects, creating a more personalized connection.

During our thirty-minute class visits, I'm all about immersing students in the world of stories. While the format may vary—from reading picture books aloud and showing book trailers to giving book talks or exploring excerpts from novels—the essence remains centered around literature. Following the storytelling, I lead students in engaging activities like conducting polls, sharing connections, or unleashing their artistic side by drawing in the style of the illustrator. Post-activity, the students have the freedom to explore the library, a haven absent of screens. Here, they can engage in a myriad of activities—playing chess, solving Rubik's cubes, building with Legos, or getting crafty with origami, to name a few.

You might wonder why our library doesn't feature computers and iPads in the mix. Once upon a time not so long ago, libraries transformed into media centers, with a significant chunk of space dedicated to computers. Back then, these spaces were often the only exposure students had to computers and digital technology within the school. However, fast forward to the present day, post-pandemic, and students have become digital natives, surrounded by technology from birth. Our library philosophy has evolved to focus on fostering creativity and imagination through books and hands-on activities, leaving digital technology to other spaces in the school.

Having a library assistant isn't just about managing the day-to-day operations; it's a strategic move that enables me to focus on other critical aspects of my role. For instance, managing a substantial budget is a significant responsibility. Juggling funds from the parent teacher association, school (federal) funds, birthday book club funds, and those raised from our annual book fair requires careful planning. Allocating resources for new books, replacements, and updated series demands attention to ensure the needs of all stakeholders—students, staff, and parents—are met. It's not just about surveying them but also analyzing the results to ensure spending aligns with their needs. This crucial aspect of my job deserves undivided attention, and the breaks in my schedule provide the ideal moments to dive into this financial planning, with another set of eyes, ears, and hands managing the circulation desk.

Collaboration is another cornerstone of my role. Most frequently, I team up with our instructional coach to ensure alignment with teaching and learning standards across classrooms. This collaboration extends beyond the school walls, involving educating parents and the community about our library services. It could mean presenting to parents at a "parent university," creating screen-recorded how-to videos for the latest educational apps, updating our library website with current information, or curating a collection of e-books tailored for instructional purposes.

But it's not all about the numbers and the collaborations; a significant chunk of my time goes into crafting an inviting, inspiring space that sparks curiosity and inquiry. Weeding out older titles to make room for more current, relevant, and desirable books is a constant effort. Designing displays that make books practically disappear, rearranging the space for comfort and accessibility, and engaging patrons with contests and interactive components that promote ownership of the space are all part of the creative process. It's about keeping the library fresh and current, ensuring it remains a vibrant and dynamic hub within the school.

In essence, my role as a school librarian encompasses a multitude of hats—educator, fundraiser, advertiser, manager, content creator, and collection curator. All these facets come together to define the role, not just as a librarian, but as a champion for books, reading, and learning in the school community.

My Favorite Things

I often describe my role as experiencing the best parts of teaching without the overwhelming aspects that come with being a classroom teacher. There's no dealing with report cards, graded papers, parent-teacher conferences, or the complexities of organizing field trips. The pressure of high-stakes testing, and constant analysis of assessment data is absent. It's a space where you can be a teacher to students who learn for the sheer joy of it.

Challenges

As a school librarian, you're essentially a team of one. While having a library assistant is a plus, the solitude can be stark compared to the collaborative environment of a typical teaching team. Building connections becomes vital.

I've forged strong relationships with teachers across all grade levels at my school but finding that go-to person is crucial. In my case, the instructional coach serves as a sounding board for ideas, a collaborator, and a friendly ear for venting. I encourage others in this solo role to seek out someone similar within their school. Beyond the school walls, the professional learning network can extend far and wide. I rely on Instagram colleagues for ideas, inspiration, and motivation, breaking the limitations of the immediate school or district network.

My Career Path

My journey into the role of a school librarian was unexpected. I was a fourth-grade teacher at a new school when I learned that the school librarian was retiring. The idea intrigued me, and I investigated further. Though lacking the required master's degree in school library media, I had time on my side. Enrolling in an online master's program in January of that year, I interviewed for the librarian position by March and was hired for the following school year. It felt like on-the-job training, with much of my coursework directly applicable to my work in the library. Graduating brought not only the job I desired but also a higher degree and the accompanying pay raise.

Advice

With eighteen years of teaching experience spanning various grade levels, I brought a toolkit of instructional strategies and behavior management skills to the library. Classroom management and delivering engaging lessons were already second nature. The curveball came in teaching younger students (kindergarten through second grade). Initially intimidating, they're now my favorite due to their natural curiosity and easy excitement for learning. When faced with working with unfamiliar grade levels, seeking advice from those with experience and being open to unexpected preferences are key. The brain has the capacity for growth and adaptation, leading to newfound enjoyment in areas with people you didn't initially think were your cup of tea.

Anything Else?

Be open to where the work takes you. I had a small following on Instagram prior to becoming a school librarian. As I continued to share books, ideas, lessons, and thoughts on being a school librarian, my account (@ thebookwrangler) grew to over 100,000 followers. It's allowed me to have a great deal of influence outside the walls of my school, hopefully expanding people's ideas about humanity, equity, equality, censorship, and the need for all to be seen and heard. Additionally, having a large audience has been profitable for me. Not only can I advertise educational products and promotional merchandise that I make and sell on online marketplaces, but I have also had the opportunity to create content for publishers and other companies in exchange for payment. I'm not telling you this will happen for everyone, but I will say be on the lookout for paths to the unexpected.

Public Middle School Media Specialist

Dale F. Harter

What I Do

To be a middle school librarian, especially if you are by yourself and do not have a paraprofessional assistant, you have to be energetic, willing, and able to perform a variety of tasks, from the highly challenging to extremely mundane. Although some in my profession are advocates of student self-checkout of books, to me this implies that the librarian is not needed. I think it's extremely important for a school librarian to be present as much as possible in the library and to be there for students, from helping them find the books that will turn them into lifelong readers to being a compassionate adult who is willing to listen to them. I also like having tasks and responsibilities that change from day to day.

I open the library each morning forty-five minutes before classes start and spend that time interacting with students and checking books in and out, while also serving as a hall monitor. I regularly host classes in the library, collaborating and co-teaching with teachers on a variety of lessons. I try to engage with teachers across the curriculum, but most of the classes I work with on a regular basis are English and history. Depending on the time of the year, and on our required standardized testing days, I might have zero classes in the library one week and fifteen classes the following week.

When I am not teaching classes in the library, I am busy with a multitude of tasks every day: shelving books, repairing or weeding damaged books, cataloging books, researching and ordering new books, preparing displays, planning for library events and upcoming classes, interacting with students who visit the library, and participating in professional development through online resources, podcasts, and webinars. In this job you also will need to be prepared to give up your library space for required testing and other non-library functions. You often will be called upon to be a test proctor.

My Favorite Things

If you want to make a difference in the lives of preteen and young teenagers every day, then you should be a middle school librarian. You also need to be someone who likes being a reference librarian in general. I love helping students find the right book and teaching them to be information literate, but I'm most happy when I can say a kind word that helps brighten their day. I decided to move from a high school library to a middle school library in part because I was seeing far too many teenagers who did not like to read and were addicted to their smartphones. I don't have a magic wand, but I do believe that middle school librarians are the key to ensuring incoming elementary school students keep reading and continue reading into high school and throughout their lives. In a time when parents, politicians, and librarians are extremely concerned with what children might be reading or might be prevented from reading, I think it's far more important to realize that many of them are not reading *anything*.

Challenges

Middle school students are normally between the ages of eleven and fourteen. They can be quirky, curious, engaging, precocious, apathetic, unengaged, and disrespectful, sometimes all within one day. There will be days when their behavior will exhaust my last bit of patience, followed by days when I know there is nowhere else I would rather be or work. There have been times where a colleague has irritated me enough that I dreaded coming to work the next day. I have never felt that way about a student. To excel as a middle school or high school librarian, you must stay flexible, be multitalented, and have a heart for working with adolescents. Many of them will try your patience, but when you see the proverbial "light bulb" come on, it's truly worth all the work and frustration.

My Career Path

I went to the University of South Carolina (USC) for their joint master's program in public history (archives administration concentration) and library and information science, after working as a paraprofessional archivist at the Library of Virginia for nearly two years. My career goal was to be an archivist, but I also saw the MLIS as a "green card" to work in other types of libraries. I did not, however, have any desire to be a school media specialist. After I finished graduate school, I returned to the Library of Virginia as a research archivist/reference librarian. When I was laid off due to a state budget cut, I took a position as a librarian at St. Margaret's School, a private girls' boarding and day school. Within days after starting that job, I realized I had a natural knack for working and connecting with teenagers. Although I later returned to the archives world and worked four years at Bridgewater College, a small liberal arts college in Virginia, I knew I was meant to be a school librarian and returned to St. Margaret's. Due to a budget cut at that school, I had to make the transition to public school librarianship, which required me to return to school to complete additional classes in education and school library science.

Advice

Because of my own experiences with unexpected layoffs, I would advise anyone who wants to be a school librarian/media specialist to earn an ALA-accredited MLIS, with a certification in school librarianship. That will give you flexibility to work in other libraries if the need arises. One of my USC professors advised us to be ready to "provide information in all formats," and that advice still rings true today.

Some of the best school librarians I know were K-12 classroom teachers who had completed formal education degrees but had become burned out and went back to school to earn degrees in school librarianship. Although I hated going back to school in order to be a public school librarian, the education classes I was required to take for certification turned me into a true teacher librarian. I also benefited from taking several school librarianship courses at Longwood University.

Maintaining an active membership in your respective professional state school librarians' association and in the American Association of School Librarians will help you immensely in your job as a school media specialist/school librarian. By attending professional local, state, and national conferences, you will learn valuable lessons and skills that you can immediately take back to your school and put into action. You also should seek opportunities to present at conferences and to publish in professional print and online library publications and outlets.

3 Academic Libraries

Access Services Librarian
Glen J. Benedict

What I Do

As an access services librarian, I'm split between two primary responsibilities—access services and reference services. Access services cover circulation, collection maintenance, interlibrary loan, and customer service. Reference services involve the reference desk, requests for research assistance via chat or email, and occasional information literacy instruction. In larger academic libraries, many of these jobs would be handled by specific librarians or staff specialists; at smaller universities, you need to be flexible in overseeing a variety of different tasks. You may also be required to supervise the access services or circulation team; I currently have five circulation technicians that report to me and no student employees.

At my university, librarians are classified as faculty, although this isn't true at all schools. This comes with additional expectations of professional development, academic achievement, and service to the university and the community. To fulfill these expectations, I serve on our faculty senate and professional committees through the American Library Association (ALA) and the Washington Research Library Consortium (WRLC).

My Favorite Things

What I love most about my job is the variety of tasks that I get to work on. A typical day for me might include going into the stacks to pull books for the hold shelf, attending an ALA committee meeting over Zoom, giving directions from the reference desk, and assisting a student with finding articles via online chat. I would recommend this position to people who already know that they enjoy an array of library jobs. It helped that I had previous experience working at a circulation desk, providing reference services, doing library instruction, supervising employees, and planning collection maintenance projects. I have a lot of leeway to be self-directed in my tasks and goals.

Challenges

Probably the biggest challenge at my job is staff supervision. This is a separate set of skills from those you learn in library school. In an academic library, your staff may be under a different union than teaching faculty, so it's important to familiarize yourself with the terms of their employment. I do annual performance evaluations, which is a time of great stress for both me and my employees.

Navigating academic bureaucracy is also frustrating at times. Expect slow response times from campus departments like human resources. Even for librarians who are technically professors, sometimes it is hard to feel included or respected by the broader teaching faculty.

My Career Path

I graduated from college with a bachelor's degree in philosophy. I lived in New England for some time working odd temporary positions, and eventually got a full-time job working the overnight shift at an alarm monitoring call center, dispatching emergency services for burglary, fire, and medical alarms. This taught me how to provide customer service, even in very stressful or traumatic circumstances.

The long hours and very limited time off wore me down, and I moved back home. I worked at a nonprofit organization that provided services to individuals with developmental disabilities, and finally decided that I wanted to go to graduate school for library science. However, my undergraduate grades were poor and I was not accepted.

I started taking night classes in an adult education program, eventually earning a second bachelor's degree in management which got me admitted to the library science program at the University at Buffalo. Attending in-person ended up being a great decision. I earned job experience working as a student coordinator at the music library on campus, volunteered to help the Pride Center of Western New York redesign their collection, completed a one semester internship at Niagara University, and attended my first professional conference at ALA Annual in San Francisco. Getting a student membership to ALA was extremely influential in helping me develop my professional interests and goals. I was able to volunteer for committees, get help with my resume, and become energized about my chosen vocation.

After graduating, I took a position as the access services and information commons evening associate at the University at Albany, another school in the State University of New York (SUNY) system. This role did not have a librarian title, but it did have some great perks. I was able to build experience working in an academic library, putting my skills from my management degree to work supervising both civil service and student employees. I got to see how new and ongoing stacks maintenance projects were planned and executed. Because I was often at the desk without onsite administrative staff during the late evenings and early morning hours, I was able to apply my customer service skills from the call center to handling emergencies and problematic patrons. Best of all, my position was under the faculty union, which provided professional development funding to attend ALA Annual every year.

I wanted to move up into a full librarian position, so I started applying at some of the other SUNY schools. Knowing that I was job hunting, a coworker who had recently made the same change sent me a posting for an access services librarian position in Washington, DC. I don't know why she thought about me, but I'm glad and I have been here for almost four years.

Advice

Think about what skills you already have that an employer might be looking for. If you want to work primarily in access services, you will probably not need a second master's degree. Instead, what you will need to demonstrate is customer service skills, experience with stacks maintenance projects, management experience, and flexibility and availability to cover other responsibilities, like instruction or reference.

If you are just starting out in your career, whether you're still in library school or just graduated, say yes to every opportunity if you can afford it. Say yes to that practicum or volunteer position, start attending professional events, and begin building connections with other library professionals at other institutions. Volunteering for committees is a great way to get experience, find chances to network, and start building a body of work. Sometimes what seems like a small choice can snowball into a lifelong passion project.

For example, growing up, I was always very passionate about the freedom to read. When I started getting more involved in ALA, one of the committees I served on was the Intellectual Freedom Committee, and I was a member during a massive spike in organized book bans. Being on the committee gave me perspective on the scope of this censorship. I decided that I wanted to share some of this information with my local colleagues, so I submitted a proposal to do an overview of intellectual freedom topics at WRLC's annual meeting. The proposal was accepted, and the morning of the presentation I found a call for chapter proposals for a volume about book bans. I knew that I could take the research from the presentation and expand it into an analysis of the current wave of book challenges. This chapter was accepted and published the following year. This has led to other writing opportunities and the success of the consortium presentation has given me the confidence to speak at other conferences and conventions.

Arts and Humanities Librarian
Sarah Elizabeth Sheridan Bull

What I Do

Like some of you readers, I was recently a brand-new MLS grad, searching for a job and hoping to end up in one that I was neither overqualified nor underqualified for. I graduated from Indiana University's (IU) library program in the spring and, after a summer spent interviewing, I accepted an offer from East Tennessee State University (ETSU) for their newly created position, arts and humanities librarian.

In an academic library, librarians are traditionally given tenure track faculty rank, though this has changed much in recent years. In my case, I have faculty status without tenure, or "clinical track." This essentially means that I am exempt from most research and publication expectations and am expected to spend most of my time teaching and supporting patrons from my subject liaison areas with their research needs. That said, as I write this, I do have a survey running that will help my department examine its efficacy in serving our student population. It might be relevant to point out that, as clinical faculty I am *exempt* from conducting research and seeking publication opportunities. Exempt, but not forbidden.

Though I can only speak to my professional experience as an academic librarian, I believe these understandings about whatever position you land in are universal. My job description encompasses several essential functions, including but not limited to "staying current with discipline-specific trends" and "developing and delivering information literacy instruction." While I strive to successfully fill all of those, I do not limit myself to them, nor do I always take them at face value, and this is encouraged by my supervisor. One of my listed functions is to "initiate outreach and marketing efforts, including presenting to academic and service departments, assessing user needs, and developing new library instruction, workshops or programs to meet the needs of the ETSU community." Through my reading of just this one function, I've justified taking charge of my institution's blog, creating a rotating virtual book display for faculty and staff, and beginning a (so far, highly successful!) campus creative writing club with another librarian in my department.

My Favorite Things

While I am a big proponent for the creative interpretation of job descriptions, there are some things that I must do as prescribed. For twenty hours of my 37.5-hour work week, I must make myself available to students through in-person and virtual reference. This generally means that for ten hours of my week, students can use the library website to make appointments to meet with me on Zoom. For another ten hours of my week, I am scheduled to be in our live reference space, where we help walk-in patrons. Fortunately, this is one of my favorite parts of my job and the reason I pursued jobs in reference, rather than in my degree specialization, archives. Because of this, I get to interact with students and faculty from all over campus, in addition to those in my specific subject areas.

Challenges

While it can be a little daunting sometimes to have a liberal arts background and often work with grad students in medicine, engineering, or physics, I enjoy the challenge and conversation that can come from these interactions, as well as the well-rounded experience they provide. As a new-career librarian in a non-tenured position, the question I seem to get asked all the time is: "Are you leaving?" I usually answer, "not any time soon," but regardless of whatever the eventual answer to that question may be, I believe it is essential to seek out challenges and to use the opportunities I have been given to get as much experience as possible.

My Career Path

Before I was a grad student at IU, I spent a gap year working in youth services at the Mishawaka Penn Harris Public Library (MPHPL). Before any of that, I was an undergraduate student, and before all of that, I was a high school student with an archivist neighbor and an interest in history. As an undergraduate, I spent a lot of time working on a lot of things that had little to do with libraries or even archives. I lost my original focus, and it wasn't really until two long, unemployed months after graduation that I began picking up part-time library applications and getting back on track. I had, in the beginning of my undergraduate experience, a vague conversation with a librarian at my university about my interest in being an archivist. She used the term "library school" to describe her training and asked if I was interested in any program, myself. As an eighteen-year-old freshman and one of the few in my family to attend college, I did not understand then that she meant graduate school, but as I went through the academic system, and as I walked into my interview with MPHPL, I spun the idea out in my mind. My undergraduate grades were good enough, and with some actual library experience to pad my CV, I regained the focus my hectic undergraduate years had fractured.

Advice

Depending on your background and where you end up (both institutionally and departmentally), prior experience in odd or seemingly unrelated jobs can play a fundamental role in how you operate professionally. From the time I was sixteen, for example, I worked in front-facing food-service jobs. This included cashiering at concession stands, working as an ice cream shop girl, and waitressing during rush seasons at a family friend's restaurant. Despite these positions providing no formal library experience, they provided me with the people skills I use regularly in my position. The ability to communicate effectively is so important when you are in a reference position, more so even than being knowledgeable about your institutional resources, journals, and databases. A librarian could know every database in the world, inside and out, but if they don't know how to properly communicate and conduct a reference interview with a patron, that knowledge means nothing.

If you have interest in becoming an academic librarian, don't discount any work or life experiences you have had that are not strictly academic. Even if you don't have them on your CV, jobs in demanding service fields like serving, bartending, or retail can add value to you as a candidate. Some library jobs are introverted, studious, and require little contact with others, but most of them require at least a degree of extraversion, the ability to reach patrons at their level, and the willingness to go out of one's comfort zone, be that socially or academically. It can take a lot to be a librarian, and maybe even more so to be a good one, but for me, the reward of seeing that "a-ha!" moment on a student's face when I pull up that perfect article or book makes it well worth it.

Collection Development Librarian

Monica Cammack

What I Do

I am lead for collection development at a community college in Texas. Although I coordinate collection development, I also participate in other domains within the library, such as instruction or online learning. My job duties include coordinating several programs to help maintain the library's collection, such as acquisitions, collection maintenance, collection budgets, and electronic reserves. For acquisitions coordination, I develop the process and make sure it is completed every year. This is a lengthy, annual process that begins with selecting books and makes sure they end up on the shelf. For collection maintenance, I create and maintain updates to the collection maintenance processes, assist in ordering materials, and work with circulation to complete collection maintenance tasks. I am also responsible for the print and e-book budget. This includes creating a formulated budget, setting up projections, and creating a budget guide. A new service the library offers is electronic reserves. I research copyright, create processes and procedures, and work with circulation to implement the electronic reserves service.

My role also requires me to coordinate several types of support. For library donations, I make sure we have sufficient storage, work with librarians to select from donation items, and assist in the acquisition process for these items. The library also offers print and electronic periodicals. I project budget costs, communicate with our Library Technical Services department for renewals, and work with circulation on annual inventory of the items.

My Favorite Things

I consider myself very fortunate in my career as a librarian. I love coming into work at my academic library and working with the collection. I feel as though the collection is a living thing that needs care, and under our care it thrives and grows. What is especially enjoyable about working with the collection is that no day is the same, and I am kept constantly busy coordinating acquisitions, donations, and periodicals.

Although I love working with both old books and new books, I prefer new books. One of my favorite aspects of this job is selecting and ordering new books for the collection. Every academic year, we order all our new books within the span of one week. When they arrive in boxes on carts, we stack them in a room. As soon as the entire order has arrived, we have a box opening party. It is like opening presents on Christmas morning.

I am always looking for ways to improve access to the collection. One such project that I especially enjoyed involved selecting, measuring, and purchasing slatwalls for the collection. Slatwalls offer a way to display books without the traditional table setup. It was a large project from start to finish, but it is very satisfying to see students walk up to the slatwalls, pick up the books, and check them out.

Challenges

One of the big challenges at a community college is that budgets are very limited. With a smaller budget, librarians must be very deliberate about what we purchase. For the collection, this means that the books we select are selected primarily to help support the courses offered on campus, as well as to help fill in gaps in the collection.

Another challenge is having a smaller staff to help with the collection. Whether it is inventory, weeding, or collection maintenance, the staff is always smaller at community colleges, so projects usually take longer to complete. With a smaller staff, we also have to wear more hats, especially as we are not departmentalized. Although I am lead for collection development, I also participate in other domains in the library, such as research instruction. However, I feel these challenges benefit me because I get to build my skills in different areas of the profession.

My Career Path

I never intended to become a librarian. When I entered college, I was undecided about what my major would be. I considered a field in nursing or even computer programming. My mother suggested teaching. She was an academic librarian at the time, but before that, she was a teacher. So, I decided to earn my degree in education. After I graduated, I became an elementary teacher and taught for seven years in public schools. I loved helping students learn and grow. However, as the stress of the teaching field became overwhelming, I decided to follow my mother's pathway once again. I earned my MLS degree and became an academic librarian. During this time, my triplet sister Noël and my older sister Lisa also became librarians at public libraries. Sometimes patrons are amused to learn that we are a family of librarians.

What has surprised me about my job is how much I have learned and grown in my profession. I have come to realize that the more skills I acquire, the more confident I feel in the profession.

Advice

The field of librarianship has so many different and interesting areas, and it is important to find an area in a field you are passionate about. For example, when I started library school, I wanted to be an elementary school librarian. Through my internship, I discovered that was not the right path for me. After I earned my degree, I obtained a position as a part-time librarian at an academic library. It was then that I knew this was the type of library where I would be happy. I loved everything about academic librarianship, even the mundane tasks. I had finally found my happy place, where I still am today. If you are interested in a certain area in libraries, I recommend an internship or volunteer work to help you determine if it is right for you.

Collections Care Coordinator
Shelby Strommer

What I Do

I oversee the preventative preservation of the library's materials. This includes collection-level activities like environmental monitoring, integrated pest management, storage and housing, and disaster planning and response. I also serve as the first point of contact for treatment and repair of our paper-based circulating collections and oversee commercial library binding.

The collections storage environment, including the temperature and relative humidity, impacts the rate of deterioration of our materials, as well as the likelihood of mold outbreaks and pest infestations. We monitor the environment in our spaces, especially where special collections are stored, to help ensure the long-term integrity of our materials. Integrated pest management is an ongoing and proactive process designed to prevent, monitor, identify, and control infestations. A wide variety of insects eat paper, glue, leather, and other organic materials, so integrated pest management plays an important role in safeguarding our collections. Disaster planning and response is another important aspect of large-scale collections care.

My role includes maintaining our written disaster plan and ensuring staff are trained and know what to do in case of an emergency that impacts our materials.

We also treat individual items, especially circulating materials from our general collection, not special collections. When circulating items need preservation treatment, we decide whether they should be sent out to a vendor for commercial rebinding, or whether we can repair the item in house. We also create and purchase custom enclosures to protect brittle and fragile items.

I coordinate the collections care activities, which means I supervise the staff and students who complete most of the hands-on work such as collecting environmental data and performing minor repairs. A lot of my time is spent writing emails, creating documentation, attending meetings, and participating in committees within my institution and in professional groups. Since I work in an academic library, there is also an expectation that I participate in professional development activities, which could include conference attendance, research, publishing, or presenting on topics related to my position.

My Favorite Things

I really enjoy working with physical collection items, performing minor repairs, and especially creating custom enclosures. I spend most of my time coordinating the collections care activities and supervising the staff who do the hands-on work, so I don't always have time to do the more fun tasks. Luckily, I have a supportive supervisor who encourages me to pursue my professional interests and make time for the parts of my job that I enjoy the most.

I've been surprised to discover one of the most rewarding aspects of my job is the chance to work with and mentor student employees. In a previous institution I primarily supervised undergraduate students. They weren't necessarily interested in libraries or information science, so we focused on developing transferable skills that could help them in any profession. Work experiences that demonstrate practicing attention to detail, communication skills, teamwork, and adaptability are useful for the students to have on their resumes, no matter whether they want to be a computer programmer, an art historian, or a human resources professional.

I've also been fortunate to work in institutions that have information science graduate programs, which gives us the ability to provide hands-on job experience to students that are actively looking to join the profession. It's been a pleasure to work with our graduate students, learn about their interests and goals, and help them gain the skills and experiences that will help them in the future. It's exciting to see them grow and develop into our future colleagues in the field.

Challenges

Working in such a large institution with so many collections means that our work is never done. In some ways, that's an advantage because I'm never bored. It can be difficult to juggle competing priorities, and some people, me included, may be more prone to trying to do too much and risk burning out. We're also constrained by limited budgets and staff time, so it can be difficult to balance the needs of the collections and wants of the collection managers with those limited resources. Sometimes there are too many fires to put out, and I have to decide what is the most on fire at the moment.

My Career Path

When I first went to graduate school, I was particularly interested in working in historical collections in museums or archives. I only applied to programs that had archives or preservation courses and ended up specializing in the preservation of information track. My jobs and internships during school were in small museums with unique collections, but after graduation I found it was hard to find full-time, permanent positions in museums. My first professional position was in an academic library, and my experiences were still helpful because there is so much overlap in the principles and best practices of libraries, archives, and museums.

I know plenty of people who find archives and special collections more exciting than circulating collections. The items I work with are not necessarily historical artifacts; they are important because of the information they contain. I've developed an appreciation and pride in our circulating materials, because they are books that people actually check out and use, and they support the teaching, research, creative work, and clinical care that is done at this institution, and they are shared with partner libraries around the world.

Advice

A lot of my coursework in graduate school emphasized the importance of project management skills, collaborating with others, and adapting to changing technology. Those are definitely important skills and I use them often in my position, but I wish I had learned more about how to supervise other employees. As I mentioned above, this can be one of the most rewarding parts of my position, but I've also often found it challenging to manage staff, especially when it requires difficult but necessary conversations. I've been fortunate to have supervisors that I can rely on for support, and I've worked for two large universities with supervisor training programs. These learning experiences, combined with actual on-the-job practice, have helped me continue to develop my skills and become more confident in my leadership abilities. I recommend taking personnel management courses and workshops, whether they are through your graduate program, your employer, or elsewhere. I know from experience that having a great boss has a huge impact on job satisfaction and morale, but being a good boss requires skills and practice.

For those interested in joining the field or learning more, I would recommend checking out some professional development organizations. I've found participating in these organizations can be a great place to become familiar with concerns and new developments in the profession. They can be expensive to join, but some have reduced fees for students and early career members, and some do not require paid membership to sign up for listservs and online communities. If you have the money to join an organization and the time to serve on a committee, that can be a great way to network, provide service and resources to other members of the profession, and gain experience for your resume. State and regional professional organizations are often less expensive to join and can provide a good entry point into learning more about the profession and meeting people closer to home who have similar jobs and interests.

Anything Else?

One of the things that has surprised me the most is how valuable my previous customer service experience has been. My customers are now curators and collections managers within the library, and it's essential to maintain strong communication and good working relationships.

Community Engagement Director
Morgan Brickey-Jones

What I Do

As the director of community engagement, I manage the staffing of four public service points, two in our six-floor central library and one at each of our branch libraries on campus. Our central library is open 24/7 (during fall and spring semesters) and the overnight team is housed within my department. Additionally, our library hosts programs throughout the week. My department helps our internal colleagues with these programs through reserving the spaces on our calendars, checking in student attendees, providing supplies, and so on. We develop the content and schedule staffing for the multitude of new student orientation sessions throughout the year, mostly in the summer months. We also support heritage month programming by developing relationships and supplementing the programming provided by other campus offices. I help provide direction for programming efforts, hire and train staff, as well as meet with the team to coordinate our staffing and deliver messaging from the library executive team.

My Favorite Things

I enjoy the fast pace of the position; there is always something going on and problems to solve. I like how much I get to interact with our student employees (we have over fifty student employees in my department) and how often I see our student users. I enjoy the hiring process for new full-time staff; most staff on my team are entry level, so it's nice to see the beginning of their journey in libraries. My department, because we are so forward facing, is a collaborator with many other library entities, so I meet with my peers often to discuss how we can best serve our student users.

Challenges

The flow of faculty, students, and staff in our building never ceases! It can be hard to sit down and do any planning for the future because there is always an immediate need. I find it very difficult to plan long-range departmental goals in the way that some of my fellow directors can for their departments. Additionally, my role is different from theirs, as a major element of my job is being available for my employees. Sometimes I need to cover shifts; other times I need to answer a facility-related question at 7:00 p.m. I need to have Microsoft Teams on my phone and need to have ample flexibility in my personal schedule.

My Career Path

My path has not really diverted from libraries since I discovered library science was a degree option. I took on internships in several types of libraries during graduate school, and after I graduated, I was fortunate to find a full-time paraprofessional job at a public library. I was quickly promoted to a librarian role and continued in public libraries for ten years. When I saw a posting for a children's librarian job in an academic library, I realized that this could provide the schedule stability (namely, fewer nights and weekends) that I was seeking. I was the K-12 librarian at the University of Texas at Arlington (UTA) Libraries for over a year, and when this director position came up, I was initially hesitant. I would be giving up that same stability that I sought out initially. Then I remembered that my community of colleagues—my fellow directors, associate university librarians, and team members—were more plentiful than at the public library. Simply, there were more hands to share and support the work. I am glad I have taken this promotion, and the shift into academic libraries is one that I have welcomed into my career.

Advice

I always encourage library school students and early career librarians to seek out professional development at the district, state, and national level. I was extremely fortunate to have a few mentors at my first library who encouraged me to contribute to the library discourse by writing book reviews, writing articles about programming, and taking part in committees. By being a member of my state and national library associations, I was able to seek out funding opportunities, find chances for career growth, and make professional connections I still lean on today.

Make the active effort to seek out joy in your work. I do not think that means you should ignore or not discuss areas in which your workplace can improve, but your customer service skills and your ability to help users are enhanced by projecting job satisfaction.

Additionally, one skill I use daily is innovative problem solving. I wholeheartedly enjoy figuring out how to make something work out—the more pieces and facets to the situation, the better. That skill has come in handy throughout my career and is one that I try to hone and develop.

Anything Else?

I was under the impression that once a librarian chose the type of library they were going to work at—academic, public, school, or special—it was a permanent decision. I assumed changing course was a task that required going back to school, getting multiple certificates, and even then, you may not be successful. That is not the case! Try to find a job that suits your pre-existing skills in the desired environment. This may require jumping in and doing a job that you are overqualified for to just get your foot in the door, but often if the job is right for you, the change can happen.

Curator
Alba Fernández-Keys

What I Do

As the borderlands curator at the University of Arizona Libraries, I am the staff member responsible for stewardship of materials related to the United States-Mexico border region: from California to Texas on the US side, and Baja California to Tamaulipas, Mexico. This means I make decisions that affect the access, availability, growth, and focus of the collections, taking into consideration the resources necessary to care for materials in the long term. I consider if and how new collections can support the research interests of university faculty, student learning, community access, and why they are important for the library to acquire. The ethical considerations of collecting are also an important part of the decision-making process.

As curator, I am also responsible for ensuring that our collections are representative of our community, and that they are visible and accessible to researchers and community members. This is done through organizing exhibitions, attending and presenting at conferences, authoring articles, creating social media posts, and answering specialized reference questions. I also teach classes aimed at familiarizing students with primary source materials and work closely with faculty and researchers on projects that use the borderlands collections.

Part of this job is very people focused. I work to build partnerships with potential donors, whether they are individuals or community groups, then cultivate those relationships in the long term as they may translate into new and important collections or other types of support. Donor cultivation is a crucial part of my job and one that may only show results many years, sometimes decades, in the future. It also means that I must attend off-site meetings and evening events on a regular basis. Donor cultivation and community networking can be institutional or external, local, regional, or international. For this reason, some travel can be expected.

There are other everyday aspects of my job like staffing the reference desk; serving on library, university, and professional organization committees; and attending staff meetings. Although less curatorially focused, these take time out of the day.

My Favorite Things

A curatorial position is ideal for someone who wishes to become an expert in a specific field and is open to getting to know members of the community and building a network. In general, I like that I'm making a long-term impact on the focus of the collections through making decisions about what will be available to researchers in, say, a hundred years. For a collection like the borderlands, that's a big responsibility because materials representing the many communities of the border have not always been included in institutional archives.

I also like that I'm able to use my creativity to find new ways to make our collections visible. My institution is exploring ways to engage the communities along the border and create a body of archival materials that represent those communities for the historians of the future.

Challenges

Building knowledge about any collection requires time and patience. This is especially challenging when one is in a new position, because the curator is expected to be the expert though they haven't yet gained that knowledge.

It can be challenging to regularly attend festivals, community events, and other external meetings. As an introvert, I need to be aware of this challenge and make time for myself. Depending on the time of year, I can expect to attend one or multiple evening, community, or donor events per week. I must remain flexible with my schedule and find balance.

My Career Path

I was an art history undergraduate and, after completing my MLS, was fortunate to find a job in an art museum library, where I started my career and progressed to leading a small department of librarians and archivists. I was not trained formally in archival practice, but I was tasked with starting an archives department. As head of a department, I was able to work closely with curators, donors, educators, and collection specialists. I was also awarded several local and federal grants.

After twenty-two years in the nonprofit world, I accepted my first academic job as borderlands curator at the University of Arizona, my alma mater. I was concerned about transferring from the art field into a new subject area but have realized that, as long as there is interest and curiosity, one can learn about collections and the history surrounding them.

There are so many differences between working at a nonprofit and an academic job that I don't think I could list them all. Most noticeable is having to go through the faculty promotion process. Although I had published and presented at conferences while in the nonprofit world, I had never been formally evaluated in this area. Transitioning to the academic world has required me to refocus and make sure I allow time for research every week.

Another transition was from collections being object focused to learning- and student-centric. In general, pedagogical considerations are more formal in the university environment. Although I had worked with classes from the local university on occasion, there is much more teaching and interaction with undergraduate students at the university.

There are defined skills that those of us with backgrounds in nonprofit work can bring to the academic environment. For one, advancement in the form of donor relations and grant writing, which is built into the work of many nonprofit staff positions. Also, the ability to complete tasks quickly and creatively under pressure.

Advice

Look for paid opportunities to gain experience in a collections environment, because you will learn about the behind-the-scenes tasks that must happen to make any collection available, either in physical or digital form. Although I now do very little, if any, cataloging or processing work, an understanding of arrangement, description, and cataloging processes is important when making decisions as it affects everything, from colleagues' workload and processes to digital and physical storage capacity to department budget.

Depending on the subject of a particular collection, the importance of language skills must be stressed. This was true in my previous job at an art museum (where I managed collections in many languages, primarily European and Asian) and it is now. In my current role, a large part of our collections are in Spanish. I communicate with donors and researchers in Spanish almost every day.

Anything Else?

Networking is a crucial part of any job. While at the museum, I always said that half of my job was knowing who could help me out in an information-related rush or emergency. Starting a job in the academic library is no different; one needs to create relationships both within the institution and outside it.

Data Librarian
Michele Hayslett

What I Do

I help people find and understand data. One thing that is unique about my job is how specialized I am. Because I work for a large university library with a long-standing dedication to data services and good financial resources, my department of six includes a variety of specializations: besides my knowledge of data management and finding and understanding numeric data, we have experts in mapping, data analysis, data visualization, and text analysis. All of us have deep backgrounds in our respective fields, and often a master's degree in that field rather than a library degree. At smaller institutions and public libraries, there might be only *one* person who works with data. In such an environment, the services available will depend on that one person's willingness and capacity to learn multiple skills.

My Favorite Things

My favorite part of my job is that I never get bored: there's always a new topic to explore, a new data source to find. I learn a great deal from patrons themselves. Plus my job involves a wide array of tasks: teaching grad students and undergraduates about data sources for a particular class assignment; buying datasets; cataloging purchases in collaboration with our technical services staff; teaching workshops about data tools like Python; assisting researchers in identifying how best to preserve their data; conducting my own research into topics that further my profession; and more.

Challenges

In my experience, librarians hear the word "data" and get alarmed. If a data librarian is in reach, they immediately get pulled in, even for questions that are not really about data. If you're reading this, I encourage you not to be scared. Data librarianship is like any other specialty. Sure, there's a lot to learn, but if you put in the work, you can do this job. If *I* could become a data librarian, *you* can.

My Career Path

I became a data librarian by accident. My first job out of library school was as a general librarian with the State Library of North Carolina (SLNC). The SLNC happens to be a coordinating agency in the Census Bureau's national State Data Center network. In that capacity, staff received many data questions from both government employees and the public for data for many different purposes: to plan local government services or businesses, to write grant proposals, to support lawsuits, and much more. We had a demographic information specialist who handled most of those questions and who taught me an enormous amount about data sources—census data in particular—but then took another job six months after I arrived. I suggested to my boss that it might be easier to hire another general librarian than one focused on demographics and she agreed, so I stepped into that role. It was a lateral move, not a promotion, but interesting work.

My only preparation was on-the-job training, mainly through colleagues and the Census Bureau's annual conferences. Library school had offered no classes in data librarianship at all, but the government information and basic reference classes provided a foundation. Really what is important in the job is doing a good reference interview, and since the US government is the largest producer of data in the world, having a grasp of how to find government information helps. While at the State Library I also gained training in how to teach adult learners, a skill I've used ever since.

About four years later, I moved into academic libraries. The questions I got from patrons became *much* more diverse. Instead of focusing mainly on census data, research topics could be about anything: statistics on recreational boating for every lake in the Midwest; the amount of coal burned in the United States in 1898; the number of farmer suicides in India between 2010 and 2020; the number of companies using a large volume of hot water across the state; and so forth (all real questions I have answered). For many (most?) of them, I had no prior knowledge of the topic, never mind expertise in it. I found that the keys to my success, though, were an openness to ongoing learning; a willingness to reach out to others who *might* know the answer; and persistence in digging into a subject. And sometimes just using common sense: it is impossible to find out how much coal was actually *burned* in 1898, but the amount sold or mined might be possible. Eventually I also developed a specialty in data management, that is, how researchers can organize and describe datasets to make them accessible to and usable by other researchers. Data curation is another subspecialty where archivists manage repositories of datasets.

Advice

Early in my career, data librarian jobs were rare. People tended to fall into that role if they worked as government information librarians or in an environment where either patrons tended to ask a lot of those types of questions or there was close proximity to a data center or research institute. Data jobs in libraries are far more common now, particularly in academe and larger public libraries. Subject librarian jobs in academic libraries have long required a second master's degree in addition to an MLS. As data librarian jobs have proliferated, employers are moving toward more formal requirements: successful applicants either need to have a library degree *plus* a master's degree in the area of specialty, for example, statistics (for data analysis) or visual design (for data visualization), or a degree in the field of specialty instead of a library degree. Job experience can be accepted instead of a degree for fewer positions; for example, with coding in a computer language like R or Python, or with demonstrated knowledge of statistical packages and data analysis through research publications or work experience in a research environment. In the past, knowledge of statistical software like SPSS or SAS was key—these days, R or Python is more important.

Most library schools now offer classes about data management and curation, and some have post-MLS certifications. For those already in the field, a bootcamp program may be enough to enable you to take on new responsibilities in these areas. For coding, though, while a bootcamp is enough to get you started, library employers will be looking for considerable full-time work experience (at least a year primarily focused on coding), or a substantial project you coded that demonstrates your skills.

Opportunities for professional engagement and development are also proliferating. For me, the best professional home is the International Association for Social Science Information Services and Technology (IASSIST, said like the words, "I assist"). Another good option is the US-based Research Data Access and Preservation Association (generally referred to as just RDAP, "R-dap"). There are also regional conferences like the Southeastern Data Librarian Symposium. These organizations can be great for getting started in data librarianship partly in terms of education from conferences about issues and sources, but also for seeing job ads on the associated web sites and email lists, and for making connections with data colleagues. Such connections can be key for new professionals, providing a "hive-mind" of knowledge and experience to consult when encountering new topics or thorny situations.

Anything Else?

There are some pieces of advice I often offer those new to the job market:

1. Be flexible: if you can't be flexible geographically, be flexible in the type of job you're seeking. You never know what a given job might lead to. Also be aware, there's little chance for advancement in academe unless you can be flexible about moving.
2. Try to get work experience before you graduate. On-the-job experience in the kind of job you're applying for will highlight your application, and such positions often connect you with people who are willing to give you professional references.
3. Research the organization with which you'll be interviewing. If they provide a list of people you'll meet during the interview (especially if you'll be meeting with multiple groups), devise questions appropriate to each person or group. Good questions make me take a closer look at a candidate.
4. Practice a presentation. If you have to do a presentation during an interview, ask mentors or librarians you may work with if you can present to them as a practice audience. You'll not only get over jitters, but you'll also see the flow of your presentation, and likely your audience will give you practical feedback you can incorporate to improve your talk.

Dean of Libraries
Linda Marie Golian-Lui

What I Do

As the dean of a research academic library system with multiple libraries, a typical day includes many meetings, numerous phone calls, rubber chicken catered meals, massive numbers of emails, a few urgent text messages, and considerable time reading, composing, and editing documents. It involves being the final decision maker for countless organizational issues.

My most important resource is time. I always need more time; thus, I need to understand my leadership values and to employ strong organization, efficiency, and prioritization skills to use my time wisely. I need assistance, and my trustworthy administrative assistant facilitates my schedule and keeps me on track. The most crucial part of my day is crafting time to talk with the abundance of people who need "just a few minutes" so that I can assure them that they are making sound decisions, provide my advice and support for the options being considered, and mentor others in their unique library leadership journey.

I work a nontraditional schedule of approximately fifty-five-plus hours, seven days a week. My annual assignment includes, but is not limited to, the following:

- overseeing all organizational operations including collection management, assessment, strategic planning, accreditation, facilities maintenance, human resources
- representing the university at events held by the chamber of commerce
- participating in service organizations like Rotary
- serving on various advisory boards
- meeting with donors
- joining fundraising affairs

- appearing at award ceremonies (including graduations)
- speaking at invited occasions
- joining community service activities (such as an Alzheimer's memory walk)

I use weekends to catch up on critical assignments, complete scholarships, and address my leadership obligations associated with professional librarianship service commitments, such as serving on the American Library Association Council. Like other university faculty, my annual evaluation combines librarianship, administration, service, and scholarship.

It is a complex and busy schedule that is modified daily. This career best fits someone with an extroverted personality style who can be flexible and is passionate about what they do. Luckily, I love being a librarian, working in higher education, creating avenues for people to engage with their library, and making an impact through service.

My primary responsibility is simple: provide quality library collections, services, and facilities that support my university's mission. I cannot control the funding levels for library collections or facilities. However, I can impact organizational morale and create a shared vision of expecting excellence and engagement from my organization's members with our resources. A great library team ensures that all users are aware of and utilize their library's collections, services, and facilities.

The most critical organizational asset is people: library faculty, staff, interns, volunteers, donors, and student employees. A successful library system cultivates a passionate and engaged team that cares about the how and why of what they do. They care about each other. My most important job is to foster an organizational culture of trust, appreciation, empowerment, respect, safety, gratitude, kindness, patron engagement, service excellence, personal responsibility, calculated risk taking, professional growth, and leadership development.

My Favorite Things

There are two aspects of my job that I especially like: engaging a wide variety of users to use their library and mentoring the next generation of library leaders.

Today's effective academic libraries embrace andragogy (adult learning theory) and support different learning needs/preferences by cultivating various spaces and services. They are a core campus learning/researching/engagement hub instead of the book warehouse filled with quiet study spaces of the past. It is my job to ensure that the physical and electronic spaces are open, inviting, and supportive of different learning styles, preferences, and needs. I enjoy hosting various engagement events, such as donuts with the dean, to draw new users into physical library spaces that showcase collections and services that users might need to know.

I also love mentoring and providing development opportunities for all employees. I enjoy supporting employees aspiring to take on new challenges and leadership roles. I create opportunities for those on a journey to become professional librarians and support librarians considering a future deanship. I have an obligation to the library profession by assisting in developing tomorrow's academic library leaders today by providing these learning possibilities.

Challenges

While academic research deans are constantly negotiating for more funding to support collections, services, spaces, staffing, and the development of their team, my biggest challenges are managing the resource of time (especially my own); developing an organizational culture that will make the library system successful; and navigating the current political world of library censorship.

I complete my specific tasks in between the necessary meetings and networking events of my full schedule. I make my early mornings, evenings, and weekends sacred when I attempt to focus on my assignments. It only sometimes works.

Creating a thriving organizational culture takes years of investment. It is a road filled with detours and potholes that one bad decision or situation can quickly destroy.

Recent political changes and censorship attempts concerning academic research library collections are a new challenge to navigate. The attacks by individuals, organized groups, and local/state legislators pushing agendas/legal changes oppose the foundational core values of anti-censorship and intellectual freedom held dear to our profession. It is an area I struggle with daily.

My Career Path

I considered academic research librarianship as a profession once I started working as a federal work-study student in college. This turned into a full-time staff position where I was promoted several times and had hands-on experience in cataloging, serials, acquisitions, collection development, weeding, binding, library instruction, reference, stacks maintenance, exhibits, accreditation, library automation, interlibrary loan, assessment, internal communications/newsletters, and library events/programming. These experiences gave me a comprehensive leadership understanding that formal education cannot provide.

The best advice I ever received was to join the New Members Round Table (NMRT) of the American Library Association. I credit NMRT with providing me with the foundational structure to eventually become a servant library leader, an effective manager, and an academic dean. NMRT provided a gateway to learning the library profession while providing unimaginable opportunities, experiences, networking, and mentoring.

As a woman trying to break the pink glass ceiling of academic leadership, the doctorate was a necessary weapon. My doctoral chair fully supported my desire to customize my higher education administration program to focus on academic librarianship.

When I achieved my first university librarian (a.k.a. dean) position, I continued to speak bimonthly with my mentor, who wisely advised me that my first deanship would be a learning opportunity and that I would make numerous mistakes. I needed to take criticism effectively and learn from my mistakes. I excelled at making mistakes!

When I wasn't looking, my dream deanship job came knocking. I returned to Florida as dean of libraries for Florida Atlantic University after a twenty-three-year hiatus from my alma mater. My library journey of over forty years of research library experience and formal education has come full circle, and I have never been happier.

What surprises me the most about the profession is how librarianship's core values and functions have always remained strong. Libraries have always been about systematically gathering and organizing information in discoverable ways for the users. The profession has always strived to provide materials that provide various perspectives on issues so that users can formulate their own opinions and preferences. Within my lifetime, academic library spaces have radically changed, but providing space for users to interact with materials is still a core function.

Advice

Many librarians aspire to senior-level leadership positions, including deanship, but few have a business perspective and experiences that enable them to be effective in these positions. My best advice to someone aspiring to become an academic library dean is to complete a doctorate in higher education administration/leadership. The duties of a dean are like those of a CEO running a multimillion-dollar company. Success requires understanding how higher education works, the essentials of educational fundraising, managing a multimillion-dollar budget, compassionate human resources leadership, knowledge of the federal grant process, and how to conduct/complete/communicate research.

Anything Else?

My journey as an academic research library dean is a continuous process of experience, education, and reflection. It is a meandering path that has taught me to incorporate strong business practices, embrace lifelong learning, lead with a servant leadership philosophy, foster an organizational culture of kindness with gratitude, value all library personnel, and live the Rotary International motto of service above self.

Digital Archivist
Andrew McDonnell

What I Do

I help my institution preserve materials that are born-digital. By born-digital, I mean materials that were never physical objects. Rather than files that are scans of a paper or physical object, the materials I work with were originally created in a computer or a "computing environment." That includes more materials than you might at first think: digital photographs, Word documents, videos, websites, emails, databases, 3D objects, and all sorts of digital files that arrive at the archives. They can arrive in innumerable forms, everything from a shoebox of CDs buried among forty-eight boxes of paper records to a well-organized donation via Dropbox.

It can be difficult to romanticize the digital, but the new historical record, the one that really tells the story of how and who we are, is digital. Preserving that record for current and future generations is the meat of my work. Tangibly, that means many things. My first few months in the profession were spent primarily doing two things: figuring out how we were already doing this work and reading more about how we should be doing this work so our institution can continue to evolve. I am not starting at square one, as our library has a significant digital collection, but calculating what square I was standing on took some work.

My day-to-day work has significant variety. In addition to the typical work of an academic archivist (such as assisting researchers at a reference desk and attending meetings), I spend time processing new digital donations, reappraising old donations by hunting down digital material that we only have on physical media (such as floppy disks or DVDs), and building workflows to clarify how we handle all of these varied materials.

I work in a dark room without much natural light, as nearby co-workers spend a fair amount of time digitizing physical items, but when I'm dealing with digital materials on network drives or conducting research, I often have the flexibility to either work from home or take my laptop to scenic parts of the campus with good Wi-Fi, so I enjoy considerable flexibility. Because my role is a tenure-track faculty position, in addition to the work of processing and in-person reference, I also have scholarly research responsibilities and opportunities to travel to conferences and events relevant to the work.

My Favorite Things

One rewarding aspect of my job is something that not all archivists look forward to: unexpected problems. Almost once a week, one or another of my colleagues will approach with a random box or item that arrived alongside a physical collection. Or they will be working with materials they thought had been thoroughly processed, only to stumble across a disk or hard drive or some other digital object that was not listed in the original finding aid. They come to me with apology in their eyes and say, "I'm sorry to do this to you." But to be honest, sorting those materials out is one of my favorite things.

During my first month on the job, my supervisor appeared with a box containing many smaller boxes, and said, "Well, we found this …" It contained over 600 floppy disks. People working at large institutions, I am told, encounter far larger versions of this with regularity.

All this work might appear to an outsider to belong more to an information technology (IT) department than to an archivist, and certainly technical skills are necessary to do the work. More important, though, is an understanding of information organization, and a willingness to learn a little about many different technical areas and communicate with specialists who are far more technically proficient than I am. As a result, the opportunities to continue learning are endless, something I truly value.

Challenges

A challenge inherent in my role is that most people consider archives to be the place where you go to encounter physical artifacts. The public fetishizes the hushed reading room, white gloves, perfect gray boxes, and the encounter with the actual objects once held or even created by the historic figure of a hallowed past. Who can blame them? I often feel the same. Thus, there can be an overarching challenge of sharing your work in a meaningful way and gathering newly created materials that most people don't recognize as possessing historical value. That is my largest abstract challenge.

More tangibly, digital storage at a large scale is expensive. I am fortunate to work at a library with significant resources, but even so, there is a misconception that the cloud offers us unlimited storage in a way that our metal shelves cannot. Digital storage is an annual recurring cost, one that is only growing, so determining what digital materials you are going to keep becomes a very real and significant challenge.

In addition, as digital archives are so much younger than physical archives, there is no one perfect method or authority that I can point to for how to handle born-digital materials. There are excellent resources, but with so many in the field working with different software, different computer operating systems, different IT staff, and different materials, the literature on how to do this work can feel scattershot. Many of the attempts to provide overarching guidance rely on abstractions to accommodate the variety of tools and files we have access to, so they can feel frustratingly vague or theoretical to someone just getting started.

My Career Path

My career path has proven helpful in ways that are not intuitive. Prior to this job I taught high school English for over ten years, helped run a digital multimedia lab at a university, and worked in communication and marketing for five years. While much of the work I now do is technical, my experience teaching and communicating concepts in a clear and appealing manner is enormously helpful as a digital archivist. Born-digital materials can be daunting to anyone, and many of my coworkers deal with them infrequently enough that they must relearn processes, software, and bits of coding every time they dip back into digital archives. Recognizing this, I have spent considerable time making my workflow not just legible, but friendly, so that my colleagues can do the same sort of work in a consistent manner.

Advice

You should definitely pursue an MA or MS in library and information science if you want this type of position, but I also recommend pursuing practical experience with a variety of software and ideally a variety of archives. Working in a staff position in a digital media lab introduced me to a wide variety of audio, video, and photo software and the sorts of media they produce. I also had an internship during graduate school at a film studio, and that introduced me to a combination of digital asset management and archival tools that I could never have garnered in a classroom nor an academic archive.

Digital Preservation and Project Management Librarian
Ira Revels

What I Do

For a significant part of my career, I had the privilege of serving as the digital project manager for the Cornell University Library (CUL) Historically Black Colleges & Universities (HCBU) Digital Project at Cornell's academic library in New York. In my role, I was more than just a manager; I was a visionary and a catalyst for change. I orchestrated a multi-institutional collaborative digitization initiative that was generously funded by the Andrew W. Mellon Foundation. But my responsibilities went far beyond oversight; I was deeply involved in the instructional design of the digitization workshops, labs, and the digitization of invaluable archival materials in both print and audio formats. My work was not just a job; it was a calling. I had a burning desire to make a significant impact on Black libraries and archives. To support one project objective to teach digital preservation, I taught twenty-first-century librarianship skills to HBCU librarians who worked on digital preservation projects that focused on the rich founding history and culture of HBCUs.

As a project manager in a matrix organization, I wore multiple hats. I was the researcher who delved into grant opportunities, the diplomat who identified and engaged stakeholders, and the bridge that forged invaluable relationships between CUL and the HBCU Library Alliance. I have also co-authored a grant proposal that successfully secured $1.225 million across three phases. Once the grant was funded, I became the steward of the project's scope, the guardian of its budget, and the mentor responsible for training HBCU Library staff. I also served as a digitization expert, providing guidance on technical, metadata, copyright, and other project issues.

A significant portion of my role involved travel. I was often on the road, visiting our partner institutions, particularly the Atlanta University Center and various HBCU libraries across the Eastern United States. My expertise was not confined to the United States; it also took me abroad, where I was invited to attend conferences and provide high-level consultation to digitization projects in Ghana and Ethiopia.

The essence of my work transcended mere technical skills; it was preserving the legacy of CUL and the HBCU Library Alliance. I was deeply involved in high-stakes fundraising, an often-overlooked yet critical aspect of project management in academia and the nonprofit sectors. My work had a ripple effect, impacting the broader field of digital preservation by fostering strategic collaborations for sustainable collections.

My Favorite Things

The role was a perfect fit for someone like me—an adventurous, quick learner who enjoys multitasking, thinking strategically, and solving complex problems. The joy I derived from uplifting people and solving intricate problems through effective communication, strategy, and fundraising was immeasurable. I enjoyed being a generalist, meeting new people, providing technology solutions, and imparting training. If you find this appealing, then I would encourage you to find opportunities to manage library and archival projects, particularly technical projects.

Challenges

However, the role was not without its challenges and realities. Work-life balance was a rare commodity; I often found myself buried in work, with little time for personal chores like laundry. I traveled almost as much as a salesperson.

The first phase of my project began during pivotal moments in US history, among them the emergence of an innovative technology known as Bitcoin that would decentralize finance. It was only two years after Hurricane Katrina and I had taken it upon myself to move my mom out of Louisiana, having left only nine days before the disaster. As a New Orleanian, my family and friends were seriously affected. It was particularly challenging facing growing demands on my time for my mom, who was diagnosed with Alzheimer's at the beginning of my project. Each of those topics and issues would have a lasting impact on my life, art, and work in the future.

My Career Path

My mother was a significant influence, nurturing my passion for technology and art. Today, I am an entrepreneur leveraging emerging technologies like artificial intelligence and blockchain to solve complex problems. I am also a visual artist, creating with technology, and at times, canvas.

My career path has been a tapestry of experiences. I was recruited by a librarian couple during my internship at Northwestern State University library while seeking an MEd in educational technology. I was encouraged to apply for an MLIS Fellowship at the University of Pittsburgh and received the E. J. Josey Scholarship. While it wasn't enough to cover books, I figured that if I got that far, I could find a job. After leaving Cornell, I moved to Connecticut and got a job as a program director of the Hartford Public Library. I had to leave that position after three months because my mom was dying. I then decided to start my own strategic management consulting company. I quickly focused on acquiring skills using newer technologies, workflow, and certifications in Agile and Scrum. I also began writing grants for clients. During the past three years, my clients and businesses have been awarded approximately $10 million dollars.

Advice

In this ever-evolving field, resting on one's laurels is not an option. In addition to having a strong educational background, I always recommend gaining certifications in emerging technologies and project management methodologies. Networking is another cornerstone; my professional connections opened doors to international consulting opportunities.

If you're eyeing a role similar to mine, remember: You are the captain of the ship. Trust but verify your resources, be it people, money, or tools. Your intuition, combined with your skills, can lead you to unprecedented heights.

Digital Scholarship Librarian
Julia Stone

What I Do

My role is a remote two-year Institute of Museum and Library Services (IMLS) grant-funded, nontenure library faculty position focused on outreach, instruction, and digital projects. My work involves outreach for CollectionBuilder, a free, open-source digital collections framework developed by librarians at the University of Idaho. I create documentation, walkthroughs, and videos for CollectionBuilder and train others on building digital collection websites. I also assist with teaching and promoting CollectionBuilder at conferences. I am working on launching additional community-building initiatives as well, including a blog, Slack channel, and Google Group.

I also assist library and information science (LIS) instructors with curriculum planning, train them how to use CollectionBuilder, and present in-class sessions on CollectionBuilder as part of our curriculum development program. I help administer our LIS Student Program in which a cohort of eight students learn CollectionBuilder, create digital projects, and document their experiences. I also oversee technical training and assist with developing digital research projects conducted by student and faculty fellows as part of our Center for Digital Inquiry and Learning (CDIL) fellowship programs.

My Favorite Things

One rewarding aspect of my position is seeing a student's research come to life as a digital scholarship project. I also enjoy meeting and collaborating with other information professionals via Zoom meetings and at in-person and virtual conferences. One of my favorite ongoing collaborations has been my work with public scholarship librarian Kate Thornhill at the University of Oregon (UO). I assisted Kate with integrating CollectionBuilder into her for-credit humanities research data management course. I created a course module about CollectionBuilder and taught the students how to use CollectionBuilder in person. I enjoyed connecting with students and assisting them with their digital collections. Kate and I are also going to partner to write a case study about our collaboration, which relates to another favorite part of my job: working with others on research.

I am grateful that my position enables me to collaborate with colleagues at the University of Idaho at other institutions on research and writing projects. Working with others helps to keep me motivated and I enjoy giving and receiving feedback from my collaborators. I am excited to continue collaborating with other University of Idaho librarians on a case study about creating a digital collection site for our library's board game collection.

In addition to the collaborative aspects of my work, I also like working on independent projects, such as creating high quality, detailed metadata for digital collections and customizing websites to ensure user accessibility. I enjoy being a part of a team that is focused on increasing open access to data, research, and information.

Challenges

One main challenge is that my position is 100 percent remote. As a remote worker, I often miss out on opportunities for casual in-person conversation. However, it helps that some of my colleagues and I have informal coffee Zoom meetings and conversational Microsoft Teams chats.

Another challenge of remote work is creating a productive process for giving and receiving feedback. Originally, I presented projects to the full CollectionBuilder team, and they all gave verbal feedback to me simultaneously. However, this approach relied on my ability to take notes quickly and I worried that I would forget things that were mentioned. Instead, I found it more helpful to have written feedback from other team members that I could refer to later. Therefore, sharing documents and giving team members the opportunity to write comments and suggestions became one of our effective feedback strategies.

Balancing many projects and responsibilities at once can be stressful as well. I sometimes struggle with context switching during the day, such as when I need to stop working on an independent project (e.g., writing an article, working on a website) to attend a Zoom meeting or give a presentation.

What helps me the most is to set aside meeting-free days so I can focus my attention on completing other projects. To manage my workload effectively, I also create to-do lists, prioritize tasks based on how pressing they are, and ask for more time on projects when necessary.

My Career Path

Before becoming a librarian, I was a nonprofit communications professional and magazine editor. I have always enjoyed writing, but I missed helping students like I did when I was a tutor during my undergraduate studies, so I began working as a writing tutor at a community college. As a tutor, I helped students outline their research papers and then directed them to the library to find information. I found myself wanting to help students with the information-seeking process, which led me to pursue librarianship. I was inspired to apply for my current position because it perfectly combined my marketing background with my library background. I use transferable skills from my communications career in my current job, such as email outreach, social media, and writing for the web.

I have discovered many things about myself and the library field during my career so far. One thing I have learned is that librarians need to stay up to date on the latest technologies and best practices. Technology changes quickly and our patrons rely on us to help them navigate new technologies. I have also discovered that I am interested in metadata and digital collection development. Although I entered the field wanting to do public service, I have enjoyed the technical side of librarianship as well.

Advice

For those who are interested in a job in digital scholarship, I recommend gaining skills and taking courses in digital libraries, marketing for libraries, web development, and metadata. I also suggest getting involved with organizations like the Digital Library Federation (DLF), Code4Lib, and library consortia. Joining organizations is a great way to build a network, learn relevant skills, and find research collaborators.

Mentoring programs also can be beneficial for an early-career librarian. I participated in the Association of College and Research Libraries (ACRL)

E. J. Josey Spectrum Mentor Program and the Asian Pacific American Library Association (APALA) Mentoring Program. My mentors, who worked in academic libraries, provided helpful career advice and empathetic support for my personal experience as a biracial Asian American.

Attending conferences and workshops is also a great way to keep up with the latest in the field. I have attended American Library Association (ALA) conferences, including the Spectrum Scholar Leadership Institute. I took a course on coding fundamentals at the Digital Humanities Summer Institute (DHSI), which helped enhance my web development skills. Many conferences have student scholarships to help with funding as well.

As a graduate student, I wish I had received advice about how to change career paths. I have learned that initially choosing one path in librarianship does not mean your career trajectory is set in stone. As someone who has already worked at many types of libraries during my career, I can verify that it is possible to switch from one type of institution to another. You also can switch from public services to technical services, or vice versa. The important thing is recognizing the transferable skills you have gained and being able to describe these skills effectively. As a student, conduct informational interviews to learn more about the work other librarians in the field are doing. Not only will this help you build connections, but it may also help you decide if a certain career path is right for you.

Electronic Resource Management Librarian
Lucy Campbell

What I Do

As library collections are increasingly born digital, management of the e-resource life cycle has become paramount to successful service delivery. Electronic resource management (ERM) librarianship is a unique lens through which to approach collection curation. As with print holdings, selection is typically managed by subject liaisons and collection librarians. However once acquired, e-resources must be organized and presented in usable engaging ways. This is the ultimate responsibility of the ERM librarian and necessitates mastery of a range of skills.

E-resource discovery requires understanding of library management systems, catalogs, discovery services, and search tools. Some common ways I improve discovery include the A-Z database list, management of discipline-specific research guides, and content metadata. There are also emerging trends in resource discovery: for example, integration in learning platforms and internet browsers, interactive gamification of resources, and the growing field of digital humanities. Increasingly, technology has become a research in its own right, and developing ways for resources to play a role in this emerging landscape is both fun and challenging.

Another critical aspect of ERM is access and authentication. Maintaining the security of electronic resources, managing user verification, and protecting against unauthorized access ensure the integrity of collections. ERM librarians do not handle these issues alone but often have specific responsibilities. For example, at my institution I manage the EZProxy configuration file and stanzas for off-campus authentication, while campus information technology administers security systems.

Operating in a huge and complex information environment inevitably results in a certain level of reactionary response work. Problems such as resource access, bad data, or lost connections are reported and then investigated. Key to this process is understanding why something isn't functioning, and who can fix it.

My Favorite Things

Two areas of ERM I find particularly rewarding are the satisfying solo achievements when I resolve tricky problem reports, and the collaborative nature of group initiatives.

Solving problem reports is very similar to serving on a reference desk, but instead of being in-person you're essentially a digital detective. It requires a deep understanding of the ecosystem in which you are operating and is intellectually stimulating, especially if approached as a game of wits. Do you like puzzles that keep your mind productive? With ERM things are constantly shifting and it's your job to stay one step ahead. Although ERM is not a traditional student-facing role in academic libraries, it is a crucial one in which you will communicate with students, faculty, and staff on a daily basis. ERM librarians provide support to users for accessing and troubleshooting electronic resources, making them essential for positive user experience. Electronic resources allow for 24/7 remote access, which is crucial for serving the needs of a diverse and often geographically dispersed academic community. If you enjoy helping people find information and overcome technical hurdles, this can be gratifying. For me it is personally satisfying when the error screen is replaced with a needed resource.

That said, you might imagine ERM to involve sitting at a computer for eight long hours each day, battling code and running analyses. Although that is undeniably an aspect of the job, the inherently high levels of camaraderie surprised me. The nature of the job necessitates ERM librarians work closely with library staff, faculty, and vendors to keep the ship sailing smoothly through ever-changing waters. As someone who leans extroverted on the personality scale, I find teamwork very energizing. Shared projects are enjoyable and foster a sense of moving in the same direction to meet shared goals. Ultimately what we do is for our patrons first and foremost. Keeping that philosophy at the heart of everything makes the work rewarding, and celebrating our wins collectively enriches the workplace. At my institution 60 percent of the library's collection is digital. It is a complex landscape of management that I do not and could not handle alone.

Challenges

Two of the biggest challenges working in ERM are directing the deluge and communicating accomplishments.

Because the work of e-resource management is often behind the scenes, communicating your work to others can also be challenging. In fact, when you are doing your job well, your work should be invisible. Patrons access content smoothly and find exactly what they are looking for with the least number of clicks possible. Finding, accessing, and retrieving electronic information should function like a swan gliding effortlessly across a pond. Your work is the swan's feet hidden below the surface, furiously paddling away. That work is required to build a functioning system, and it is almost limitless. There are always tweaks and improvements to be made, and new products to be trialed and integrated. Unlike an instruction librarian who can directly assess their teaching, it can be challenging to tell this story, or to bring the human factor into the work. Although you might be impacting thousands of library users every day, it is hard to capture how exactly your work improved their experience. Project management tools and before-and-after assessments are your best bets for telling these stories meaningfully. Befriend an assessment librarian and learn some data visualization tools. Nevertheless, the reality of fixing problems and putting out fires is that we often seek to resolve quickly rather than stop and thoughtfully capture the process. My advice would be to slow down and direct the deluge.

I won't lie: the curve is steep coming out of the MLIS degree. Although there has been significant progress in recent years, the academy lags behind practice in addressing e-resource management. New graduates are often underprepared for routine work expectations, and heightened requirements for on-the-job learning are exacerbated by institutional quirks. Although systems and concepts may be universal, every institution will fudge things to fit their unique characteristics and needs. As ERM librarian it is my job to not just understand this landscape, but also understand why it is so, and communicate that to other stakeholders.

Rapid technological change means ERM is an area of librarianship requiring dedication to lifelong learning. The tools I use today will not be the same in five years' time. So there's a lot happening all the time and you must pick and choose your battles. For many in the field, this is what draws them to academic librarianship—that desire to research and learn throughout their career. If that's you, ERM is a great area to consider.

My Career Path

For the first decade of my career, I was a solo librarian in a small academic library. One of the positive aspects of that was the chance to try my hand at all kinds of library work and realize what was rewarding and where I thrived. The sudden move to remote work during the pandemic necessitated a focus on electronic resources that really grabbed my attention. I always wanted to work in academic libraries but wasn't so keen on teaching. Technical services has been a great fit and I would argue it has great job security.

Advice

E-resource management takes the essential principles of librarianship and applies them to the digital landscape. The values, ethics, and competencies we learn in library school are just as relevant but require additional considerations. The personal qualities commonly seen in those interested in librarianship are just as applicable—a love of knowledge, strong organizational skills, and a core belief that information wants to be free.

Electronic Resources and Cataloging Librarian
Daniel Stevens

What I Do

Despite my title, I am essentially the "technical services department" for Edens Library at Columbia College. Most of my time is spent purchasing, cataloging, and processing physical resources; researching, purchasing, and managing electronic resources; and ensuring the accessibility of our resources by working with database providers on setting up single-sign-on authentications and making sure the links are available and active on our website. I also pull usage statistics for databases and electronic resources when deciding whether to renew subscriptions, as well as retrieve statistics for these and physical resources for annual reports that assist with accreditation. In South Carolina we have Partnership Among South Carolina Academic Libraries (PASCAL), a consortium with a shared library services platform, rapid physical resource sharing within the state, a shared e-book program, and collaborative collections. PASCAL assists consortium libraries with inputting new database purchases into our cataloging system and assisting with access issues as needed.

I recently started working on ensuring that some of the electronic resources we have had access to on our campus for several years are actually in our systems. Because of past transitions between several library systems and changes in technical services library faculty over the years, we discovered that some items fell through the cracks when swapping platforms. This proves that when you start a new job, you can't always just assume that everything was squared away and set up perfectly for you. Working through these things may also allow you to find better, or newer, ways to do the process, which may not have been possible before.

Another smaller part of my job is teaching. My position is a tenure-track faculty position and I have been teaching first year classes that focus on information literacy, which are held every spring semester on our campus.

As a part of my job duties, I work closely with our access services manager and student workers on stacks maintenance, call number and cataloging corrections, shelf reading, book covering, and other collection management duties. I have also been weeding our physical collection in an effort to reduce the square footage of shelving in our building to allow for more collaborative spaces for our students, and have also been relocating books that should be in our oversized books, juvenile collection, or our newly created "leisure reads" collection.

Due to the changing roles of libraries, and the small size of our institution, I have also added a duty that lies outside the scope of electronic resources and cataloging. This new duty considers equity of resources and environments with the student in mind. In this role, I help promote student academic success by ensuring equitable access of resources (whether that is physical books, electronic books, technological items needed for their academic success, etc.) across the entirety of our campus community, as well as equitable access to our library environments, including virtual library space for our online learners. Libraries must stay ahead of the curve by reshaping librarian roles as technology progresses and needs change.

Favorite Things

A favorite part of my job would have to be the processing and organization of the books in our system. Another current favorite thing of mine isn't something most libraries/librarians go through. Our library is currently undergoing renovations on one of our floors, and we are using this time to remove books, create more space for our students, and clean up our archives room. During this project I started finding gifted books from a notable name from our campus's history, and because of these finds, I decided to create a special collection in our archives room that holds all gifted books from this notable name. We haven't found all of the books yet, but at this time it looks like this special collection will have at least 500 titles. The opportunity to learn the history of an institution you're working at while doing something special for the institution isn't something you get to do often.

Challenges

When deciding to work in a small academic setting, you need to be aware that you'll be wearing many "job hats" (and often trading hats with others as needed). I wouldn't necessarily say that this is a downside or struggle, but, depending on the person, it can be a hurdle. I could almost say this is also one of my favorite aspects of my position, as I enjoy the opportunity to try my hand at other tasks around the library as needed, gain some insight on other aspects of library roles, and see what new skills I can learn and help with.

My Career Path

After finishing my bachelor's degree in West Virginia, I moved to the Raleigh, North Carolina area, and after a year there I found the circulation assistant position at Campbell University. It was my amazing colleagues and the friendly atmosphere at Wiggins Memorial Library that inspired me to go back to school to get my MLS. This was when I realized how much interest I had in the cataloging processes and the organization of the information that you process through the online library platforms. I finished up my master's program two years ago, and a few months after graduation I received an offer for my current job at Columbia College.

Advice

It can be difficult to find library science programs that offer in-depth classes about the various technical services duties and the actual process of working with vendors and third parties for databases and electronic resources. So find practicums, internships, and/or volunteer opportunities that will allow you to learn the skills in a hands-on environment. Being able to practice the varying techniques used by different libraries can give you a more well-rounded experience, will allow you to truly understand the ins and outs of the field, and let you figure out what you are more comfortable with doing.

Games and Media Arts Librarians
Diane Robson, Steven Guerrero, and Emily Pojman

What We Do

The UNT Media Library, one of four special libraries at the University of North Texas, houses non-print, audiovisual, film, tabletop, and video game collections. This collection is used for student and staff programming, coursework, and university initiatives related to film and gaming degrees.

Diane Robson (Games and Education Librarian): I am responsible for overseeing the management of game collections, cataloging, and processing in the Media Library. My duties include subject librarianship, budget management for game-related purchases, development of documentation for cataloging, processing, and usage, and overseeing cataloging processes.

The workload in the library and on campus varies depending on projects, coursework, and activities. Yearly tasks involve tracking usage, loss, and damage to effectively manage budgets and purchases, as well as planning for classes, events, and collaborations. Monthly tasks include managing events and processes and collaborating with faculty to support coursework and research. Daily, I may be involved in cataloging materials, performing record maintenance, or working on collection-related projects with my staff. Daily space management can involve facilitating classes, managing events, or troubleshooting general usage issues. On Fridays, I work from home and dedicate my time to catching up on orders, documentation, or scholarly pursuits.

Steven Guerrero (Media Arts & Digitization Librarian): I serve the media arts department as their subject librarian and provide digitization services for magnetic tape-based video formats. My tasks vary from day to day but often involve providing instructional assistance for resource equipment; subject librarianship; supervising of staff and students; management of digital video streaming rights; events and programming; committee work; and digitization projects for the university.

Emily Pojman (Media Circulation Manager): As the media circulation manager, I am responsible for managing and maintaining our physical collection of video games, gaming equipment, tabletop games, and film. Additionally, I manage media spaces and handle reservation requests for our classroom and game spaces. My duties also include library communications, such as overseeing the Media Library email account, handling fines and overdue items, and coordinating the booking of materials for faculty and student organizations. In terms of space and equipment maintenance, I troubleshoot technical issues and escalate them to library information technology (IT) as needed. I am also responsible for handling discarded library items and subsequent replacements, responding to disruptive students, and engaging in social media outreach and event planning.

Our Favorite Things

Diane: One aspect of my role that I particularly enjoy is interacting with students and faculty as they utilize games for research and recreation. The library is a vibrant space where people actively engage in play. Supporting this play, while managing gaming equipment and software in a networked environment, can have its challenges and stressful moments, but I find controlling the chaos enjoyable.

Steven: The aspect I enjoy the most is the variety of the workload and the collaborations that result from being able to be a part of so many different projects. I am lucky to combine my love of film and video games into the work that I do. I have found that my varied work experience has been a great help in my career as a librarian.

Emily: Each day in the Media Library presents new challenges and opportunities for learning. I enjoy working with our gaming collection and exploring new ways to interact with and make it more accessible to our patrons, such as leveraging platforms like Discord to promote video game content through streaming events. Through this position, I have gained a wide range of technical and interpersonal skills that I believe will be an asset to my career going forward.

Challenges

Diane: Some of the challenges in our work involve handling technology and managing rights related to media collections. It is important to be aware that there is often a learning curve when dealing with any technology, as sometimes an item may function perfectly one day but encounter issues the next. Developing the ability to maintain composure while troubleshooting is a valuable skill to cultivate. Another challenge we face is licensing video games, which is a relatively new undertaking. However, we can draw inspiration from the successful path paved with film licensing.

Steven: The most pressing challenge is the phasing out of physical media. As streaming distribution proliferates through studio-owned platforms with a consumer paywall, academic access to content has reduced, leaving institutions locked out of valuable resources. Companies are now only selectively releasing titles on physical formats, leaving institutions advocating for access. Coupled with rapidly changing technologies and obsolescence of older formats, academic libraries must remain vigilant in advocating for distributors to continue making physical copies of their content.

Emily: Aside from technical troubleshooting, establishing expectations for how patrons should interact with and behave in the game space can be challenging. Wear and tear on our equipment occurs faster than in other collections due to high use, and as a result requires staff intervention to model appropriate use. The ideal scenario is when regular patrons begin to communicate space rules to newcomers, creating an organic system of self-regulation.

Our Career Paths

Diane: My career in this field began as a student assistant responsible for filing shelf list cards. Over the years, I have worked in various paraprofessional roles in technical services, focusing on database maintenance, cataloging, and ordering. I transitioned to the Media Library, taking on responsibilities such as managing the circulation desk, student hiring, reserves, bookings, and cataloging. Several years later I was asked to obtain an MLS, and I became a librarian. In this role, I established the game collection and have overseen its growth since then.

Steven: I first started working seriously in libraries as a front desk student assistant. That shifted to a staff stacks manager position at Texas Woman's University and then circulation manager back at the UNT Media Library where I remained until I received my MLS and was hired into my current position. Throughout that time, I took part in many workgroups, committees, and task forces that exposed me to many aspects of library operations and the people who run them. It was a valuable experience that I often call upon in my daily work today.

Emily: I have a background in television and digital media production, having worked in that industry for almost a decade. When I decided to transition to a career in libraries, I began working as a paraprofessional at a high school library. This experience allowed me to directly connect with students and inspired me to pursue my MLS degree. I was hired by the University of North Texas to my current position one year ago and have since enjoyed learning about the unique aspects of special and academic libraries while building valuable professional relationships within this community.

Advice

Volunteering in a library or for library organizations is vital for picking up skills related to library services. Familiarize yourself with current library trends and technologies, new and old. Media libraries provide opportunities for librarians to curate collections of specialized materials, often allowing them to cultivate an assortment of items that align with their interests and passions. Media librarians interact daily with patrons engaging in research, recreation, and technical endeavors. Therefore, strong interpersonal skills and the ability to effectively communicate and cooperate with others are highly valued in this role.

Human Resources Director
Laura Blessing

What I Do

As the director of libraries human resources for North Carolina State University Libraries, I manage a small team that is responsible for the human resource needs for all library employees. This includes employee onboarding, position classification and compensation, policy interpretation, employee recognition, training and professional development, employee benefits, and payroll and leave coordination. I also provide leadership support for equity, diversity, and inclusion as well as for talent management (recruitment). In short, my team's purpose is to ensure that the employee experience for all of our libraries' employees, starting at recruitment and continuing past separation, is a positive one.

The university has a campus-wide human resource department that I consult with on various human resources (HR) topics. I often tell new library employees that while the University Human Resources (UHR) office has employees who specialize in specific aspects of HR (recruitment, training, benefits, etc.) the Libraries' Human Resources (LHR) department has a team of HR generalists, and our "area of specialty" is the human resource needs of library employees. For instance, I specialize in classification and compensation of librarian and library staff positions, but I may need to consult with UHR for information on the university's current salary bandings, and on policies on reclassifications and salary increase requests. UHR also serves as the final approver for all human resource matters on campus. So, for instance, all of our recruitment and compensation recommendations must be approved by the appropriate division in the UHR department.

My Favorite Things

The main thing that attracted me to working in HR is the same thing that attracted me to librarianship: I love helping people find information. In my current position, I spend a great deal of time helping library employees find HR-related information (benefits, personnel policies, etc.) and teaching them to find this information on their own. Many of my responsibilities are similar to what librarians do when they assist patrons. I often say that my "patrons" are all of the employees in our library, as well as potential employees (a.k.a. applicants) and former employees.

I also enjoy the counseling aspect of human resources. Early on in my life, I wanted to become a counselor or a therapist, so I majored in psychology in college. I eventually felt that this was not my true calling, and I ultimately decided to go to library school. In my HR role, I often counsel employees on various matters that can have effects on their work and personal lives. Whether I am talking to an employee about what leave options are available to them for the upcoming birth of their baby or coaching a manager on a difficult personnel matter, I get that same feeling of satisfaction from giving guidance to employees and helping them make better decisions. However, I appreciate the fact that there are a lot of other responsibilities in my job so that the counseling part doesn't become overwhelming.

I should also note that it's possible to be an HR practitioner anywhere, but I love working in libraries because I get to work with so many lifelong learners. Library employees also tend to have a variety of interests and are likely to give you great recommendations on the latest music, movies, and yes, books that have come out recently. And most of all, they are committed to doing good work because they know everything they do has a big impact on many of their patrons. The people are definitely what makes my job amazing.

Challenges

One of my biggest challenges in this position comes from having to navigate restrictions or other policies that have been enacted at levels beyond our organization—which could include those at the university, university system, or even the state level. For instance, the university system may impose a new threshold (across all institutions in our system) for internal salary increases in a year when funding is tight. At other times, we may have our requests denied due to misunderstandings about the type of work that a specific library position is responsible for, or misunderstandings over what the appropriate market rate is for a certain position. We are normally able to resolve many of those cases, but it can sometimes be discouraging to have to re-clarify and justify our requests as we continue to advocate for our employees and the work that they do.

Another challenge of my position is having to navigate and explain policies or procedures, especially those that I don't fully agree with. I am responsible for interpreting and helping to enforce a wide variety of policies and procedures that come from federal or state-level legislation, community or university-wide policies/procedures, and library-wide practices. It can be difficult recognizing that some employees may end up associating me with these policies, guidelines, and practices, including those that I also want to critique.

My Career Path

I began my career as a librarian in circulation in a small university library; nowadays, we would probably call that position an access services librarian. In that position, I had the responsibility of hiring approximately thirty student employees each year, overseeing the student employee budget for the unit, training the students, and occasionally disciplining or terminating students. The work in that position prepared me for some of the responsibilities that I now have in HR.

Although access services can be a common career path for library human resource managers, I also know library HR managers who began their careers as instruction librarians. The focus on training can be a natural entryway into human resources. Finally, I have spoken to a few library HR managers who began working in HR in the private sector and ended up later working in libraries. As I have noted before, this is a job with a lot of variety in it, so it's not surprising that nearly any area of librarianship (and beyond) could be a good entrance point into HR work.

Advice

I would hesitate to recommend this type of work to someone who doesn't like analytical work. Yes, there is plenty of "people work" in human resources—"human" is in the title, after all! But you also need to be able to analyze trends that affect people. Whether examining recruitment and turnover trends, developing a presentation for administration based upon a recent employee engagement survey, or analyzing salary compression data, HR practitioners make frequent use of their analytical abilities.

In addition to my analytical skills, my ability to be flexible and roll with the changes has helped me significantly in this line of work. You never know, for instance, when you might be told that the campus-wide freeze on recruiting for vacancies is over, so you need to start recruiting for several positions—now! Flexibility can also be needed when dealing with novel situations. There simply is not a blueprint for every single situation that you may encounter. Just like our patrons, employees are human, and therefore, they can be unpredictable.

Anything Else?

Many HR positions in academic libraries also oversee the promotion and tenure process. I have not worked in a library that has tenure available for library faculty, so my knowledge about that process is secondhand, but I am told that it can be stressful at times for everyone involved. However, it may also be a positive experience as the process is related to continuation of appointments and oftentimes related salary increases. In addition, it's one of the few times where librarians get to "toot their own horns" about their many career successes, so HR managers tend to have both positive and negative thoughts about the process.

HR positions in libraries often focus mainly on recruitment. Regardless of whether you are more interested in that aspect of HR, or if the idea of employee engagement or other aspects are more appealing to you, you will likely do a significant amount of work in recruiting, so even though HR is a good profession for many people, make sure that you are comfortable with the recruitment aspect before entering this line of work.

Information Literacy Librarian
Joy Oehlers

What I Do

As an information literacy librarian in a community college, I create lessons and assignments to help students select and use the best information sources, be it using artificial intelligence (AI) apps, Google, or library databases. I collaborate with instructors and test-drive these lessons and assignments with our library student assistants before rolling them out to face-to-face or online classes.

On-the-fly assessments (observing how students respond or carry out the tasks) and formal assessments (written or oral feedback from students and instructors as well as analyzing students' assignments) help me re-tweak and make the lessons meaningful and the tasks relevant. I want students to find value in library lessons, not to perceive them as useless busywork. If you work in an academic library, assessment is required.

While the *ACRL Framework for Information Literacy* guides my work, in reality, it's about translating that framework to be appropriate, engaging, and somewhat novel for students. Most students are already savvy searchers, but by observing what they do, we can discover what they need to know to be even better researchers. One challenge is developing lessons that are different for each course, as a student will often attend more than one library class during their time at college. So if you enjoy teaching, or if you have ever attended a boring course and felt that you could make it better, this job would provide a great opportunity to develop your pedagogy philosophy, assessment toolkit, and instructional design.

My Favorite Things

Before we can be successful instructors, we need to connect with our students. We must help students feel safe in the library and comfortable talking to librarians. Part of my job is to run orientation and events in the library throughout the semester. This is the part of my job I enjoy the most. Together with our team of creative librarians, I design breakout rooms and interactive exhibitions, screen movies, find freebie giveaways, organize games day, and even throw pizza parties. I often apply for university or outside funding for these events. Creative grant writing can be fun. Asking for community donations is also fun as long as you remember the worst they can say is "no." All this effort is worthwhile when students tell you how much fun they are having and how glad they are to be at this college, making new friends, taking a break from studying, and winning prizes.

Mostly I love this job because there is so much room for growth and flexibility, space to try new ideas, and support from my colleagues, because we all share the same passion for our students.

Challenges

People often ask if I have anything to do during summer or if I get the summer off as there are fewer students on campus—I wish! Time management is quite important, as you often juggle a lot of projects, meetings, instructional classes, and reference requests at once. You might find that you are more productive in the mornings or late evenings; as faculty, you may be able to arrange your work hours to complete your tasks.

Community college libraries are slower paced than many public libraries; most students are independent researchers or are just looking for a quiet study spot. When I worked in public libraries, the volume of transactions was huge and the range and needs of library users were diverse.

As much as I love to update myself on new technology trends to keep up with my students, our library sometimes has difficulties keeping up with our students' requirements. We sometimes get feedback like "What, you don't have a charger for this phone model?" or "Why is this laptop so slow?"

In recent years, there are so many more professional development (PD) opportunities online that I don't have to travel for conferences. However, sad to say, I think I'm less "professionally developed" from attending online conferences because I end up multitasking during these times instead of focusing on the PD. If your organization is unable to support all your conference requests, do carve out quality time to sit back, read some professional literature, and sign up for online courses. School might be out, but you will need to keep on top of what is happening in your field as well as in related fields (you never know when you would like to change jobs!).

My Career Path

As an MLS student in New Zealand, I enjoyed volunteering at my local public library so much that they hired me as a weekend supervisor and later as a copy cataloger. After my MLS, I transitioned to a liaison librarian position in a brand new academic library. It was very exciting, conceptualizing and designing new services from the ground up, and trying out new ideas to connect with undergraduate and graduate students. Don't be afraid to take up a position at a new, rural, or small library. They offer many opportunities for you to grow and experiment.

When I moved to Honolulu, there were no job openings near where I lived, so I volunteered at my local public library and community college library. It is hard for library students to find time to volunteer but I think it can be worthwhile. Volunteering helps you decide if you really like the type of work and it also helps the library decide if you are a good fit for them and their community. Don't turn down boring tasks; you may even find a way to improve them. Don't be afraid to put your hands up for unpopular tasks; supervisors will eventually assign fun tasks when they see that you are serious about volunteering.

Throughout my career, I have looked for mentors and coworkers who supported me. They might be non-library faculty who will tell their peers about what I do or librarians who are skilled in areas that I'm weak at. Whether you work in a small or large environment, look within your library and outside to related communities for partnerships and camaraderie.

Advice

Join your local or state library association and volunteer for committee or subcommittee work. They always welcome volunteers, including student volunteers. Don't let yourself suffer from imposter syndrome. You don't need to be an expert. You just need to be willing to contribute your enthusiasm, talents (yes, *you* have unique talents), and time. The connections you make there are for life, and it is one sure way to find out about job openings and get references for your job applications. Your prospective employer wants to see that you care enough about the profession to contribute to their professional association.

No matter what job you take, even jobs that are not library-related, knowing your major stakeholder—the reason why you go to work—will help you succeed and love your job. If you don't enjoy students, you are unlikely to see the library-related problems or understand the challenges faced by your students. I have a lot of respect for our students as I watch them trying to combine school with work, and for some, family commitments and/or health issues. Your attitudes toward your students or clients or patrons can't be faked; they will eventually see through you. So obviously, don't be a children's librarian if you can't understand kids; and don't be a community college librarian if you don't enjoy mixing with students from all levels of socioeconomic backgrounds with a wealth of life experiences that might be very different from yours.

Instructional Technology Specialist
Lara Taylor

What I Do

I teach software workshops for the library. Instructors and professors rely on me to teach the students how to use the software that they need for class. I teach workshops both in-person and online. I also give one-on-one tutorials in software. When I am not teaching, I am working in our makerspace, digital media center, or on committee work. I am also in charge of overseeing our virtual reality studio. I work with professors and instructors to incorporate software lessons into their curriculum. I also teach how to create e-Portfolios and online syllabuses.

My Favorite Things

I love the interaction with students. This semester, I am working with a technical design class to update our instructional booklets. This is something that I would not get to do in any other library position. In workshops, I also enjoy watching my students have "light bulb" moments where something just clicks in their brain.

Challenges

The biggest challenge comes from trying to connect in an online environment. I offer a lot of online workshops because they are convenient for the students, but it is easier to anticipate questions or struggles in a face-to-face environment. When I am in a classroom, I can see the questioning look on a student's face and offer to help. Often in an online environment, students are reluctant to interrupt or ask questions. It is something that I try to encourage during my workshops but is harder to achieve online.

I teach several workshops on various Adobe software and Adobe has recently incorporated generative Artificial Intelligence (AI) into the software. This is challenging because so often, I must teach background on AI and generative AI before I can even get to the software program we are using that day. It's exciting because I get to have these relevant and interesting conversations about an emerging and rapidly changing technology. It can also be frustrating to encounter the fear or the distrust that people have of generative AI.

My Career Path

I spent over thirty years working in live television sports production before turning to this present career. I took a part-time job at my local library when it reopened (long story) and fell in love with library work. I was surprised that I loved working in a library as much as I loved working in live TV. They are opposites, to say the least.

I started in a public library and moved to an academic library. I worked toward a certificate in special collections and archives while earning my MLIS, thinking that preservation would be my area of interest and study. But I had two opportunities in my academic career that influenced my direction. First, I was allowed to catalog rare books as my practicum experience. This made me realize that I wanted to be in front of students in some capacity. Second, my current job became open. I had never considered working in the makerspace/digital media center, and I had certainly never considered teaching software instruction full time, but it was a good opportunity. And it brought my focus back to technology, which has always held an interest for me. This current position is a combination of many likes, talents, and experiences I have had over my career path.

Advice

Get out there and have as many experiences as you can. One of the things that has benefited me greatly has been the diversity of cultures and people that I have encountered in my life. I have worked with groups of all ages, ethnicities, and socioeconomic backgrounds. Learn as much as you can about everything that interests you. You never know what skill you will be able to use in a future job. I never imagined that my TV experience would help my career in a library, but we have a full TV studio inside our makerspace and digital media center. So, my best advice is to cultivate those skills and experiences! You never know how your passions will serve you in the future.

Anything Else?

While I spend most of my time teaching software workshops, I am on several library committees, which I also thoroughly enjoy. I am in my second term as the chair of our libraries' Emerging Technologies Committee. We work with different units in the libraries to figure out how we can help them. We received a grant this year, which has helped some of those departments and units. We are also working with the libraries' Hackathon committee on this year's event. I have also spent the last year with a dedicated group as we have rewritten the library's five-year strategic plan.

Metadata Librarian
Chad Deets

What I Do

I work at a large research university that has a digital repository environment used for storing and accessing digital library collections as well as the scholarly research products of university faculty and graduate students. As metadata librarian, I make sure that all content going into the repository environment has the appropriate metadata, meaning the objects are described and discoverable by users. My job duties include oversight and management of all metadata, as well as the processes and workflows surrounding them. A typical set of routine tasks might include the preparation, ingestion, quality control, and remediation of contributed metadata (i.e., working with many spreadsheets), training colleagues and users on how to enter metadata, establishing or revising workflows for getting metadata into the repository environment, consulting with prospective contributors on metadata requirements, coordinating remediation projects of legacy metadata, and creating training materials/documentation.

Beyond the list of job duties, this position includes a lot of continuous education and upskilling. It is important that metadata are inclusive and respectful. To ensure this, I keep up to date on current industry-wide conversations and practices on using inclusive language in description, and I work to establish relationships with colleagues who represent users from diverse and underrepresented communities. I am also responsible for ensuring that all of our metadata are interoperable (i.e., shareable, exchangeable, and ready for migration to different systems) and I work with a team of colleagues who help with the design and evaluation of our repository environment.

As an academic librarian, my job also includes participating in scholarly activities related to my field of study, as well as accepting service/volunteer assignments for the library, university, and community at large. This can include things like publishing, presenting, serving on committees, and representing my position or department at various panels and events. These activities are required, as we are expected to make scholarly contributions to the field.

My Favorite Things

Positions like mine are well suited for someone who enjoys solving problems and optimizing workflows. People who gravitate toward cataloging and metadata work tend to have an innate curiosity. We enjoy tasks and activities that include learning rules and systems, recognizing patterns, investigating discrepancies, organizing, and labeling. Metadata often functions as a system (almost like a language). My role is to learn and eventually master the system, design workflows and processes around it, and then train and disseminate that information to colleagues and staff who help execute the work. In essence, I serve as a subject matter expert, setting standards and providing guidance.

I enjoy the freedom that comes with learning something new and then sharing it with others. I also enjoy opportunities to learn and serve in a variety of different ways. When I work on materials submitted by our faculty, I get to learn about a wide variety of topics, often in fields I have no exposure to otherwise. In addition, many graduate student projects are completed in partnership with organizations that serve the community, and it is fulfilling to see this work. As I create and revise metadata for projects, I get to see how the scholarship benefits its intended audience and then I determine the best ways to make it discoverable so that other people will see it too. I also enjoy chances to improve our internal processes and collaborate with staff. I believe that as higher education and the needs of library users evolve, we need to evolve with them.

Challenges

Metadata for digital materials shares a lot of the same challenges as metadata for print materials. There is always more work to do than time or people allotted to do it. Metadata standards change over time, causing a perpetual need for maintenance and remediation projects. In addition, repositories have the added complexities of a digital-only world. The technology challenges can compound in the sense that the system not only houses the metadata, but also the collections themselves. Any glitches in technology can temporarily restrict discovery entirely.

Also, repository metadata is often a team effort and is created and managed by a lot of different user groups, including faculty, graduate students, and community members who are not professionally trained in metadata and who may have no experience with describing information. I am faced with the complex challenge of designing processes and documentation that make it as simple as possible for anyone to do this, without compromising the integrity of the final product or creating a massive amount of work for library staff afterwards. Good training practices and open communication are essential. In addition, there will always be cleanup work to be done, which can be frustrating for people who don't like the idea of unfinished work.

My Career Path

I came into librarianship midlife, having previously worked in law enforcement records management for seven years and then in a private industry for two. I really enjoyed the service aspects of government work, but I found that I wanted something that was more educational and cultural. After finishing my undergraduate degrees in history and political science, I found a job working with government documents at a government library. Although I wasn't considering a library career at the time, I was happy with the prospect of working with historical materials at a cultural institution. In that job, I fell into technical services and metadata out of necessity but found that I really enjoyed the organizational and cataloging aspects. I have always been interested in languages and systems, and cataloging is its own language of sorts. Since that job, I've continued to upskill in MAchine-Readable Cataloging (MARC) cataloging while also expanding to non-MARC digital metadata. As with all languages, if you don't use it, you lose it!

Something that initially shocked me was how much cultural institutions have to fight for survival. Law enforcement agencies don't often have to justify their existence or fight for funding, so I definitely felt a culture shock in that sense. In library school, I read about the changes the field has undergone over the past two decades (collections moves, renovations, reallocation of space, and so on) and have subsequently experienced them in every job I've had in the field. In libraries, we are always expected to do more with less—in physical spaces, staffing, and budgets. In addition, we're constantly forced to prove that we are worth the financial investment we get, even as that repeatedly shrinks.

Advice

First, the degree will teach you the theory, but the vast majority of your education will happen on the job. Libraries want people who want to make contributions. It's important to take ownership of your work, which includes being curious and looking for opportunities to collaborate. Second, remember that libraries are ultimately here to serve users. Although working with and preserving resources is a part of that, without the users, there is no point to that work. Finally, recognize that change is inevitable. User needs, budgets, administrations, and technologies all change over time. Be flexible and adaptable. Learn as much as you can and stay open to doing new things. You will make yourself an asset to your institution.

Music Librarian
Marci Cohen

What I Do

As an academic public services music librarian with a focus on popular music, I worked at Berklee College of Music, a conservatory focused on training professional musicians and those pursuing other music-related careers including music therapy and music business. I now work at Boston University (BU), a research university with a small conservatory program. As part of a large library system, I have duties supporting all libraries, not just my own branch.

I provide reference services. I have one virtual reference shift each week, answering questions across all subjects via email or chat. I also answer music-related reference questions that come to me directly or are transferred because of my subject expertise.

I establish connections with patrons through instruction activities. Last year, I met with sixteen classes, a mix of music-specific and other courses, typically first-year writing classes where students learn basic academic research. I prepare for each session by familiarizing myself with resources related to the course topic. I find relevant examples and either identify an appropriate subject research guide or create a course guide. In music classes, we delve into music-specific resources such as RISM, a database documenting the location of music manuscripts.

Collection development has always been part of my job, but the details have changed dramatically. Physical media circulation has dropped off considerably in the past decade. I now rarely buy physical recordings. We now prefer to buy e-books. Use of scores (printed music) has also declined, but not as sharply as other materials because musicians still use them for scholarship and performance. Scores are trickier to collect than text sources. Typical library vendors don't carry scores. I have to choose the right edition for our needs, starting with parts for individual performers versus scores that show what all the performers are playing. I may have to differentiate by vocal range, arrangement for certain instruments, editor, or critical edition with commentary. When selecting piano scores for popular music, I need to avoid simplified arrangements for beginners.

I supervise paraprofessional staff. This includes mundane tasks such as approving weekly time submission. I also check on their work, assign projects, and answer their questions. I identify areas for skill development; for example, recommending software training. I recently mentored an early-career colleague to help him qualify for career advancement.

Professional service is a notable component of my work. I've held leadership positions in the Music Library Association (MLA). I write a monthly music column for a Charleston Hub blog and reviews of music-related books and databases for *Notes* and *Music Reference Services Quarterly* once or twice a year.

My Favorite Things

The best part is working with students. It is invigorating when I have a lively instruction session and can see the students grasping new information literacy skills. Even better is when I incorporate my music expertise. I've had research consultations with students interested in grunge and Riot Grrrl that drew on my experience as well as scholarship. In the broader view, I tap into my love and knowledge of music in a stable, rewarding profession. I relish the thrill of the hunt in reference services, tracking down just the right source to meet the patrons' needs, ranging from an article on U2 and Irishness to the precise edition of performance parts of a musical work.

Challenges

Library systems are built around text, which creates challenges in making systems work well for music materials and users. Thankfully, music catalogers have advocated for cataloging rules and display options to support music discovery, and our discovery staff listen to our concerns. I advocate for my patrons to ensure our collections truly meet their needs. This is particularly important for e-scores compared with e-books because musicians use them in different ways than patrons read text.

The shrinking specialty is an existential challenge. Academic librarianship is shifting from subject specialties to functional roles such as e-resources and user experience. When music librarians leave jobs, the positions often face elimination. My advocacy pitch is that we are format specialists as well as subject specialists.

My Career Path

My pre-library career as a music journalist landed me a public library job as a multimedia librarian, where I assisted with music, videos, audiobooks, and videogames. When I relocated for family reasons, a colleague suggested earning a music degree. Most music library jobs are academic, and most academic jobs expect a subject degree; my bachelor's degree is in business. I embarked on a master's in musicology, which also required auditing an undergraduate degree's worth of music history and theory.

Pursuing the music master's helped me qualify for the position at Berklee. I also emphasized my transferable skills, especially my experience teaching internet skills to patrons. My MLA involvement, including several conference presentations, raised my profile with the search committees at both Berklee and BU.

My online MLS program didn't offer a music librarianship course, so some surprises have been in the details. My general cataloging class didn't address uniform titles, which function as name authority for musical works that can be referred to in different ways. I also hadn't previously realized that different score editions aren't interchangeable. However, on the job I developed enough expertise to design an instruction activity at Berklee involving assorted editions of Beatles scores, including a piano jazz arrangement, excerpts for theater auditions, a drum play-along, and the typical piano/vocal/guitar version.

Until I got to BU, I didn't recognize the difference between a conservatory and a research institution. The culture at Berklee emphasized musicianship over scholarship, so librarians tried to squeeze in information literacy despite indifference from many faculty. Research is integral at BU, so the library is essential to the institution's mission. Even if the stellar musicians aren't interested in the library, the musicology and ethnomusicology faculty and students find us vital, and general reference and instruction are core values.

Advice

Some aspects of my job are common for all subject liaisons. Learn how to answer reference questions, do collection development, and conduct library instruction. Get familiar with the *ACRL Framework for Information Literacy*. Customer service and supervisory experience in any setting provide transferable skills. Use your reference skills to research potential employers so you can explain why you want the specific job in the specific institution.

Other aspects are particular to music librarianship. The field has shifted away from expecting an advanced degree in music, but you'd be wise to enter with an understanding of music research tools and methods and how to read a score. Beyond my coursework in music, I read a lot about music for both my professional development and leisure, which builds a knowledge base that enables me to do my job well.

Finally, connecting to a professional community is invaluable. Get involved in MLA. Avenues include regional chapters and MLStEP, the Music Library Students and Emerging Professionals interest group.

Open Educational Resources Librarian
Kate McNally Carter

What I Do

In my role as an open educational resources librarian, I assist faculty with finding, adopting, adapting, and creating open educational resources (OER). OER are teaching and learning materials that are free and openly licensed in a way that allows them to be retained, reused, revised, remixed, and redistributed to fit a variety of teaching needs. Most commonly, OER have a Creative Commons (CC) license that enables the copyright holder to grant specific permissions for the reuse of the OER. In my role, I help faculty navigate the differences between the CC licenses, helping them understand how an OER can be reused and, if possible, adapted to fit their specific context.

There are many benefits of using OER. The most commonly cited benefit is the cost savings to students. Because OER are free, this can alleviate the substantial burden of commercial textbook costs. For this reason, many OER programs measure impact through cost savings. Another benefit of using OER is the fact that they can be modified and customized by the instructor to fit the needs of their course. Unlike traditional course materials under copyright, the open license applied to OER allows more flexibility for instructors to adapt and combine relevant materials to more closely align with their learning objectives.

I work in the Open Education Services department at University of Houston (UH), which includes myself and the department head. Though we are a small department, we are fully dedicated to the work of open education initiatives at UH. Typically, most institutions include OER duties as an add-on to other positions, so UH is unique in that we have dedicated time and resources to work in this area.

My Favorite Things

One aspect of my job that I particularly enjoy is the opportunity to support faculty in adopting open pedagogy. Open pedagogy has a wide variety of definitions and applications, but most commonly it involves an assignment in which students are invited to openly license and publish something they create for the course, whether this is an essay, a presentation, a podcast, and so on. This extends the value of student work beyond the classroom by benefiting other learners and empowering students to view themselves as information creators, not just consumers. It's an exciting teaching practice that has a lot of potential to reinvigorate classes and enrich the number and variety of openly licensed resources that could be used as OER in other courses.

Challenges

The field of open education has several challenges. First, sometimes there is hesitancy for faculty to make their courses open because this is usually time-intensive work. Often, academic departments and colleges don't recognize or incentivize the labor involved in open education. This additional work is usually uncompensated, and promotion and tenure review processes typically exclude any type of scholarship outside traditional peer-reviewed or commercial channels. This can make it difficult for librarians to advocate for OER adoption.

Another major challenge on the horizon for the open movement is the proliferation of institution-wide inclusive access (IA) programs, which is a textbook sales model that adds the cost of course materials to tuition and fees; digital content is then delivered to students through the learning management system. Many of the benefits of OER are appropriated by the publishing companies to advance IA, namely cost savings and first-day access to course materials. However, these programs are highly problematic due to their lack of transparency and overall cost. Though cost savings is a major selling point, IA programs can in many cases cost students more over the course of their education, and students lose access to the digital material at the end of each semester. When instructors use online homework packages, this can further complicate a student's ability to opt out of an IA program, effectively removing their choice. Sadly, IA undermines prior work in open education and puts librarians in a precarious position to continue advocating for OER when its impact seems to be diminished. In response to this, it's important that open educators look at other ways to measure the impact of OER beyond cost savings.

My Career Path

I find challenges to be personally and professionally motivating, and this position has driven me to seek out new opportunities that take me out of my comfort zone. The work has helped me develop more specialized skills and expertise that have enabled me to acquire a more marketable skill set. In my first professional role as a Research & Instruction Librarian in a smaller academic library, I handled a wide variety of job responsibilities, including staffing the research desk, teaching information literacy classes, performing collection development and liaison duties, as well as managing social media and events. Though I didn't have as much time to develop specialized skills, I was able to explore a wide variety of different paths of librarianship. I was drawn to open education because of its core principles of equity and access. I also enjoyed the more nuanced aspects of open licensing and publishing, which connects my work to another interest of mine, scholarly communications. One of the things I enjoy the most is the opportunity to work with faculty in-depth to integrate OER and open educational practices into their curriculum, and to see the benefits of this work trickle down to the students. When faculty use OER and open pedagogy, students realize that their instructors care, and this can in turn lead them to be more engaged and successful in their courses.

Advice

One benefit of entering the open education field is the wealth of resources available to help you. Though there are formal, paid programs to help you develop professionally in this area, such as the Creative Commons Certificate and the Open Education Network's Certificate in Open Education Librarianship, there are many more training programs that are openly available at no cost. The open education community itself is also a very welcoming and helpful resource. For example, the SPARC Open Education Forum (https://sparcopen.org/our-work/sparc-oe-forum) is an active community that serves as a channel for open education advocates to connect, share resources, and ask questions.

For aspiring open education librarians, passion for the core principles of open education can help keep you motivated in this work. The challenges facing open educators can be dispiriting, so it is important to balance this with self-care to avoid burnout. I would also recommend developing expertise in instruction, as I believe that open pedagogy is a pivotal aspect of my work that will sustain open education endeavors more broadly across my institution. Many LIS programs do not include robust instruction training, so developing yourself in this area professionally is important, and can also help in many other types of librarianship. Most importantly, it is very common for open education or OER duties to be "added on" to a particular position in the library. My role as a librarian solely focused on OER, in a department with two dedicated librarians, is unusual in this field. Approaching your work with feasibility and an understanding of your capacity can help you develop sustainable strategies for OER advocacy and support.

Part-Time Librarian
Emily Weak

What I Do

My main responsibility as a part-time librarian at a technical college is to be the sole library staff member on campus on Saturdays. We are generally open for half a day, starting just before the first class and ending just before the last class of the day. We have a single desk for reference and circulation, and because I'm the only staff person in the library, I sit at the desk for my entire shift. Saturdays are pretty quiet, but I do usually help a double handful or so of students and campus visitors by phone, in person, and over chat. The school prefers to staff Saturdays with a librarian rather than a library assistant because of the special training librarians have for answering research and reference questions. But most of the questions I get are straightforward, with the top questions being "Where is the bathroom?" and "How do I print?" I also frequently help students who are actually looking for the bookstore instead of the library.

The reference questions we do get tend to be students who need help using our online resources. This may be the first time they've been asked to find and read a scholarly article, and many need additional help in finding articles on their topic, limiting to articles available in full text, and citing what they find. Citation is another big topic for the library. Students are asked to use either MLA or APA style, and in addition to being confused by the minutiae of formatting, they often need help understanding the basic definition and use of citations.

As a part time librarian, I can work up to nineteen hours a week, so I work two days in addition to Saturday. During those two days I spend a few hours on the desk, but I also maintain a third of our print book collection (ordering and weeding books) and I am the chair of our library system's instruction committee. Our instruction committee maintains and creates content such as videos and lessons using the Softchalk platform. We also run a series of virtual workshops on research, library resources, and citation styles. I usually instruct a few virtual workshops each semester, which I do remotely from home after the library has closed.

My Favorite Things

I remember when I interviewed for my first nearly full-time public library job, I asked the interviewers what they liked about working in the library. I was a little taken aback when one person (who was nearing retirement age) said that she really liked that she could work part time. But now I get it! I spent nearly a decade working a full-time position at a public library until the pandemic let me finally admit to myself how burned out I was. Public libraries are wonderful, but they can also take a lot of your time, passion, and good humor. They are full of the need to "do more with less." Many patrons come to the library in crisis: they have lost their home, are getting divorced, need to ask a family member to donate a kidney, and so on. I am glad that the library is a place that so many people in need can rely on, but the demand is very hard on staff.

So, I really like my new part time job at a technical college. Our patrons do not need the intense, high-stakes help that is more frequent in public libraries. And I really love working a part-time schedule. I can stay in practice as a librarian working in a library but I still have time to do other things that keep my creative and intellectual juices flowing: I do contract work as an equity advisor helping California libraries with Library Services and Technology Act (LSTA) grants, I run the website HiringLibrarians.com, and I have just started teaching yoga.

Challenges

Part-time workers can sometimes be treated as second-class citizens in a number of ways. I don't get health or retirement benefits. I am not invited to campus-wide training. I don't have a performance or wage review process. And I don't get tapped for the same kind of work that full timers do; for example, when I asked to be the Instruction Committee Chair, it took a little convincing for my boss to realize that a part-timer could take on this responsibility.

My Career Path

Before I worked in libraries, I worked in grocery stores. I actually really liked it; I love food and I (mostly) enjoy customer service work. But after I had been in that industry for about a decade, I realized that at the bottom line I was always selling something. I was interested in going back to school, I was interested in working in more of a public service role, and I had always loved reading. So, I decided to go to library school. This is not a path I generally recommend to others! I think it's preferable to have actual experience working in a library before you decide to start your MLIS. But somehow, it worked out for me. I worked briefly in a museum library and then in public libraries for nearly a decade, primarily in adult programming, outreach and engagement. I was surprised to realize that libraries are so much more than books. Libraries are a lifeline, a bridge builder, a gap-filler, and a third place for so many. They are a main provider of social services and are truly the people's university.

Advice

Customer service skills are deeply important in any library job. Folks who are interested in library work should develop their ability to work with others, including their ability to maintain their own emotional health while providing great service.

Anything Else?

When I was a brand new librarian, getting my first full time job felt very difficult. Government and academic jobs have several differences from the private sector. Because their processes felt so mysterious, I started a blog called hiringlibrarians.com to gather and present information on how library hiring works. Over a decade later, I am still running the site. In addition to mostly anonymous survey interviews with people who hire, I post job hunter perspectives, guest posts by researchers, and highlight other LIS hiring and career resources. This project has really changed my perspective. If someone tells you they have the "secret to getting a library job," don't believe them! There is a tremendous diversity in what we are looking for and the processes we follow.

Research Services Coordinator
Emerson M. Morris

What I Do

Here at Colorado Mesa University, our mission is to provide affordable and accessible education, with meaningful and enriching partnerships. To fulfill our part of the mission at the library, we work to meet students where they are by keeping a fully staffed research help desk (RHD) and virtual chat service. We staff our RHD with professional librarians and student assistants.

I arrange all the training for new librarians on the RHD. I hire, train, and supervise all the student assistants for the research help desk. I work closely with our checkout and reserves desk so that our students understand and have a clear sense of our expectations for service and behavior at work in the library. I then work with them individually to review the specific expectations we have at our desk. Our student assistants help with triage both in person and on chat. If it is a simple question like whether we have a specific book or article or basic information such as library hours, they are free to answer. Anything else they are to pass along to the librarian on duty.

I also run our 24/7 virtual chat service, which includes scheduling and training librarians. All librarians and students that help cover the desk also cover chat when they are on reference duty. We have the 24/7 service built in as a backup to cover our chats when we get busy and for after-hours coverage. As part of this, I help staff the Academic Global chat service, where I assist patrons from colleges and universities around the United States and the UK.

I am also the chair of our safety committee. This committee works with the members of the police and university to make sure we keep our patrons safe and comfortable. We have members on this team from all three floors of the library as well as other departments housed in the building such as our information technology (IT) department. We keep ahead of any issues that come up in the library that pertain to the safety of the people, the building, and our collection. We arrange training for our staff and student employees covering topics such as active shooter, fire, and so on.

I also do some instruction for our first-time students at the beginning of the year, as well as for our criminal justice department. I provide collection development for the criminal justice department and our reference collection. And finally, I mentor library school students and manage internships for our students on campus looking for experience in a library setting.

My Favorite Things

I love working with our faculty and students. The service part of my job is the most fulfilling. The university is very supportive of the library, and we receive a lot of gratitude from both faculty and students. I also love to talk, and this position is very social. I have formal and informal meetings regularly with my colleagues to keep up with the day-to-day work of covering the desk and chat and keeping up with trends in instruction and technical services. I spend a lot of time on the desk myself and get to chat with all kinds of students at different places in their research and their academic journeys. I learn a lot by helping others with research. And, as a dedicated lifelong learner, this is a great way to be introduced to so many interesting topics and ideas.

Challenges

The challenges that I have tend to revolve around wearing too many hats at once. On the one hand I love it; on the other hand, if I fail to say no to things, I can get overwhelmed. When I get overwhelmed, I need to prioritize tasks more seriously and work through things one at a time until I am caught up. Sometimes this means putting projects I am really excited about aside while I handle more important tasks with tighter time constraints.

I also struggle with statistics. I am not a numbers person. Thankfully, the programs that we use through Springshare make statistics a lot easier to keep and look up.

My Career Path

My career path was a bit of a winding journey, but it shows that any goal can be within reach if you are willing to persevere. I started by earning my MLIS before getting on-the-job experience. Many of my colleagues started in paraprofessional positions and then got their degrees to move into professional positions. When I decided that librarianship was what I wanted to do, I went to school first. I volunteered in a couple of archives because I initially studied to be an archivist. After getting my degree it was hard to find an immediate job, as employers looked for experience. I managed to get a temporary job shelving books at my local public library. Once the head of the children and teen library section found out I was degreed, I was invited to help with reference and programming a few hours a week. I loved it and discovered that the reference desk was where I wanted to be!

I then got a permanent position at an academic library and through a series of events ended up being the technical services and special collections librarian. It was here that I learned the importance of cataloging in being a good reference librarian. It was a small library, and everyone helped with reference, so I kept up my reference skills. When I decided to move again, I took a paraprofessional cataloging position. The library was short-staffed on the research help desk at the time, so I offered to help. Again, this was a great way to keep up my skills and make myself an even more valuable member of the team. When the library decided to restructure the positions in the library my position was created, and I was excited to take it.

Advice

Familiarize yourself with what is being taught in library instruction classes if the library offers classes. Learn to catalog and make friends with the technical services staff. Above all, for any position dealing with reference one needs to be a people person, introvert or not (and I do consider myself to be something of an introvert). You should enjoy and truly care about the people walking into your library.

Join an association, be it local, state, or national. This offers a sense of community especially if you are the only person in your institution that covers your area. There are also a lot of great ideas being generated by these groups and it is fun and rewarding to be directly involved in the conversations.

Anything Else?

Don't be afraid to try something new. If I hadn't accepted the technical services and special collections librarian position at my first university, I would not be where I am today. Say yes to things that might seem hard or scary. I said yes to a few things that I was unsure of, and it helped me get into my position, grow my position, and be happily productive.

Resident Librarian
Elizabeth S. Blake

What I Do

My mission as a resident librarian at the University of Pennsylvania is to gain experience and knowledge as an academic and medical librarian.

My primary responsibilities are answering reference questions through Springshare's LibAnswers and LibChat platforms. I also create library guides for the library and the library section of the critical writing program. I partner with STEM and other subject librarians on projects, including impact metrics for departments. I am involved in Penn's patient education meetings; write for the medical library's blog, *Biomeditations*; and participate in Philadelphia's Community Engagement Alliance project (CEAL). I have also worked on exhibits, digital programming, and forums with the chemistry, dental, math, physics, and astronomy libraries at Penn. My first exhibit involves ex-votos, a collection of paintings offering thanks to patron saints. I enjoy researching databases for consultations to assist patrons with their projects. I also created bibliometrics and altmetrics reports for different departments at the Perelman School of Medicine.

My Favorite Things

I love continuing to learn about academic and medical librarianship and to develop strategies to help medical professionals find information. I have exciting opportunities to try new projects with different science librarians and the freedom to choose which projects to focus on.

Challenges

One of my challenges is explaining my position to people, even those in the library science field, as many librarians have not heard of library residency programs. When I mention residency, many people think that I am a doctor. My purpose as a resident librarian is to gain experience as an academic librarian. A residency program offers new graduates from underrepresented groups the chance to gain professional experience. It can sometimes be frustrating to describe my position to others, and I hope that more people become aware of career opportunities in academic and medical librarianship.

My Career Path

My original career goal was to work as an occupational therapist but while getting my undergraduate degree, I decided not to pursue that career path. After graduating, I took some career assessment tests at Temple University's Career Center. The first career at the top of the list was pharmacist, but I didn't want to take the Pharmacy College Admission Test and more medical courses. However, the second career was health information specialist, and another career on the list was a librarian. At the time, I was working as a library assistant and I enjoyed the job, so I decided to become a librarian. During library school I was surprised to learn that there are different types of librarians besides public librarians. When I was a library assistant, I thought that librarians only worked for the public, but my library director told me about some of the different places librarians can work, such as hospitals, government organizations, schools, and law firms.

Advice

Look at the job that you are interested in, the duties and responsibilities of the position, and the skills that the job is looking for. Set up informational interviews with people who work in the jobs you are interested in. Ask them about what they do and what their day-to-day activities look like. Network as much as you can through sites such as LinkedIn. Visit library associations' websites to learn more about the different types of librarianship and decide which interests you the most.

Anything Else?

You do not have to fit the librarian stereotype to be a librarian. Be your unique self and be the most fabulous librarian you can be. As an African American woman, I do not fit the stereotype of being a librarian. I was initially discouraged not to see someone that looked like me in my local library, but that did not stop me from becoming a librarian. I am working diligently to encourage others to follow my career path so that others will see more people like me in libraries and in higher education administration. Use your unique personality, experience, and skills to show others that anyone can be a librarian, and encourage others to continue diversifying the profession.

Resource Sharing Librarian
K. Zdepski

What I Do

I coordinate the interlibrary loan (ILL) unit at the University of Massachusetts Amherst Libraries, which entails managing five full-time staff, designing workflows; troubleshooting and improving a variety of resource sharing systems, web pages, and related technologies; creating policies; maintaining statistics; creating reports; and searching for particularly difficult-to-find materials. I work closely with other areas in the library—for example, referring patrons to liaison librarians for support, and providing anonymized information about frequently requested materials for Acquisitions.

We share through OCLC, RapidILL/RapidR, and ComCat, as well as via email or web forms if the library we're working with doesn't have a system in common with us. We use ILLiad as our Resource Sharing Management System, tracking all types of requests in one place.

At my library, librarians are in the same union as faculty. There is an expectation of service and professional development—it's part of my job to engage in library, campus, consortial, and even national and international committee work.

I'm also a member of our access services managers team, which meets once a week to collaborate on departmental level planning and coordination, and the content and discovery leads, which does the same at the division level. My library is a member of both the Five College Consortium and Boston Library Consortium, and I collaborate a great deal with these colleagues. Note that my library is very large. Where we have six people doing interlibrary loan work, a small college might have only one person.

My Favorite Things

The community of interlibrary loan and resource sharing practitioners is incredible. There are people doing similar work all over the world, excited to support each other not only by sharing materials for patrons, but by answering questions, sharing documentation, and more. I see these conversations happening most on email lists related to the resource-sharing communities I am a part of: Boston Library Consortium, OCLC ILL, RapidILL, IDS Logic users, ALA RUSA STARS, and IFLA. There are many other regional and consortial groups. While resource sharing with these groups requires full memberships, many discussion lists (including IFLA Resource Sharing and OCLC ILL) are open to anyone.

I love the detective work involved in tracking down obscure materials and love seeing how delighted researchers are when we're able to provide something they had almost given up on accessing.

I also love getting to work with evolving technologies to try to improve user experience for both staff performing interlibrary loan work and patrons making use of interlibrary loan services. I really enjoy creating process maps and acting as the connection point between various vendors, library and campus information technology (IT), ILL practitioners, and others to make our processes work better.

Interlibrary loan work is an important piece of supporting affordable education. I see enormous relief from many students when they first learn the service is free. This is a major factor that drew me to libraries in the first place.

Challenges

Fragmentation of resource-sharing systems and lack of interoperability: the number and scope of resource-sharing systems is growing, and while most espouse a vision of interoperability in the future, many are siloed. It's difficult to keep up to date with the status of systems currently under development and what it means for the libraries using them.

Bureaucracy and communication: My institution is large and bureaucratic. I struggle to get all the information my team and I need when we need it, and things like hiring a new person after someone retires can take a very long time.

International sharing: In the past five years, we have worked with libraries in more than forty-five different countries. There are amazing resources within IFLA and the International Toolkit, but international shipping will always be a challenge, as will export restrictions and the unique licensing and copyright restrictions in other countries. For example, after a change in German copyright law in 2018, German libraries can no longer share digital scans of newspaper articles. Before that, if a researcher needed primary source information on pre-Second World War Germany, they could easily receive digital copies of articles; now, if the newspaper isn't held by a library elsewhere in the world (and it usually isn't) the articles have to be printed out and sent through the mail if they can be shared at all.

My Career Path

I started working in libraries as a student assistant in circulation at my college's library. I loved the work, and it led me to start library school immediately after graduating college. While in library school, I worked at both public and academic library circulation and reference desks, then as an interlibrary loan assistant, then as an electronic resources and serials access librarian, a position I was lucky enough to get a few months before finishing my MLIS.

Having a strong background in patron services, reference, and e-resources has helped me a lot, as has being curious about technology and how different pieces of libraries work.

Advice

I highly recommend taking classes that cover:

Copyright and Intellectual Freedom: There is a lot of misinformation about what copyright and fair use actually means when it comes to interlibrary loan. Interlibrary loan is explicitly authorized by Section 108 of the United States Copyright Act, as well as applications of 107 (fair use). It's well worth spending time to learn more of the nuances.

Reference: This job involves a lot of bibliographic searching. A reference class will cover both the kind of strategies necessary to succeed and skills for reference interviews, which become necessary when working with a patron on particularly odd requests.

Databases: Because of what I learned through a class on database design, I have a better understanding of how our systems work, and I can apply that in everything from customizing our patron-facing request forms to doing SQL searches to get significantly more detailed data out of the system for various reports. Right now, there are many new resource-sharing management systems in development and a strong technical background will serve you well.

Management: Even a small institution has student workers. It can be difficult to get support and mentorship around managing others, so take advantage of whatever you can learn in library school. Additionally, my management class included a section on project management, which is highly relevant wherever you go.

Languages: Knowledge of languages other than English is extremely helpful. At my library, after English the main languages requested are German, Spanish, French, Italian, Chinese, and Japanese. This will depend on your institution's program areas and community population. Even small pieces, like recognizing different transliterations to match Japanese titles accurately, are useful.

It's an exciting time in resource sharing, with a lot of ongoing change. You'll need to be ready to navigate quickly evolving systems and advocate for what you need to do your work well.

Anything Else?

Nothing compares to real-world experience in libraries, and you deserve to be paid for your labor. I highly recommend looking into temp agencies such as Bibliotemps, which can allow you to gain job experience in a variety of positions and get a stronger sense of what kind of work interests you most.

For more specific information about interlibrary loan work, I recommend checking out the recently revised *ALA RUSA STARS Interlibrary Loan Code for the United States* (https://www.ala.org/rusa/interlibrary-loan-code-united-states-explanatory-text) and the *Professional Competencies for Resource Sharing Practitioners* (https://www.ala.org/rusa/guidelines-professional-competencies). On an international level is the International Federation of Library Associations and Institutions (IFLA) *International Resource Sharing and Document Delivery: Principles and Guidelines for Procedure* (https://www.ifla.org/files/assets/docdel/documents/international-lending-en.pdf).

Scholarly Communications Librarian
Elaine Walker

What I Do

My main responsibility is to manage the daily operations of our institutional repository (IR). This includes adding and editing content; managing documentation, workflows, and interface updates; collecting, analyzing, and reporting IR usage data; and promoting the benefits of the IR to the campus community. The IR is a platform, or a web-based database, for collecting and preserving scholarship produced by the faculty, staff, and students of our institution from scholarly articles and research data to presentations and theses and dissertations. My top priority is to promote IR services to the campus community and recruit appropriate and sustainable content for it to support open access publishing. Another priority is to maintain a high standard of quality control for metadata that is used to describe the contents of the IR to enhance the visibility and discoverability for researchers around the world to access through their web browsers.

I also offer instruction sessions, workshops, and individual or group trainings to share my knowledge and raise awareness of scholarly communications topics and issues related to both traditional and open access publishing, open educational resources, and the institutional repository. I attend faculty department meetings to address questions about navigating open access publishing and scholarship specific to their discipline, and to explain how they can contribute and promote their research by utilizing the IR. I also serve as the libraries' resource for copyright and fair use, licensing, and intellectual property. Most of these consultations happen over email but I also have virtual meetings and face-to-face meetings. All these scholarly communications topics are wrapped up into several educational sessions during the annual International Open Access Week. These events provide an opportunity to establish a sense of community and start conversations around the importance of open knowledge sharing systems and the changes we can make to work toward more equitable and sustainable open access publishing practices.

My Favorite Things

This position requires a continuous balance between technical service and public service. One of my favorite aspects of the position is the outreach. I regularly check the campus calendars to stay on top of current events happening around campus like the Undergraduate Research Conference, the Faculty Research Showcase, lectures and workshops, and more informal occasions such as the Multicultural Coffee Hour. I try to attend or volunteer to serve at as many events as my schedule will allow. I have learned along the way that this is the most effective strategy for establishing connections with colleagues beyond the university libraries and for raising awareness of the services we offer to our campus. I am always thrilled to receive new submissions from faculty, which is usually an indication of successful outreach efforts.

Challenges

One of the biggest challenges I face is capacity. I am the only librarian at my institution whose role is fully dedicated to scholarly communications work, and there are times when I wish I could be in two places at once or when I find myself overwhelmed with emails and scheduling requests for consultations and meetings. Another challenge is battling the misperceptions that surround open access publishing and increasing faculty buy-in for using the IR. They may not always see the benefits right away and sometimes view submitting content to the IR as extra work that they do not have time for. I try to make the submission process as easy as possible with clear documentation, quick responses to email inquiries, and an offer to upload content on their behalf.

My Career Path

Once I started my MLIS, I knew I wanted to work in academic libraries. Experience is extremely valuable when getting started in this field. I have had internships and part-time positions in archives, public libraries, university libraries, and private research institutions, which allowed me to develop transferable and unique skills that can be applied in almost any library setting. Just after graduating, I accepted my first full-time professional position at a small university that serves about 3,000 students. During the first two weeks, in what I now see as a pivotal moment in my career, I volunteered to manage the new institutional repository even though I had no experience with database management. This responsibility was not explicitly listed in my job description, but I recognized it would be valuable experience to have. I quickly learned how to navigate both the user and back-end interfaces, learned the basics of HTML to customize the website with the university's branding, and created workflows and documentation for individual submissions and batch uploads for both internal employees and external users. Learning how to manage an IR also required me to learn about academic publishing. At that point in my career, I did not have any formal publications and was not familiar with open access and open educational resources, but I quickly set off to learn as much as I could by attending free webinars, subscribing to email listservs, looking at other libraries' open access library guides, and following conversations on social media (Discord, X). This set the stage for transitioning into my current position as a scholarly communications librarian.

Advice

If you are just getting started in this area of librarianship, do not be afraid to say "yes" to taking on new tasks and responsibilities even if they are a bit outside of your wheelhouse. Tackling a learning curve results in valuable experience and wisdom. In addition to the formal coursework of the degree program, I recommend learning the basics of copyright law and Creative Commons licenses. Study the ins and outs of academic publishing by becoming familiar with publishing models, publisher names (Elsevier, Taylor & Francis, and Sage), the reputable journals in your area/discipline with which you are most familiar or that you would like to work with, and their open access policies. Through my research in analyzing scholarly communications job descriptions, I have noticed an increasing demand for computational skills such as a working knowledge of website design (HTML, WordPress), programming languages (JAVA and Python), and data formats (XML and JSON). These skills are important for the technical services side of the position for managing the IR—which can be hosted on a variety of platforms like Esploro, Digital Commons, or DSpace—and for working with structured metadata. The benefits of my current position include a subscription to LinkedIn courses for professional development where I learned the basics of Python, which is required for part of the workflow for depositing batch uploads of theses and dissertations and open access articles into the IR. I also recommend learning the basics of database management, data analytics, and both qualitative and quantitative research methods and software (NVIVO and SPSS). There are other websites like Coursera that offer free introductory courses on copyright, licensing, and intellectual property that equip you with the resources and tools to expand your knowledge.

Social Sciences and Government Information Librarian
Amanda McLeod

What I Do

As my title suggests, I wear several hats. My two main functional work areas are as a reference and liaison librarian and as a government information librarian. These areas complement each other quite well. As a social sciences liaison, I work with patrons associated with the departments of psychology, sociology, anthropology, and criminal justice, and I often find myself drawing on my knowledge of US government information resources to support my liaison work.

While there is no such thing as a typical day, there is a certain flow and seasonality to being a liaison librarian. The beginning of each long semester (fall and spring) is often quite hectic with instruction, research consultations, and general reference work. During the latter part of the semester, I can typically give more attention to collection development and other projects. Summers are almost always taken up by special projects that can vary widely in scope.

My Favorite Things

My current role is a perfect fit for me. I really enjoy my liaison work, and it allows me to use my previous educational background to support my librarianship. I have always preferred the public facing side of librarianship, and I truly enjoy getting to work with students to connect them with the resources they need. In addition, in my liaison role I am able to provide greater support for faculty and graduate students. I get to constantly learn and explore new ideas—which is a wonderful aspect of my job.

As for government documents, it is something I never expected when I was in library school, but I have found it to be a fascinating niche in librarianship. My work as a documents librarian aligns well with my own orientation as an information professional. I feel strongly about breaking down barriers to accessing information, and the current ecosystem of government information in the United States is one way I can further that work. In the United States, at the federal level particularly, most publications and other information produced by government agencies and entities is available freely for anyone to access. While I am currently working at an institution with the resources to provide several subscription databases that support my work in government information, I always keep up to date with the freely available resources available. This allows me to serve community patrons and users who may not have access to a library's electronic databases.

Challenges

On the government information side, one of the biggest challenges is awareness. There are so many incredible items in our collections, but not many people know about us. It's also challenging to keep up to date on all of the different government resources. Particularly as the Federal Depository Library Program (FDLP) is shifting strongly toward a digital first/digital only model, there is so much information that it can be a bit overwhelming at times. Because of that, outreach and promotion are a huge part of the job. There is also a lot of internal outreach—within your institution, it can sometimes feel a bit like being on an island where you have to continually explain what you actually do.

As a liaison, awareness is also a challenge and trying to make connections with faculty can be tricky. Aside from that, one of the biggest challenges I have faced has been teaching. Like many librarians, I never received any formal training in teaching or pedagogy, so especially early on in my career, teaching was a huge stressor in my work. I used to dread teaching because I knew I was not at my most effective there. It has taken years of trial and error, shadowing more experienced teachers, and a lot of personal research and exploration for me to feel more confident as a teacher.

My Career Path

I never expected to become a government information librarian. My original plan when I went to library school was to become an archivist, but I also knew that was a tough field to break into, so I kept my options open and tried to gain a variety of experiences through internships, assistantships, and volunteer work. By the time I graduated, I knew that I wanted to pursue a career in academic libraries. My first position was as a library assistant handling serials and government documents. While my heart has always been on the public services side of librarianship, I am grateful for this experience because it helped me understand the work required to make our collections discoverable. It also introduced me to government documents librarianship. From there, I moved into a role as a government information librarian that also allowed me to develop my liaison skills before settling into my current role.

I think one of the most surprising things so far has been just how much I can use my government information experience to support my liaison work. There really is a government information resource for everyone!

Advice

With liaison work, it's very important to be open to different areas of work. If you are working with an academic department you're less familiar with (which is common), there are a lot of different options for learning. Look for opportunities to collaborate with faculty within your departments. If you can make a strong, positive connection with one or two faculty members in your departments, they can be an invaluable asset to promoting your work. In addition, while outreach is critical, it's important to consider your own bandwidth and workload to avoid burnout.

Don't be afraid to ask for help. When I was trying to improve my instruction, I asked more experienced teachers if I could shadow their classes as well as seek feedback on my instruction. It can be nerve-wracking to be observed, but it can be extremely helpful. Also, you will make mistakes, and that's okay. Trying out different ways of doing things or changing your approach to your work is how you learn and grow.

As a government information librarian, you often end up needing to work in areas that may not be your primary job. For example, even if your role is primarily public facing, you may still need to know basic copy cataloging to make sure that new shipments of documents are processed correctly. The good news is that there are a lot of free professional development opportunities that can help support your work. The Federal Depository Library Program (FDLP) Academy is a great resource, and the Government Publishing Office (GPO) has tools for new depository coordinators. The government documents community is very supportive as well, so reach out to other coordinators.

Anything Else?

If you end up in a faculty librarian role, it is critical that you try to build a community with others in similar roles, especially if you have to engage in research or go through the tenure process. When I moved into a tenure track faculty role, I was incredibly nervous about research. I did not have a lot of formal research training or experience, and I wasn't sure how to get started. Having "research buddies" has been so valuable—both novice researchers who understood the nerves and experienced researchers whom I could ask questions.

As a helping profession, we librarians can often take on too much because we want to help our patrons. Even in the face of the refrain "do more with less," it's okay to say no, and sometimes you have to let things break. Taking care of yourself needs to be the top priority.

Student Support and Engagement Librarian

Mary Kamela

What I Do

As a student support and engagement librarian, I participate in student success initiatives both inside the classroom and out. My main instructional duties center on first-year education. I am part of a small team of librarians who coordinate, plan, and conduct embedded library instruction in ENG 105, the first-year composition course at my institution. In addition to teaching up to four instruction sessions per section of ENG 105, I also teach a one-credit information literacy lab for ELI 105, my institution's first-year composition course for non-native speakers of English.

While I am not currently a formal subject liaison, I have been assigned liaison duties with student support units on campus. Previously I was liaison to the English Language Institute, which supports non-native speakers of English, and I am currently the liaison to the University Honors College. In this role I coordinate and provide in-class instruction for honors courses upon request, and I also meet with honors college students one-on-one for research consultations and other information literacy support.

In addition to these assigned duties, I may also teach other one-shot information literacy instruction sessions for other courses as needed. My position also grants me the freedom to pursue other projects related to the engagement and support of students across campus, so I usually have a few side projects underway. These could include anything from planning a library event to investigating innovative instructional technologies and new teaching platforms.

My position is tenure-track, so I also spend a good portion of my time on research, scholarship, and service requirements. I serve on committees on the university, regional, and national level, attend professional development whenever possible, and am usually working on at least one writing project and one professional presentation idea. My research interests, helpfully, relate to my job duties and center on the role of academic libraries in student success.

My Favorite Things

My favorite aspect of this position is the freedom it grants me to explore new possibilities and pursue passion projects. When I started, I felt like my team focused almost solely on instruction and was missing potential opportunities to engage students outside of the classroom. With my supervisor's support, I established a working group focused on increasing student engagement through library programming. This group has been able to foster connections between students and the library by planning and facilitating programs such as scavenger hunts, book clubs, and stress relief events. I have been continually encouraged to pursue opportunities that push me to become a better librarian and faculty member, including seeking leadership positions on committees and even applying for (and receiving!) a grant from ALA to establish a new book club partnership between the University Libraries and our campus's Educational Opportunity Program. Having both the freedom and institutional support to seek new opportunities encourages me to be self-motivated and ambitious in the projects I pursue.

Challenges

My biggest challenge has been taking on a tenure-track position. I came to this position after starting my career in school libraries, and making the switch really challenged my way of thinking at first. In a school library, I was often working in a very practical, solution-oriented way; my goal was to meet the day's needs and succeed in the scheduled lessons. Accepting a tenure-track position and feeling the push to formulate innovative ideas and write about them seemed completely foreign to what I was used to doing. It took about a year to feel like I had a grasp of what was required of me and to make the requisite mindset shift. I found that the best way to navigate this was to just dive into the world of academic libraries by getting involved with professional organizations and seeking out training opportunities. Once I found my footing within my new position and began to build professional connections, writing and research ideas began to form organically.

My Career Path

I began my career as a school librarian, first at an elementary charter school for two years, then as a public high school librarian for three. I then began wondering if school librarianship was where I wanted to spend my whole career. While there were aspects of the position that I loved, namely reading promotion, collection development, and library management, the working environment proved particularly challenging in the return after pandemic closures. I wasn't job searching in earnest when I saw the posting for my current position, but it seemed like the perfect transition point between library types—though it was moving into academic libraries from schools, it centered on information literacy instruction to first-year students, and I had ample experience teaching these topics at the high school level. I decided to apply and, as I learned more about the position and institution through the interview process, realized that the position would be an excellent fit.

As I navigate academic librarianship, I am continually surprised at how many different positions there are for information professionals. Though we all may describe ourselves to outsiders as "academic librarians," there are numerous specialized areas that come together to make academic library systems thrive. Since my path has focused on instruction and pedagogy, I find it fascinating to have opportunities to connect with librarians who work in areas like cataloging and metadata, archives, and delivery to see how our services come together to create an optimal learning environment for our campus community.

Advice

Many positions are cropping up that use the buzzwords "student support" or "student success" in the job title. Take a close look at individual job descriptions to ensure that the duties of these positions reflect your interests. Some positions are very instruction-based, like mine, while others may focus on library support and programming for specific student groups. Regardless of specific job duties, student support librarians should be willing to conduct outreach, connect with students, and advocate for resources that support student success initiatives. Even if the position description does not explicitly mention instruction, be prepared to teach, in both formal and informal settings.

Student support/success positions may or may not be tenure-track, depending on the institution, so I also recommend noting this and weighing how tenure and the reappointment process factor into your job selection. Finally, if you are seeking an academic librarian role, familiarize yourself with the application process, which can include a full day, on-campus interview. Coming from school libraries I was completely unprepared for the rigor of this process, but thankfully found a wealth of helpful guidance online and would encourage others to do the same.

Anything Else?

Do not be afraid to try out different library types or move between positions, even if you've got a few years under your belt in one specific setting. Skills you build in one library job will absolutely have transferability to another position or library environment. Though I was not anticipating moving from school to academic libraries, I found that the switch I made allowed me to continue the work I love in a different, more personally suitable environment.

I often hear from other academic librarians that they wish they were more prepared for the teaching required of their position. As you prepare for the job search, if you are interested in this type of position, seek out opportunities to gain experience. If your graduate program offers a teaching course, sign up even if it is not a requirement, or seek professional development opportunities online. For real-world experience, practicums, internships, and volunteer opportunities are an excellent way to practice instruction techniques.

Systems and Discovery Librarian
Emily Wros

What I Do

In a nutshell, I manage the integrated library system (ILS) and related software. Libraries of all kinds rely on multiple software and content packages that may or may not work well together. I troubleshoot problems that pop up, prepare the library for software updates, and pay attention to vendor communications. Sometimes I get to shop for new technologies. Every fifteen years or so there's a major ILS migration that can take a year or more, while smaller, more targeted software changes are happening almost all the time. Whenever there's a software change, I inform the affected parties and request their input, offer training, and update documentation.

I also have duties that are common to most academic librarians: I sit on committees, go to conferences, write grants, put on workshops, and conduct scholarship. Most of these tasks are technology-related in some way, but they don't have to be.

My Favorite Things

My favorite part of the day-to-day work is helping patrons with their technology problems. Ninety percent of issues are recurring and easily fixed, so it's easy to look smart and delight the patron with your friendly competence.

I appreciate that the systems and discovery field is relatively uncrowded, which makes it easier to get a job and to conduct scholarly research. It's not difficult to come up with a unique idea for a poster presentation or article because hardly any work has been published on systems librarianship.

Challenges

The biggest challenge is clear communication. Relating technical concepts to patrons, decoding vendor emails, talking to administration about what exactly you do all day, and negotiating with your coworkers about changes to the software are some examples of what this position does every day. Being good at communicating is harder than learning to code and probably more important.

The position is not typically patron-facing, which for me is the biggest downside. I enjoyed patron interactions (well, most of them, anyway) in my jobs before library school and I often miss them, but others may appreciate the lower social demands.

My Career Path

I stumbled into being a systems librarian. Originally, I wanted to be an adult services librarian in a public library. Since those jobs can be pretty competitive (especially in desirable locations) I thought I'd increase my chances by picking up some technology skills. To demonstrate that I was comfortable with computers and would be useful to have around when the printer inevitably stopped working, I minored in computer science in undergraduate school. That got me a graduate assistantship in library school, working for the state academic library consortium as they managed a big migration from one ILS to another. The assistantship required that I become certified in the big shiny new ILS that all the cool academic libraries were switching to, and that certification helped me get my first systems librarian position.

Advice

I got two good pieces of advice when I first decided to become a librarian: read library blogs and pay attention to job ads. Reading blogs and otherwise following librarians on social media will teach you a lot about conditions and trends in the field. Paying close attention to job postings will tell you what employers are looking for, especially when you see that multiple institutions are looking for the same qualifications. This will help you learn which skills are the most important to develop to get a job.

To become a systems librarian specifically, you're going to have to learn how to program—PHP is the most common language used at the time of writing, but Perl, Python, Ruby, and so on are all fine. You should also learn how to use Linux and APIs and ... actually, there's a long list of technological competencies that would make a hiring committee's eyes light up. You're not going to be able to learn them all, so the best thing to do is to find a few that you enjoy, get good at those, and be able to demonstrate what you know.

Take advantage of any access to library software you already have. Do you work at a library circulation desk? Start by reading the ILS vendor's documentation about the circulation functions (you can find this online through a basic web search), then expand into reading about adjacent areas, like interlibrary loan. Learn how the ILS works with other software. If something goes wrong with the ILS, ask the systems person (who may be in your library or may be at the consortial level) if they can walk you through their troubleshooting process.

Taking these and similar actions will not only help you become adept with your library's ILS, but it will also demonstrate to hiring committees that you're proactive and able to learn. Only consortial support offices and the largest universities have more than one systems librarian, so it's important to show that you can self-train.

If you're in library school, try to get a job or internship working with your university library's systems librarian. If there doesn't seem to be a preexisting position, email the library and ask about it—they might have some leads for you, or they may be able to create a position if you sound sufficiently motivated and there's money lying around. Almost all systems work can be done remotely, too, so you don't have to be an on-campus student.

Technical Services Director
Susanne Markgren

What I Do

I am the head of the technical services department of a college library. While technical services can involve different things in different libraries, mine includes acquisitions, cataloging, electronic resources, interlibrary loan, and systems. I supervise five people who work in the aforementioned areas. I work with the executive director of the library and two other directors (of access services and research and instruction) to formulate and assess annual goals and objectives for the library as a whole and for my department. Some recent objectives have included redesigning the library's website with a focus on accessibility, usability, and simplicity; collection assessment with regard to diversity, equity, and inclusion; serials review based on faculty members' "wanted journals"; and the implementation and migration to a new integrated library system.

My main tasks are to manage the library's collection budget; oversee projects and progress within my department; assess usage of the library's collections; process renewals, new subscriptions, and cancellations; review licenses; communicate and negotiate with vendors; and troubleshoot access issues. In a nutshell, my job is to ensure that students, faculty, and staff can seamlessly access the resources they need, both on and off campus based on the collection budget allotted per year.

On a lesser level, I participate in reference and research services providing online and on-call assistance, individual research appointments, and—occasionally—course instruction. As the subject librarian for the English department, I interact with faculty and review and purchase materials to support their teaching and research. The tasks I do vary by day and by time of year (annual renewals, fiscal year end, midterms/finals, summer projects), and the variety keeps my job interesting.

I also participate on committees and sit on boards, both at my institution and for local and national organizations like the Association of College and Research Libraries (ACRL) as well as its New York chapter. I write and publish and present on topics that interest me, such as career exploration and development, identity and reputation, informal leadership, and collection development. While my role is not a tenure-track one, I (luckily) am encouraged and supported to contribute to the profession and participate in professional development activities.

On any given day I might be signing off on invoices and purchases, updating budget spreadsheets, answering research questions, ordering materials that someone needs immediately (for a paper due tomorrow!), fixing an online access issue, cataloging a digital thesis, updating our OCLC holdings, communicating with a vendor, attending an online board meeting, identifying materials for deaccessioning, working on a writing project, and strategizing with colleagues about the timing and logistics of next the big project to tackle.

My Favorite Things

My favorite part of my job, or why I like coming to work every day, is the connections I have with my colleagues, my director, and all of the library staff. We work across departments—and as a whole—extremely well, and together we address challenges and develop solutions and think about how we can best support the campus community. In a few of my past positions this wasn't always the case. Silos still exist in many libraries, with little collaboration or communication between departments or among staff, which can often lead to isolation and a lack of motivation.

Another aspect that I enjoy, which I never really thought I would, is wearing a director's hat and being able to focus on bigger-picture projects that will affect not only my staff, but also the library and the campus, such as: what areas of the collection should be moved or weeded in order to create more student space? And how do we accomplish this, collaboratively?

Challenges

One big challenge for me is time (and task) management. This is probably true for most people in any position but may be more challenging when managing a department, and people in that department. I am not only attempting to manage my own day-to-day tasks, but also manage (or oversee) what others do, as well as make sure that tasks get done, goals get met, and things run as efficiently as possible.

Technical services roles have changed a lot in the past few decades, as we've moved to an online world, and technical services departments have shrunk with outsourcing, consolidation, and budget cuts. My library is no different, and I've had to move people into different roles, and have a single person take on the role of two, which involved a bit of retraining and lots of cheerleading.

Another challenge is managing expectations (and emotions) from below, across, and above. This is best done—in my opinion—with effective communication and transparency. One-on-one discussions, departmental meetings, and all-staff meetings have worked well in my library to establish a strong sense of community, understanding, and empathy. I strongly believe that everyone should know what their colleagues are doing and what they have accomplished.

My Career Path

Before library school, I worked in both public libraries and special libraries. While in library school, I got a job in the university library and realized pretty quickly that I wanted to be an academic librarian. And, in the past twenty plus years, my career path has taken many turns. I've worked in four different academic libraries, with varied sizes and organizational structures. At these libraries, I held many roles: reference, instruction, systems, electronic resources, and access services. And I realized that my preferred role and expertise lie in technical services. I also recognized that I prefer working in smaller libraries where I can do more things, wear more hats, take on more projects, and participate in public services roles with direct contact with students and faculty.

I'm a huge proponent of "more"—the more jobs/roles you can do, the more skills you can acquire, the more people you meet, the more environments you experience, the more questions you ask, the more risks you take, will help you choose the best pathways to build and shape your career. Each position has led me to the next, and the next. Along the way, I've never stopped learning, or challenging myself, or trying new things. I guess *this* has been the surprise, that my career is a cumulative and ongoing process—and I'm not done yet. I originally imagined I would be a special librarian, working in a theater or art library with books and plays, supporting artists, historians, and performers. But here I am, working primarily with digital materials and systems, in a small academic library, as a director. Who knew?

Advice

During library school I learned HTML and I took a digital design class and a database design class, and these probably helped me the most as I entered my professional career (sorry, LIS professors). I learned how to be a librarian on-the-job, and applied my technical skills to all my roles.

Curiosity on how things work, and a tenacity to identify problems or fill a need, has helped define my career. In one of my first positions (working as a reference and instruction librarian), I questioned why students couldn't renew items through the online catalog. So, it was tasked to me—with support and training, I must add. This was my first real foray into technical services and I was hooked. Adaptability is key to working in technical services. As previously mentioned, there has been much change, and there will continue to be as new technologies and systems emerge and replace others. If this seems exciting to you, then perhaps you should explore technical services roles. And if you do not believe you are qualified, think about past experience and skills (we call these transferable), or figure out how you can get some hands-on experience, and don't be afraid to go for it.

Finally, can someone develop a library course on curiosity, tenacity, and adaptability, please?

University Librarian

Rick Anderson

What I Do

My job can be summarized pretty simply but takes a lot to fully explain. The summary version is that I direct the work of a large academic research library. But it's important to understand that this doesn't mean I "run" the library. I have a leadership team of four associate university librarians (AULs), each of whom oversees a division of the library (research services, collections services, metadata and information technology services, and administrative services). I work very closely with my leadership team to set strategies for the library and then to ensure that their divisions are helping us move in the right directions. My AULs and the managers they supervise are really the ones who run the library; one of the challenges of my position is to maintain the right balance between being actively involved in the library's day-to-day work and keeping out of my managers' way so they can do their jobs.

Having just said that I don't really "run" the library, an obvious follow-up question would be "Well then, what do you do all day?" It's a question that I'm often asked, and I feel kind of self-conscious answering it—because while I know I'm very busy, I nevertheless have kind of a hard time explaining how exactly I spend all my time. I certainly spend a lot of time in meetings—probably 60 percent or more of my typical working hours. These are leadership meetings (in which we discuss policy issues and strategic direction, as well as how to implement both) as well as one-on-one meetings with my direct reports (in which they bring me up to date on developments in their areas and we strategize together) and with others in the library. There are also meetings with campus administration; although my title is "university librarian," I'm considered the equivalent of a college dean, and therefore part of the university leadership, which means I attend quite a few meetings with the other deans and vice presidents. And I have a variety of other meetings with individuals and groups that arise based on what's happening in the library at any given moment. The time that I don't spend in meetings I mostly spend writing and responding to email messages, drafting or reviewing policy and guidelines documents, and performing the myriad other random tasks that constantly come up.

Because Brigham Young University (BYU) is very well supported by The Church of Jesus Christ of Latter-day Saints, its sponsoring institution, I am not required to spend time cultivating donors and securing financial donations, for which I'm very grateful. This frees me up to spend virtually all of my time doing the work I genuinely love: helping to ensure that our library is serving BYU's students and faculty as well as we possibly can.

My Favorite Things

I love the process of determining strategy and figuring out how to implement it. I believe passionately in institutional alignment—in other words, working to understand what our host institution is trying to do and then figuring out how our library can best act as a strategic partner in making that happen. Two things about our host institution make my job a particular pleasure:

First, we are a religious institution with a fundamentally religious mission. Because I'm a dedicated and believing church member, I get a lot of satisfaction from helping to further BYU's religious mission, and being able to do so by encouraging and facilitating deep learning and high-quality scholarship is very satisfying.

Second, BYU is a university with a strong focus on undergraduate education and a secondary focus on applied research. I spent the first two-thirds of my career working for "research first" universities, which was wonderful; it was exciting and fun and those universities were doing outstanding things. I'm very happy, now, to be concluding my career in a "students first" institution.

Challenges

My answers to this question won't be surprising: personnel issues are always a major challenge, not because we have more such issues or because ours are more difficult than anyone else's, but simply because every organization has personnel issues, and they're always very tough.

My second answer is that setting and carrying out a change agenda is always difficult, especially in libraries. Libraries weren't designed to change easily; they were designed, in fact, *not* to change but instead to be consistent and reliable, and a lot of people who work in libraries came into the profession expecting (quite reasonably) to be in the business of consistency and reliability. Now they're being asked to be "nimble" and "flexible" and "responsive," and that's not an easy shift. Helping them through that process can be very difficult and is a major part of what's expected of library leaders right now.

My Career Path

My path to leadership was a little bit unusual in that I came up through acquisitions, collection development, and scholarly communication rather than through public services. Otherwise, my path has been pretty unexceptional: I rose through the ranks of management like pretty much anyone else. To be completely honest, not much about the job of library director has really surprised me—maybe because I spent thirteen years as an associate director before becoming a director, which meant that I got to see the sausage being made for a long time before I was put in charge of making it.

Advice

Decide early on how comfortable you are with making people unhappy. It's not that causing people distress is the index of a good director—far from it—but if you're being a good director, you will nevertheless inevitably make at least some people unhappy, if only because you will always have people in your organization who want mutually exclusive things. If you can't stand to have people mad at you, you shouldn't pursue leadership. Leaders who can't stand to be disliked are very ineffective, and, ironically enough, end up making many more people much more unhappy.

Also, recognize early on that what you're doing as a leader is not about you. It's about your institution, your patrons, and the people you work with. The less you care about being seen as the smartest, wisest, and most capable person in your organization, the happier both you and your organization will be. Quickly get in the habit of shining light on the work of your people rather than looking for ways to get the light to shine on you.

Anything Else?

Don't assume too early in your career that you fully understand what interests you. I've been surprised multiple times by the things I never thought I'd be interested in, but that really captivated me when I was required to undertake them. One example: early in my career, I was assigned to become the library's copyright and licensing expert. I groaned inside when I got this assignment, thinking that copyright and licensing sounded absolutely dead boring. But I accepted the assignment because I was on the tenure track, and you don't get tenure by declining such opportunities. To my great surprise, I absolutely fell in love with copyright and with license negotiation—and my involvement with both ended up altering the whole course of my career in ways I've found very enjoyable and fulfilling. I ended up writing a very well-received book on scholarly communication and publishing it with a major international publisher, which greatly enhanced my career prospects and wouldn't have been possible if I hadn't accepted that assignment early on. So try things and do keep your mind open; you never know what might turn into a passion for you.

User Experience Research Librarian
Beth Filar Williams

What I Do

User experience, or UX, are words that have meaning and application within and beyond libraries, generally with the implied word "design." People tend to associate UX with web design or product branding and usability. But in general, a UX focus is on having a deep interest to seek understanding of users—their needs, values, and barriers—beyond usability only. The UX honeycomb (https://semanticstudios.com/user_experience_design/) is a useful visual that shows that the interconnectedness for a user's experience must be useful, usable, desirable, findable, accessible, and credible. All these factors relate to library services and spaces, designed with a user focus in mind or a UX mindset.

My library has been growing in this mindset, but we did not have anyone with a role or position focused on this specifically. For over seven years I was head of the Library Experience and Access Department (aka public services and including spaces), which was a new combination of units when I arrived. This department's name was intentional, and I strove to create a UX mindset for public services. When I chose to step out of management, it was perfect timing for our library to create this new role: user experience research librarian (UXR). Reporting to the dean and housed in library administration provides the right location for me to lead the library holistically into a new phase of user experience research.

Officially my role is "to inform improvements of the Oregon State University Libraries' services and spaces through research and analysis." Since we know that the needs of library users are continuously transforming, my role is to collaborate with library workers in all units, to develop a culture of curiosity with how our users interact with services and spaces, what behaviors they exhibit, and what needs and barriers they face. Through my work I offer various levels of support, from informal brainstorming with staff to collaborating on focus groups and analysis. Fifty percent of my position is this "user research coordination," where most of my work focus falls. Collaborating across the library, I apply both qualitative and quantitative methods, ethnographic theories, and observational approaches to balance onsite services and spaces with remote services and to enhance service design. About 20 percent of my role consists of strategic communication, which dovetails with the UXR side nicely. Focused on library-wide communication both inside and outside the library, I apply my user-focused lens in assisting with outreach and promotion, which varies depending on the audience. Considering new ways to communicate to various user groups on campus is the other side of UXR.

My Favorite Things

Working across a library with many units and people is one of the best aspects of my position. It's the next best thing to working directly with our users. I am intrigued by the library ecosystem and how all our users intersect with us–their journeys, their touchpoints and barriers, their behaviors. I have always been a generalist in libraries, working in a vast number of areas, interested in how all units interact with each other. In this role, I have that bird's eye view of all of this, along with our campus intersections. The opportunity to work with so many people and personalities is very enriching—it's never boring, always interesting, and new. On a college campus our users change often, bringing shifts or new needs or behaviors. Working with college students also means you can hire student interns for projects or work with an academic professor on collaborative research or with a class for a course project. Being in a learning environment, a living laboratory like the library, can offer so many exciting opportunities within this role.

Challenges

Working across the library with many units and people is also one of the challenges. Not only are you working in areas you might not know well content-wise, but you're also working with various personalities, styles, and expectations. There are positions in libraries that span several units, but not many positions that can work within every unit as a UXR librarian can. Seeking user input on a project or service is always challenging; you have to approach a person/unit tactfully, so that they do not feel defensive (about the fact that you thought there was a problem) and want to collaborate. In the same way, it can be challenging to share user feedback to that person/unit. Spending time to build trust, sharing some small but positive experiences with others, and setting the tone as a collaborative one, can help alleviate these issues.

Balancing user input (and sometimes users say one thing while actively behaving differently) with the expertise of library staff, while staying flexible and agile, can be challenging. Determining which projects to pursue—a variety but not too many—takes thoughtfulness and time. Sometimes cost or people, timing, or capacity, can hinder making the feedback changes. Not every user input method will work; you might flop on some, or not get anything useful, or just end up with more questions. Stay curious and try another method or at another time.

My Career Path

Starting at age fifteen working in Baltimore County Public Library—when I swore I would never be a librarian—to receiving my MLIS, I have worked in all types of libraries and roles. Embedded throughout my whole journey was a curiosity of our users' experiences from online to in-person—how users interact with the library, seek help, and face barriers. I have used this lens in *all* my roles. I have also been able to apply and translate aspects of every position into my next role; I believe many librarians can do this as well.

Being privileged to be able to move really helped me explore librarianship, move up or laterally, and gain increases in pay and opportunities. Working in different libraries, especially in various regions and states, helped me to better understand the issues libraries and users face firsthand, and how that varies. Working in different library roles helped me to better understand how the whole library system interacts and works (or could work better). Now toward the latter part of my career journey I feel I am in a role I can truly enjoy and still learn something new every day.

Advice

A good UX mindset is to constantly notice how people are doing things or moving through your spaces. And then, not simply show them how to "do it right" but ask questions or observe in order to understand why/where/how they're struggling. Though there are many similarities, our users are not the same across libraries. Taking the time to understand *your* users, wherever you work, is a lens to adopt now and apply in any role you have in libraries. Having the curiosity to seek understanding of your users is what draws someone to this role.

Just because one person is in charge of UXR doesn't mean they have all the solutions. This is not about only observing or interviewing, it's *about building solutions together* to have an impact on our users' experience in the library. If you can, find allies, create a team of any size, or simply find project collaborators to work with. UXR is a powerful facilitator of teamwork because everyone's at the same level facing the user. Through the preparation and analysis, you explore as a team, put together the tools, collect data, confront the data, collaborate to draw conclusions, and take participatory action within the whole process.

4 Special Libraries

Adult Services Librarian, Library for the Blind and Print Disabled
Jami Livingston

What I Do

The Wolfner Talking Book and Braille Library provides braille materials, large print materials, talking book players, talking book cartridges, and braille e-readers for our patrons. We also facilitate the delivery of audio magazines and help patrons use Newsline, a telephone service that provides audio files of most newspapers. The Braille and Audio Reading Download (BARD) app is available for patrons to use on smart tablets and phones as well. Our patrons communicate with us on the phone on a regular basis. The National Library Service is our parent agency, and we follow their directives. Our services are 100 percent free of charge for our patrons. We serve the print disabled only patrons. Patrons must fill out an application and be qualified for our services.

As the adult services librarian at the Wolfner Library, my job is divided into three areas. I answer the phone and talk to patrons when I am in the office. I also catalog digital records and large print materials for our library. I manage the summer and winter reading programs. I also help with our weekly book clubs. We have a Zoom book club every Thursday afternoon. I help pick out titles, promote, and oversee some of the meetings. The third portion of my job is outreach. I contact public libraries, send them promotional materials about our services, provide onsite training opportunities, and attend senior health fairs and conferences to promote Wolfner. I travel all over the state and talk to people about what we offer.

My Favorite Things

I love that the job is not too repetitive. I feel like I am actually making a difference and helping people with their reading lives. I love talking to people on the phone. This job is more hands-on and fast-paced than my previous public library job. This job is really all about serving the patron. I love that I don't have to worry about managing budgets, writing grants, or calling a plumber—those director duties are not my problem anymore!

Challenges

We send out all materials by mail. Many of our patrons live in large metropolitan areas. We spend a lot of time talking with them about delayed mail, lost mail, missing mail, and so on. But we have no control over the materials once they leave our building! Also, we cannot have every single title that patrons ask for. Not all books are published in large print. The National Library Service picks which titles will be recorded talking books. Some patrons want items that are not available as talking books.

My Career Path

I started working in public libraries in my teen years. I knew I wanted to be a librarian. I earned my MLS from the University of Iowa. Before taking this position, I previously worked as a library director at county libraries. I was interested in working at Wolfner because my grandma used the blind library when I was a child, and I remember helping her order her tapes and return them to the library in Des Moines, Iowa. I feel like this is finally the right place for me. I traveled to a conference this summer where I met other people from other libraries for the blind and print disabled (LBPD). I really liked them, and it was great to meet people that shared the same goals as I have. I am often surprised at how passionate I have become about advocating for the disabled.

Advice

Embrace the awkward. Sometimes you have to do things that may make you feel uncomfortable or awkward, but that is the path to an authentic life. This job requires attention to detail, creative thinking, general friendliness, and patience.

Find your place. If your job doesn't satisfy you, keep looking. Network, even if it feels forced. Knowing people and appearing as a friendly individual will benefit you in life. Don't give up or settle.

Art Museum Library Director
Jon Evans

What I Do

Art museums, such as the Museum of Fine Arts, Houston, are special environments that bring together rich cultural objects, diverse audiences, and knowledgeable staff. Having spent the past three decades at this institution, I recognize that it's a privilege to spend my days surrounded by incredible works of art, curious patrons, and deeply committed staff. Overseeing an art research library and archives has evolved over the years given the changes in technology and cultural shifts. That said, most of the fundamentals have remained the same, as I still spend much of my time involved in four primary areas: communication, staff support, relationship building, and collection development. Our institution has 650 employees, including administrators, curators, conservators, educators, art handlers, registrars, development officers, and security personnel. Among my key roles are communicating effectively up, down, and across the "food chain." This means speaking the language that is most applicable in each environment, whether that be articulating our value in support of the institution's mission and financial imperatives to administrators, helping to create a positive research environment for staff, docents, and the general public, or welcoming academic classes to our facilities.

Coordinating and collaborating with my library and archives colleagues is another vital part of my role. I spend much of my time ensuring that they have the support and resources that they need to be at their best in order to carry out our goals for service, access, and preservation. Building relationships both within the institution and externally has been an increasingly active part of my job, enabling us to play a more central role in the museum's activities and to make a bigger impact in our community. Over the past decade, we've established formal partnerships with academic institutions, nonprofit arts organizations, and foundations in order to expand access to analog and digital resources for the museum's research staff and to enable our own physical resources to be shared beyond our campus. Circulating collections beyond one's institution might not seem like a radical action, but within the art research field it's a rare practice. We continue to lean into this in order to make our resources accessible beyond the ivory tower and to meet members of our community at their point of need. Lastly, collection building is something that I'm engaged in on an almost daily basis, ensuring that we have the "goods" when scholars and the general public come calling, whether these be the latest exhibition catalogs or rare illustrated volumes from the fifteenth century.

My Favorite Things

As mentioned above, I'm passionate about collection building and then putting these resources into the hands of community members where they can be used and appreciated. As my role has shifted over the years, I've tried to stay connected to what drew me to the field in the first place. While I'm less engaged in public service than in years past, I still make it a point to serve at our reference desk once a week to gauge the pulse of our patrons and to better appreciate how we can support their needs. Collection building has remained a constant throughout my tenure. Developing strong research collections that mirror our institutional holdings is central to our mission and enables us to support the information needs of our professional staff and those outside the institution. My approach has been to develop collections through an individualized selection process, rather than using approval plans. This is no doubt time and labor intensive, but it has allowed us to cultivate a much more intimate knowledge of our collections. Consequently, our colleagues have found that we're reliable partners in providing research support for their own collection building and exhibition planning needs. This has proven true not only with secondary research materials, but also when pursuing special collections materials. With a modest degree of coaxing and encouragement, these rare materials then frequently find their way into the museum's galleries where they complement the narratives that our curatorial staff want to tell our museum audiences.

Challenges

Among the challenges of working in an art museum environment is the need to advocate for our value within the institution, and the constant challenges related to space. More specifically, it is often necessary to advocate for positions that might seem self-evident to information professionals working in an institution where one is surrounded by other information professionals. For example, museum administrators have suggested that we consider digitizing large portions of our collections, such as our 40,000 auction catalogs, with the goal of then withdrawing these materials to free up space for non-library assets. While a not unreasonable request, it is one that is more complex than one might presume. Thus, it has been necessary to diplomatically advise our leadership on occasion that projects such as these require significant financial, personnel, and technical resources, not to mention the legal and technical hurdles involved. All the while we must continue to work diligently not only to maintain our existing space, but also to strategically expand our footprint to accommodate the continued growth of our collections, as space challenges are endemic to art museum libraries. It should also be noted that art history is an accretive process, and as a result, weeding collections is not as easily achieved as it may be in fields such as the hard sciences.

My Career Path

Thanks to my parents, regular visits to museums throughout my youth in cities like Pittsburgh, Chicago, and Philadelphia forged a lifelong interest in museums. After pursuing an undergraduate degree in studio art, I might have pursued my own creative path, but knew instinctively that a career in art museums was a better match. That said, my road to art librarianship was not a direct one. It took me several years in the museum's retail department to recognize that this was a viable option. As the museum's bookstore manager and book buyer, I began selling books to the museum's art librarians, which presented an entirely new career avenue. Once I realized that I could merge my interests in art, books, and public service, I was hooked. This would allow me to go beyond the transactional to help build something that would make a lasting impact in my community, which has remained a driving force for me. While still working in the bookstore, I began volunteering in the library. Within a year, a position opened up in the library and I made the leap, starting as a library assistant while simultaneously enrolling in a library science program that would keep me busy during weekends over the next four years. Patience, timing, and much good fortune found me leading the institution's research entities after fourteen years of work in virtually every position within the library.

Advice

Take as many art history classes as you can manage, as it will provide a solid foundation for your work. Visit museums, galleries, and libraries as often as possible when traveling to a new city or region. This exposure will pay dividends in the future, as there's no substitute for active engagement with art and art documentation, regardless of your role within an art library. Study other languages to expand your skill set, as the field is grounded in a multilingual foundation within an increasingly global environment. Don't forget what drew you to the field in the first place and continue to find ways to feed that passion as you cultivate new ones.

Associate State Librarian
Michael Golrick

What I Do

As associate state librarian for the State Library of Louisiana (SLOL), I am responsible for the library development department. In that role, we provide support to the public libraries across the state of Louisiana. Most of the public libraries in Louisiana serve the whole parish (county).

The support we provide includes offering advice on issues related to service to the public. One of the staff in the department is specifically responsible for providing support for youth services staff. Continuing education is an important part of what we do. In 2009, the SLOL was part of the pilot program of the American Library AssociationAllied Professional

Association (ALA-APA) to establish a certification program for library support staff. The program is the Library Support Staff Certification (LSSC). The SLOL currently offers six approved courses that have been taken by over 600 people. Louisiana has more certified support staff than any other state.

When I think about it (and what motivates me to get up in the morning), not every public library building has a degreed staff member present at all times. How can we make sure that every person using a public library receives excellent public service? That is accomplished with training. That is the inspiration for the state library support of library staff. My job is to help teach and do the administrative work that is required.

My Favorite Things

To be successful in library development, it helps to have a variety of experiences in different aspects of library work. I have worked in suburban and in very urban libraries, which has been a huge help. Having a broad range of experience allows me to be able to offer suggestions. I think that this is a culmination of all that I have learned from my years of working in the field, and from the many and varied acquaintances I have from my professional activities.

Challenges

One of the hardest things to deal with is the uncertainty in many situations. Starting post-pandemic, the public arena has changed dramatically. The challenges to library materials and the actions of legislatures are one of the biggest issues I face. Part of what I do is track legislation that could affect the libraries in my state. Legislation has required a lot of reexamination of library policies and practices, and the state library is the entity working to help libraries deal with those changes. At times, it feels like the staff in the public libraries around the state are "blaming" the SLOL (and sometimes it feels personal) over these changes that came from the legislature. Being able to separate personal feelings and realize that the questions are not personal, is important.

My Career Path

I started working in the public library in my hometown while in high school. My childhood children's librarian became the director and hired me. She served as a mentor, and we met for lunch at my first ALA conference. I worked in university libraries as an undergraduate and graduate student. I worked as a reference librarian in public libraries, was a public library director, ran a multitype library consortium, and have been at the SLOL for the past fifteen years. I started doing public library statistics, became head of the reference department, and a year ago, I became the associate state librarian.

Advice

Moving to different parts of the country has broadened my horizons about what library service can mean. My first real professional job was in a county that was larger than the state I grew up in. It was a shock for a New Englander to move to the Southwest. However, the exposure to the distances was critical in understanding what was happening in the library world. Going on the bookmobile opened my eyes to the rural nature of some library services (even after having worked on the bookmobile in my very suburban hometown). Seeing the reservations and incredible challenges faced there changed me in many ways, and at the same time let me be aware of and sensitive to the urban poverty that I later saw. In some ways there is more commonality than differences in those communities.

A different formative experience involved finding data. In my second graduate program (MBA), I worked in a research department of the business school. I worked in their small, very specialized library, which exposed me to the vast array of data that is available. That knowledge is still useful to me today and was useful as I did planning as a public library director.

One thing that had not been emphasized enough to me, although I think it may be done more now, is the importance of building relationships with community organizations, for example, making them aware of what the library can provide and also enlisting their support for library services. Use groups like the chamber of commerce and the service clubs (Rotary, Kiwanis, Lions, and others) as a place to identify potential board members for both the library board (however it may be constructed) or your friends/foundation. It is critical to build relationships with your funding authorities. In one job, I had a champion in the city finance director because I approached her early on to ask her to explain all the intricacies of the budget and funding process. I also asked what we could do better and was able to implement some of those changes.

In the public library and state library agency world, there are many, many moving parts. It is a challenge to pay enough attention to all of them.

Anything Else?

Librarianship is a small profession. Be careful of burning bridges. You never, never know when someone will return in your professional life, even in a different role. I have had this happen to me more than once in the course of my career. People from twenty or more years previously have become part of my world again, with both of us in very different roles.

Audiovisual Archivist
Ari Negovschi Regalado

What I Do

As the technical director of Texas Archive of the Moving Image (TAMI), I am responsible for overseeing the digitization of audiovisual (AV) material—think VHS tapes, 16mm film, and so on—for the organization. TAMI aims to preserve the history of Texas by preserving moving image media with the goal of making it accessible to the public via our website. Working together with a part-time archival media technician and a digitization intern, we are able to digitize approximately 500 items per quarter, which then go into our digital repository.

A large part of my job involves managing our digital repository, by transcoding footage, working with an outside information technology (IT) agency to manage our cloud storage, and working with our operations manager to prepare archival footage for licensing requests.

Considering how niche the audiovisual archiving field is, and how new (relatively speaking) audiovisual technology is, I also spend a fair amount of time researching analog technology, mentoring my technical staff, and troubleshooting our systems. As you can imagine, there's not a whole lot of standardization within the audiovisual archival field given how quickly technology changes, so it's important to stay in tune with your organization's need to determine the best course to move forward.

On a regular day, I could find myself doing a media preservation assessment, digitizing Betacam footage of old news broadcasts, baking U-matic tapes, or repairing a broken tape. This job never gets boring; there's always more than enough work to do!

My Favorite Things

Collaboration is one of the huge benefits of working at a small organization. TAMI relies heavily on collaboration, both internally and externally, to fulfill its mission of preserving Texas history. Internally, I am frequently collaborating with our curator to generate digitization priorities and metadata, which allows us to work through a vast expanse of archival material more efficiently. As an organization that does year-round public outreach, I'm able to bounce ideas for programs around with our managing director.

Externally, through our collaboration with the Texas Film Commission, we are able to host two home movie collection events per year. These events, operated via our Texas Film Round-Up program, allow us to offer free digitization services to the public and generate a crowd-sourced archive of Texas history. Organizing these events requires a fair amount of collaboration with outside stakeholders such as film centers or community-based archives that have roots in the communities we are tapping into. In doing this work, we've been able to generate a network of archival contacts across the state.

Another wonderful aspect of the job is learning every day from the wealth of material our archive holds. TAMI aims to digitize as much content as possible each year with the goal of posting it to our website and making it viewable for free. As the person who does quality control of every digitized file before it gets accessioned permanently into our digital repository, I gain exposure to unique archival materials that haven't been viewed in decades. Whether it's getting a first pass at handling a Kodacolor film from the 1930s or a U-matic tape from NASA dating back to the 1970s, this job keeps me intellectually stimulated.

Challenges

Undoubtedly the rapidity of technological obsolescence is the biggest challenge we face as audiovisual archivists. Unlike traditional book and paper conservation, which has been standardized through scientific research over the course of decades (or centuries, depending on how you view it), audiovisual archiving lacks standardization due to two major factors: time and intellectual property (IP).

Archivists, scientists, conservationists, and others are fighting against a short lifespan for most media (e.g., VHS tapes can be rendered obsolete and unplayable in as little as twenty years, depending on storage conditions), and a short period of research on the technology itself, given that film and video technology can range from 15-plus to 100-plus years old. Historically speaking, we are looking at a very new invention.

What information we have regarding the conservation of physical media has been determined by a combination of anecdotal evidence and scientific research in a brief span of time. Not only that, IP varies among film/video tape formulas *and* playback deck manufacturers. For example, even if a U-matic tape is in good condition, you'll have to source a functioning U-matic deck for playback. Decks were churned out from factories as disposable commodities with a limited lifespan (i.e., planned obsolescence) under warranties that only allowed the manufacturer (or approved repair technicians) access to factory repair manuals. So in the case of our U-matic tape, if you are lucky enough to source a deck from the 1970s, how do you preserve this deck to allow for full functionality? Analog deck repair, preservation, and mechanical engineering are not skills that are typically taught in library science or conservation programs; this is inherited knowledge learned through apprenticeship, experience, and independent research. All that said, our field is truly playing a game of catch-up that leaves audiovisual archivists at a huge disadvantage.

As if that wasn't challenging enough, after you digitize a film or video, you'll likely encounter issues related to storage. It's rare to find an archive that is not pressed for digital storage space. On top of the cost (e.g., a 100-terabyte server partition can cost $10,000!), you'll be looking at the maintenance of the repository itself, which can include backup copies, cloud-based integrations, and security.

My Career Path

There's no one path to becoming an audiovisual archivist. You'll encounter people who started as sound engineers, media makers, and film projectionists, to name a few. It's really a varied field, although it's becoming the norm to see job postings requiring an MS/LIS degree.

I began my career as an undergrad in California Institute of the Arts' film/video program. I took a course in video art, taught by John Hawk, and worked at the school's video production studio, which specialized in the digitization of analog video formats. Between the two, I got to learn about the history of analog video, experiment with video synthesizers co-constructed by Nam June Paik, and gain experience digitizing videotapes for students in the program. While I thoroughly enjoyed the work, making money as a video editor was a more practical pursuit out in the real world, so I hustled to work in the production field. I gained knowledge of organizing digital media assets for postproduction during this time, which I would later come to understand as a form of digital archiving in and of itself.

I left California for Chicago and eventually found myself working at a boutique digitization vendor that specialized in digitizing home movies and analog broadcast formats. Our firm was frequently hired by corporate archivists to digitize large volumes of audiovisual media, which led me to begin researching how I could formally advance my career into the archival sphere. I intentionally sought out MS/LIS programs that were affordable, were accredited by the ALA, and offered courses in audiovisual archiving. Living in Illinois at the time, I was fortunate to find that the University of Illinois at Urbana-Champaign offered exactly what I was looking for and was hiring a media preservation graduate assistant, which positioned me as a paraprofessional film archivist in the Rare Book and Manuscript Library. All the skills I learned working in postproduction and at a digitization vendor gave me a strong foundation to begin working in the vault on day one, given my familiarity with analog media.

After graduate school, I was extremely fortunate to receive multiple offers for audiovisual archivist positions, given my unique experience working in media prior to entering the archival field. I chose TAMI based on our aligned values, culture, and interest in home movies.

Advice

Get as much experience with archival media as possible. Participate in internship opportunities that will allow you to gain hands-on experience, learn as much as you can about traditional archival best practices, join local professional associations for archivists, and volunteer at a local archive if possible. You'll be more than well-situated to grow a career in the audiovisual archive field by doing some or all of these things. In many ways, hands-on experience with media far outweighs the master's degree, so prioritize learning about AV above all else before you take the leap to pursue a graduate degree. You'll be a highly desired candidate if you bring a strong media foundation with you. And remember, there's no one path to becoming an audiovisual archivist.

Conservation Librarian
Megan Burdi

What I Do

As the national librarian for United States Fish and Wildlife Service (USFWS), I'm involved in every aspect of the library's operations and work with a small team of many talents. My title, national librarian, refers to the scope of our library and my position, but on any given day I act as a systems, metadata, acquisitions, outreach, reference, or instruction librarian. I enjoy the generalist nature of my job, and because there is so much project-based work, I'm never bored.

I spend much of my time doing reference work and assisting our scientists with literature search requests, which often center on Endangered Species Act protected species or their habitats. My colleagues and I collaborate on our distance learning efforts, and quarterly we host new staff for library tours and education sessions. We develop internal resources like library guides, microlearning videos, and job aids so USFWS staff can get information they need to use the library at point of need. I also work on collection development for print and electronic resources and compile and report out our usage metrics. I maintain our catalog and do some cataloging work, but because of limited staff resources, much of what I do is copy cataloging.

The USFWS Library has also been working for several years to migrate our National Digital Library online media repository, which features over 30,000 digital objects, to an updated platform. Our collection features contemporary and historic imagery of wildlife, public lands, and the work of the USFWS, mostly in the public domain. I spend a great deal of time working with photographers, digital communicators, web managers, and other staff to design and implement a system that we hope will allow field staff to contribute their public domain imagery to a user-friendly and accessible platform.

The USFWS Library also hosts a public and internal book club, America's Wild Read, which focuses on engaging with conservation literature. We host quarterly online book discussions that aim to inspire our readers to connect with nature and conservation.

My Favorite Things

Working for the federal government offers unparalleled job security, and my work as a public servant gives me a sense of honor and purpose. My agency's mission is to work with others to conserve, protect, and enhance fish, wildlife, and plants and their habitats for the continuing benefit of the American people. I feel that in my small way, I'm making a difference in supporting conservation with my skills and background.

I also enjoy the variety of my duties, and my program, the National Conservation Training Center, has a culture of growth that encourages me to develop professionally. I have the pleasure of working with many talented, passionate people who care deeply about our environment and all its inhabitants.

I would absolutely recommend working for the federal government for those who feel a call to public service. Working as a generalist "jack of all trades" librarian is exciting work for those who crave variety.

Challenges

The biggest challenges of my position are also its strengths. Our library has a small team, so we can be flexible and nimble, but at times our capacity does not match the amount of work to be done. Because of this, it's important for us to prioritize the most important work and look for opportunities to work on the project backlog.

We are embedded within a larger program and organization that reaches across the United States to stations in the field, so it has been a challenge to ensure we reach those we serve wherever they work and ensure busy people know what resources we offer.

The federal government can be slow to adopt new technology, especially as cloud-based technology becomes the norm, because of important software security requirements such as the Federal Risk and Authorization Management Program (FedRAMP). Confirming that we comply with requirements while meeting the needs of our users is critical but challenging for a small library.

My Career Path

As an art history undergraduate student at West Virginia University, I was inspired by a fantastic mentor, the creative arts librarian. My mother is also a retired school librarian, and I was a regular at my public library throughout my childhood, so I had some inclination toward libraries. Librarianship seemed like a natural fit for my interests in research and information; I often cared more as an undergraduate about the process of research and writing than I did the outcome of my papers!

I enrolled in the MSLIS program at Simmons University with an archives management concentration. My program had a practicum requirement, and I had the opportunity to intern at the Smithsonian Institution's Archives of American Art. When my practicum concluded, I accepted a job in the digital operations department, where I worked with metadata, mass digitization, and research assistance. After a few years in my "dream job," I felt the desire to grow into a leadership position and find a way to live closer to nature and close to family.

From a neighbor, I learned about the National Conservation Training Center in Shepherdstown, West Virginia. She seemed so happy at her job there, so when the librarian position was advertised on USAJobs, I took a leap of faith, applied, and was offered the job.

The reference and metadata skills I developed at the Archives of American Art (AAA) have been critical to my work at the USFWS. I gave many professional presentations at the AAA and now do a great deal of public speaking for USFWS trainings. I've had to learn a lot about federal acquisitions and electronic resources management, but my comfort with learning new technology has been very helpful.

Advice

Although my work serves patrons in the field of wildlife conservation, my background in art history and archives did not exclude me, because my skills were transferable. I made sure to emphasize this throughout the application process. Librarians should learn to advocate for themselves and confidently communicate their strengths in resumes and interviews.

Take advantage of internships and practicums whenever possible and connect with colleagues and leadership. The network I cultivated helped me progress just as much as the skills I developed.

I also encourage those who want to work in a special library or government library to apply for positions based on interest and potential for growth, rather than on being the perfect fit on paper. The federal application process is unique, and sometimes intensive. Take advantage of online resources explaining the nuances of applying via USAJobs.

Flexibility is critical to working in a government library. Priorities and projects can change quickly, as can the budget. Patience is also key. Sometimes important, groundbreaking projects can take a great deal of time, but are worth persevering.

I wish someone had told me, when I was a student, to pursue a career path based on my vision for my life as a whole, not just on my professional interests. I loved working in the archives field, but I wanted to raise my children close to nature and be near family in my rural hometown. I am grateful I've been able to find a job that fits my lifestyle.

Anything Else?

Don't be afraid to change course and try a different area of the field, or even jobs you aren't sure you fully qualify for. Transitioning from archives to libraries, and subject-wise from art history to conservation, was at times challenging, but has been so worth it.

Corporate Librarian
Eileen Davenport

What I Do

As a research librarian at an investment bank, my department serves users across varied departments. We are charged with getting relevant data to the appropriate audience at the optimal time. To find this data, I look for answers to incoming questions, using open access and subscription databases. The sources used are determined by the question posed, and they range from "please send the full text of this article" to "who are the largest companies in (whatever) industry, and how big will the market be in ten years?" These subjects are determined by our client's needs, and those are spread across industries and geographies. Anything and everything can be the topic of a question. Most, but not all, materials are electronic; only a few print sources are still used.

My Favorite Things

The variety of topics is the most interesting: I never know what I'll be working on when my morning starts. And the job offers constant learning opportunities.

Challenges

When I started, electronic information was still developing; a lot of research relied on print sources. What is now available in online databases (like equity research reports) was only available on CD-ROMs mailed out by a vendor. I can remember spending hours digging through multiple CDs to find reports that are now retrievable in seconds. But this presents a new challenge to business information centers: the perception among users that we can retrieve all data in a short period of time, for no or low cost. If only that were true!

The sheer amount of data floating around also affects our work. What is readily available is widely known, or, at least, it should be. In addition to making sure our internal clients have all the same data as our competitors, we work to find additional info that is still relevant, yet possibly overlooked by others. And we check the validity of what we pull from open access sources. The only thing worse than not finding an answer is spreading wrong information. Trust takes years to earn but can be quickly lost. If you don't know or can't find reliable data, you *must* be upfront about it.

The number of corporate libraries has declined significantly since I've been working. Offshoring information centers is a real job threat. When I became a corporate librarian in the late 1990s, there were many opportunities to network with other corporate/financial librarians at events sponsored by our local Special Libraries Association chapter. Now the remaining members are mostly academic or legal librarians.

My Career Path

I began my MLIS program with the goal of becoming a school librarian, and held part-time positions and internships in public libraries, archives, and school libraries while earning my degree. My first reference and instruction course was taught by an adjunct faculty member who worked full-time in a corporate library. The workplace descriptions mentioned in class were intriguing, especially compared to my own experience in other settings. That introductory course was followed by a business reference class, and my goals changed as I found this track much more engaging. I do regret not taking business or accounting classes as an undergraduate; they would have provided a stronger understanding of some of my first research topics. I have picked up a lot on the job; I just wish the financial topics had been more familiar from the start. For those just starting out, corporate libraries are great places to work, but you should prepare for other roles, as you may not retire from one.

Advice

The three most important characteristics are curiosity, attention to detail, and a good memory—each is irreplaceable. It is also helpful to read the news daily; sooner or later, most stories will be relevant to a work request. But, given the number of peers who have lost jobs to offshoring, I would encourage all who are interested in the corporate path to earn other business credentials. When I was earning my MLIS, I remember discussions about the usefulness of the degree, hearing professors claim that training and experience would easily translate among different library types, making it possible (and not unheard of) to work in academic, public, and special libraries over the course of a career. In my experience transfers among library types are the exception, which is a shame. Each type of library has a unique culture, but any new hire must adjust to the new environment, and the value of experience shouldn't automatically get overlooked because of a different setting.

Anything Else?

Offshoring hangs over my head like the sword of Damocles. I once heard a speaker say that business information needs to be accurate, obtained quickly, and at little cost, but in her experience, most patrons can get only two of those three characteristics. When costs need to be cut, the easy accessibility of information seems to be perceived as an abundant constant, while the ability to identify the relevant, updated, and pertinent items never seems to be addressed. And the offshoring firms have great sales reps. Information professionals have many skills, but it is hard to compete with those who promise everything budget-conscious management wants to hear. A friend lost two good positions in banking information centers when those departments were outsourced. Three years after the second elimination, she's still searching, even with two decades of experience.

Curator and Archivist, Historical Association
Laura Kathryn Nicole Jones

What I Do

While my job title only includes curatorial and archival work, my actual position encompasses everything included in the entire collections department of a museum: exhibits, collections management, accessions, research, reference, conservation, preservation, and more. If you can imagine something being done by someone who works with library, museum, or archival collections, it is likely part of my job. However, working with collections is not my *entire* job; because we have so few employees, I am often helping with various other tasks and events. I wear so many hats—when I think about it, it reminds me of when I saw Cher on her "Farewell" tour, and she walked on stage wearing a giant stack of hats.

For the most part, my typical day consists of operating one of the museum desks and attempting to complete other tasks between visitors. We get quite a few research requests, so I am often working on those between helping visitors. My current main project is organizing our collections storage, so when I am not assisting visitors or researchers, I am decluttering our collections storage and developing policies and procedures, as well as a project plan, for getting everything organized and housed according to best practices. If I weren't an organizing fanatic, I would have run away after seeing how much work needs to be done with collections storage.

My Favorite Things

Working for a small institution is not the kind of job you want to get if you like sitting in an office. This job gets physical and requires creativity, innovation, and experimentation. This is a job for jack-of-all-trade types. You can't be afraid to get down and dirty: spray painting, fixing doors, constructing picnic tables, exterminating rodents, gardening, building sod-roof sheds, and so on.

I am often doing something new, and that is exactly why I pursued a position at a small institution. When I worked at a university archive, I felt siloed and bored because I only did a select few tasks every day. I'm a creative person who loves to learn and try new things, even things that don't seem related to my position. I'm a kinesthetic learner, so having a job where I'm constantly doing things with my hands helps me stay engaged.

This position also provides a good balance of independent work and teamwork. I never feel like I'm unheard by others because there are so few of us, but I also never feel isolated because we are constantly working with each other throughout the week on events and larger institutional goals. I have immense freedom with my time and can choose which projects I want to engage with, based on my mood, but with that high level of independence comes the challenges of managing my own tasks and time. It requires self-discipline, motivation, and determination to keep going and keep on top of all the various projects that are occurring simultaneously. As I previously mentioned, I'm an organizing fanatic, so I love the flexibility and ability to be my own "boss" while also working for someone else. I grew up homeschooling myself through most of my adolescence, during which time I learned a lot about managing projects, time, and myself; those skills are vital in my current position.

Challenges

The biggest downside of this position is the lack of benefits; the only benefit my employer can offer is unlimited paid time off. I also live in an expensive area, so while people outside this area see my salary as decent, it is actually low. If I did not have a partner who was also working full-time with benefits, I could not afford to live in this county.

The museums don't get enough traffic, and we struggle with getting grants because our population is not very diverse. We are constantly over budget, and that influences how much staff can get paid and how well we can update the museums from their 1980s format. I desperately want to help improve the museums so they can attract more visitors, but some days the task feels overwhelming. I must constantly remind myself to just try my best to keep from getting depressed; this is not the right environment for people who struggle to stay positive and excited about their jobs without external motivators.

My Career Path

Like most college students, I started college clueless as to what I wanted to do, so I tried a variety of courses that eventually led me to American Sign Language interpretation; however, after attending courses for a year I did not feel it was the right path, so I switched to English for my bachelor's. While in my final year, back to being clueless about my path, I got a job at the university library. My supervisor suggested pursuing library science, so I did and found archives by volunteering at my local library.

I've always loved museums, so I chose a university that offered both an archives and museum studies program because I wanted to broaden my skills as much as possible. Throughout my program, I attended as many extracurricular events as I could: webinars, workshops, lectures, conferences, informational interviews, and so forth. I joined the Society of American Archivists and got matched up with a mentor. I volunteered in the local library archives and did both physical and virtual internships at as many different types of institutions as I could. All this information and experience guided me toward the exact type of work and institution I knew would make me happy, make me feel like my job was more than a job, and make me feel like I could wake up even on my worst days and feel motivated to go to work, because I wanted to be there. It was specifically volunteering at my local historical society that made me feel that way, and I knew that I wanted to work in a place like that, but back home in Colorado.

Advice

Learn everything: if it sparks an interest, pursue it. So many things I learned for fun have been incredibly helpful throughout various positions, school, and especially in positions like my current one where you have to think outside the box. Here is a brief list of skills I have learned and found useful: American Sign Language, writing (all types), public speaking, website design, sewing, paper conservation, bookbinding, papermaking, photography, and sociology. Here are some skills that I wish I had learned: carpentry, building conservation, psychology, textile conservation, debate, and nonprofit management.

Create an online portfolio of all your accomplishments and skills. My portfolio impressed a lot of employers and got me several positions, including this one. Link it on your resumé and cover letter and add a link to your LinkedIn account.

Pursue all opportunities. Apply for all the scholarships and internships you can, even if you think you don't stand a chance. I applied for a virtual NASA archives internship and got it, even though I never expected to succeed. The internship alone improved my resumé significantly and impressed a lot of people. Filling out all those forms feels like having another full-time job, but it can pay off.

Anything Else?

I got my dream job right before I graduated because I knew exactly what I wanted to do, and that dream was realistic and niche. Most people don't want to work the hard jobs at small institutions that pay little and are in rural areas that don't even have a Walmart. Think about what it is that you really want to do for the rest of your life and narrow down your search to those positions; just do whatever you can get until then that will support you. If you can't get a position in the field right away, get a different job and volunteer in the meantime to keep your skills fresh and your resumé up to date. Employers can tell when you are passionate about the position you are pursuing. They will hire that type of applicant over people who have all the skills but none of the passion.

Library Development Consultant
Reagen A. Thalacker

What I Do

I work with a team of six to provide continuing education, resources, support services, and consulting to public libraries across Virginia. My particular audience is the public library directors, trustees, friends of the libraries groups, and foundation members. Any one day I could be answering questions regarding the Code of Virginia, hosting a webinar on fundraising, adding books to our professional development collection, onboarding a new public library director, building a new spreadsheet of data, conducting a board training, traveling for a library site visit, or building new partnerships that will benefit the libraries. My role was created quite recently and I'm the only one to ever hold it, so I have a lot of autonomy and am getting to create its parameters and increase those boundaries each year.

My Favorite Things

Working in a library development role is perfect if you're eager to serve the librarians themselves versus the general public. Our entire existence is to make the lives of those who work in public libraries better. While my role isn't necessarily available in all fifty states (it's sometimes wrapped up in other roles), there is usually a library development team for each state library. It's also a good fit for someone who is keen to get on the road and visit library locations across the state.

One of my favorite parts of my role is building data spreadsheets for library directors. This was born out of seeing the same questions get asked over and over on the directors' e-mail listserv and wondering why we didn't have a one-stop shop for the answers. It began with a fine-free spreadsheet (i.e., who is fine free, when did they go fine free, etc.) and now the files include other things like holidays, directors' salaries, per capita spending, and so on. Additionally, we've built resource folders with all of the bylaws, strategic plans, job descriptions, and policies, as well as maps to show all of the library buildings across the state, who has passport facilities, and so forth.

Another favorite part of my role is doing new director orientation. I began right as the world shut down for the pandemic and was given the task of revamping our orientation process for new directors. Our previous orientation had been done completely in-person over a longer time period, but the pandemic prevented that from occurring. Our new process includes a welcome message, a direct welcome from our team, a chance to chat with each of our team's consultants so that directors can better understand what we can assist them with, a peer mentor, quarterly check-ins with me, quarterly virtual meetups with other directors, and basically whatever we can do to let them know that they have our support.

Challenges

The biggest challenge for my role is not having direct contact with the audience I serve: the trustees, friends, and foundation members. Almost everything I do and or send out is relayed through the library directors, so sometimes that third party communication works well, and sometimes it doesn't. It can also be a challenge when you have folks step into those roles who aren't as familiar with how a library operates. This is not uncommon since we as library folk have done a bang-up job of making it look like the library operates like magic. So, explaining the roles and where those boundaries are, how they can support the library, and how not to violate the law when it comes to book challenges, can lead to some interesting conversations.

My Career Path

If you had told my graduate school government documents intern self that I'd be consulting for public libraries across the state of Virginia, I'd have questioned a lot of things. My first role after getting my MLIS was as a solo librarian for a federal wildlife research center in North Dakota. When the funding for that ran out, I was a library clerk at the local public library, and then moved to Minnesota where I was the executive director of a multitype system that served public, school, academic, and special libraries across nineteen counties. In addition to that role, I was also an adjunct reference librarian for the university library in which our offices were housed. From there I became a regional librarian for eleven counties, where I did everything from training to delivery to youth services to web team to regional statistics. After a brief transition to a different position there, I moved to Virginia to take my current role. At each stage, I wasn't looking for any defined job, but took advantage of the opportunities along the way.

Oddly enough, I learned about librarianship from a book literally titled *Jobs for People Who Love to Read* that I found in my local library. Chapter one was about being a librarian. I read it and thought, "That sounds like me." As I was doing more research, I attended a wedding and accidentally ended up sitting at a table of librarians who allowed me to pick their brains about their jobs. After doing all that, I decided to take the leap and the rest, as they say, is history.

When I look back at what I wrote for my application essay, I cringe a little bit. It was full of mellifluous words that sounded like an ode to the written word.

After all these years, I realize that libraries are always going to be less about the things they contain and more about the people, both those who serve as employees and the public that they in turn serve. Most folks outside our library world don't get that, hence the evergreen comments of "it must be nice to just sit around and read all day." One thing that has surprised me as I've gone along in my career is that the longer you're in an area of librarianship, the harder it is to shift to something else. While you might advance, you also become more locked in. Our profession doesn't exactly foster gaining a breadth of knowledge of librarianship, but rather a singular niche depth. This means that the longer I work in the field, the fewer opportunities I feel there are to explore all that the field has to offer.

Advice

My work focuses a lot on the infrastructure beneath library work—policies, procedures, human resources, bylaws, budgets, strategic plans, state and federal laws, hiring, job descriptions, board education, and the like. These are often things that are overlooked. My knowledge was gained over many years of going through files or looking for answers about why something operates the way it does in a library. I was curious about the underpinnings that make everything possible. This curiosity stemmed from the fact that almost nothing I did was covered in graduate school. There's always a basic management course that covers bits here and there, but it barely scratches the surface when it comes to things like friends groups that decide to go rogue or a board who is micromanaging staff, and so on.

These underpinnings don't fall on the "flashier" side of librarianship. If you work in this area, you're unlikely to win accolades or be touted for the work that you do, but you will be essential. You will be the person that folks turn to when they have some of the toughest questions to answer or who can provide support in the most challenging of times. It's good work. It's rewarding work. But it's seldom acknowledged.

Anything Else?

View the world of librarianship as broad versu deep. Gain skills in everything that interests you, not just what's most relevant to your job. I consider myself a utility player in the library world. When I entered graduate school, I'd never worked in a library before, so I knew that I needed to gain a large skill set. I took courses on XML and law librarianship, worked in government documents, and did fieldwork at a public library. With every job I've taken, I've always looked at what opportunities and skills will be available to me in that new role.

Also, if you're interested in a particular role or place to work—for example, the United Nations headquarters, the CERN supercollider, or the Supreme Court—seek out those folks who already do that work and ask them how they got there. Pay attention to the open jobs that are out there, not just when you're looking, but also when you're not, because you can see the skills that are up and coming, and you just never quite know when that new opportunity for your career could show up.

Marketing and Outreach Librarian, Library for the Blind and Print Disabled
Ashley M. Biggs

What I Do

I am the marketing and outreach librarian for the Maryland State Library for the Blind and Print Disabled. My primary job duties include but are not limited to creating, finding, and engaging in outreach opportunities, community engagement, creating marketing materials for both the State Library Agency and the Library for the Blind and Print Disabled, creating content for all social media platforms, website administration and maintenance, and adult programming. I act as an agent of the library, performing digital outreach and creating community engagement opportunities.

My Favorite Things

My favorite part of this position is communication. I love communicating about the library's services through digital, print, and in-person means. I love showcasing the library's materials and unique customer base and creating community engagement opportunities. I would recommend this position to someone who loves building connections, has a good grasp of digital and print marketing, and is willing to learn about people with differing abilities.

Challenges

The biggest challenge of this position is learning to ensure American Disabilities Act (ADA) and Web Content Accessibility Guidelines (WCAG) compliance while still making print/digital materials aesthetically pleasing. I had to learn this on the job, and it was a huge learning curve. This job's biggest stressor is ensuring that the website, our printed documents, and digital media are accessible to screen readers for nonvisual access.

My Career Path

I started my library career as a reference librarian, though I studied to become an archivist. I eventually became a genealogy librarian and then branch manager of a large regional branch. After a few years, I had an opportunity to take an outreach position. Over time, the position evolved to include marketing, website maintenance, adult programming, and more.

The skills that I learned on the job have been invaluable both in the library field and in my personal life as well. For example, I now know how to ensure nonvisual access to websites and documents. Additionally, the work environment encourages growth and professional development, so I've learned skills I never thought I'd need or use.

Advice

My best piece of advice to someone looking at taking on a position like mine is to be as adaptable and open-minded as possible. While my MSLIS helped me get the job, I took numerous courses in marketing, community engagement, and public relations. Ideal skills would include having strong writing, graphic design, Adobe Suite, and research skills. People pursuing this position should have an interest in working with adaptive technology, working with people from all walks of life, and have strong communication skills.

Media Library Specialist, Department of Public Health
Alicia Zuniga

What I Do

My role working at the California Tobacco Control Program within the California Department of Public Health was fact-checking its multimillion-dollar communications and advertising campaigns in a variety of media formats. I reviewed television, radio, social media, digital, and out-of-home (e.g., bus stop and billboard) advertisements, as well as public relations materials, to make sure what our program was communicating to the public was supported by the most up-to-date research. During my reviews, I corrected out-of-date statistics or suggested alternate wording that correctly interpreted the study being cited. In addition to reviewing content for accuracy, I also reviewed it for tone and language choice, suggesting changes to use plain language in place of jargon for the general public.

I also created and managed the digital repository for research that we used to support messaging in campaigns and research that we may consider for future campaigns. I devised the tagging and folder structure to organize our literature in this repository, which included updating tags when a piece of literature was used in a specific campaign. This allowed easy and quick recall of what studies were cited for a given communications campaign.

My Favorite Things

My favorite aspect of this job was being part of the review process to make sure Californians received accurate and accessible health information. I am a big supporter of transparent and accessible government information getting to taxpayers (since they're paying for it!), so making sure that they were getting their money's worth was important to me. I also greatly enjoyed working in the public sector and felt like I was truly contributing to making a positive change for the health of Californians.

I would recommend this type of position to someone who is incredibly detail-oriented, not afraid of saying no or correcting someone's work, and able to do so with tact from an educational frame of mind.

Challenges

A large part of my role was telling people no. "No, we can't say this." "No, this interpretation of this study isn't correct." "No, this information is outdated." Saying no can be difficult for some people, especially if the colleagues you are communicating with are more senior. It is important to have reasons to back up your decisions, and not to take it personally if your suggestion is overridden.

Another challenge is that public health research, like research in general, is always evolving, and you need to stay abreast of these developments to make sure anything you're communicating to the public remains accurate. In the midst of developing a campaign, a new report could come out with data that affects it, and you would not be able to simply ignore a new statistic. You would have to update it and adapt.

A challenge in my role specifically was being a solo librarian, in a way. I was the only person in my program of eighty employees who had any library-related education or job duties, so there was sometimes a misconception about the type of work that I did within the organization. The vast majority of my work was completed independently. If you are someone who needs more of a team structure with colleagues that deeply understand your role, this type of position would be difficult.

My Career Path

I served as a Literacy AmeriCorps member for two years, and one of those years I worked in a public library delivering adult literacy programming. This solidified my interest in libraries, and I subsequently earned my MLIS. I worked in similar adult literacy roles in public libraries before my first position at an open access publisher, where I worked on two public health/biomedical peer-reviewed journals. This was a game-changer for me, because it opened my eyes to the world of scholarly publishing and open access. I credit this role with the development of my in-depth knowledge of academic publishing and the peer review process, which is critical for a librarian who wishes to work in a special or academic library. From there I worked on digital roles in government and a public library. Aspects of all of these roles prepared me for this job, including the transferable skills of academic knowledge, instructional and training experience, and strong written communication.

Advice

In my MLIS program there was no requirement to take any coursework in instruction, but I wish there had been. All of my instructional experience was learned on the job as an AmeriCorps member, which I built on through subsequent roles. Having a solid foundation in principles of teaching would have been very valuable, even in this role where there were no explicit teaching responsibilities. Instructional training would have benefited me when explaining information literacy and source evaluation concepts to my colleagues.

Being well versed in the scholarly publishing landscape as well as research methods was also a necessary skill to have in this role. As an undergraduate I was a research assistant in several labs, and I also took a course in research methods in my MLIS program; these greatly informed how I approached evaluating individual articles and studies to be included in campaigns.

Anything Else?

One of the unique things about working in the public sector is that you may be called upon in emergency situations. During the Covid-19 pandemic, I was redirected from my regular role for six months to serve on the statewide response. I was a member of the Safe Schools team, which was tasked to coordinate the safe in-person reopening of K-12 schools during the pandemic. Our team worked with multiple state departments and agencies to coordinate this effort. My role was largely the same as my regular role where I fact-checked and reviewed communications to the public, just on a different topic than I normally worked on. It was a stressful, productive, and rewarding experience to work in that capacity.

Mental Health Hospital Library Director

Lona A. Oerther

What I Do

I get asked what I do a great deal, actually, and my answer is nearly always, "Everything." Seriously, I do everything as I am a solo librarian who is working in and running three libraries on campus. I work on the budget, write and apply for grants, schedule patron workers, set times for different groups to come to the library, order new materials, curate collections, weed, process donations, create metadata specific to my facility, and help doctors/nurses/nursing students with research.

My facility is a high-security, forensic, mental health hospital. I have three libraries and an archive. I try to split my time between the public library and the high-security library. The professional library is where the nursing students from the local universities spend some of their time while on their psychiatric rotations. I only pop in there when they need help, or to introduce myself at the beginning of the year. The public library is my biggest and requires most of my time.

I guess it is easier to think of it as a community. There are several security and competency levels among my patrons, and they are housed together. Each patron group has a set time that they come to the public library. If they are patrons that have been deemed capable of going unescorted, they can visit anytime that the library is open. The high-security building is for mental health patients who have committed a crime and are either awaiting trial or have been deemed not guilty by reason of insanity (NGRI). That building is also organized by security level, and patients come to the small library inside the high security building on a set schedule.

Along with the obvious patrons, there is also a children's high security building for patrons between the ages of twelve and seventeen. The children here are in the same situation as the adults, but they are required to attend an on-campus school. Every school should have a library, and I hold in-person meetings with the kids. Speaking of schools, our teachers and I also work with the adult patrons who are attending college either online or in person.

My Favorite Things

Anyone that has worked with mental health patients or dealt with mental illness understands the need for acceptance and understanding for members of that community. Libraries are welcoming, safe spaces, and it is no different in the spaces where I work. I treat each and every one of my patrons with respect, and in a place where they are often being told what to do and when to do it, that means a great deal. Every day I get to be a librarian and make someone's day better. You would be surprised at the way helping someone find something new to read, giving them a selection of DVDs, or just providing a quiet space to think without any expectations other than they treat me and my other patrons the same, can affect their mood and change the way their day is going.

I get to be a different type of librarian every day. One day, I'll spend most of my time as more of an academic librarian helping students and doctors do research. Another time my work is focused more heavily on public library service and providing materials for my patrons. On a different day it could be more administrative, and I'll spend time weeding, ordering new materials for my ever-growing graphic novel collection, and creating metadata that is specific to what the doctors/nurses are publishing for the mental health hospital. If you want to do something different every day, this is an ideal place for it.

Challenges

It is still difficult to believe that people do not know that I am there or understand exactly what I do. This is not a problem that is specific to me, as many librarians encounter this on a day-to-day basis. For me, a challenge is reminding people that I am there not just for the patrons, but for the workers employed there as well. Everyone gets access to my libraries and to my help.

What about book challenges, you may ask? This is one of the few aspects of librarianship where I have far less to worry about than most. I choose what goes into my collection with the guidance of my patrons and other librarians.

The administration gets no say in my collection development. I once had a doctor tell me *1984* upset a patron, and he wished for them not to have access to it. I politely reminded the doctor that the book is supposed to upset people. That is the point of the book and unless there was a medical reason, I would not restrict it. There wasn't, so I didn't.

As a side note, this can be a very stressful place to be a librarian. People are unpredictable, and some are seriously ill. Many of them have done things you do not want to know about. All employees are required to take training in de-escalation and restraint techniques. We are Red Cross CPR certified every two years as well. The work is not for most people, but those who come into it with an open mind and with some awareness ahead of time may find they really love the work, as I have.

My Career Path

I have known since a young age that librarianship, in one form or another, is what I wanted to do. Without getting too in-depth, librarians helped me, and I wanted to do that for others. I went to a state school for both my undergraduate degree in English literature and for my MLS. Near the end of graduate school, I had the opportunity to intern at an academic library and moved across the country to do it. I thought that being a scholarly communications librarian or an open educational resources librarian is what I wanted to do, and for a time it was. Something to be prepared for in the academic sphere is budget cuts, and sadly, libraries can take the brunt of them.

My next academic librarian position after my internship was removed after two years. I had to scramble to find something new in only a few months. I interviewed and got hired for my current position. When I applied, I had not realized that these types of facilities had libraries or recognized the impact a librarian can make on this type of population.

Advice

Be open minded, be compassionate, have a love for people, and remember there will be bad days. You should have a desire to stay busy and a need to do many things at the same time. This kind of librarianship can be so rewarding if you go into it with the right mindset.

Anything Else?

The questions my patrons ask me are far different than the ones students in an academic setting ask. My favorite was when one of the patrons in the high-security library asked me to Google him. "Why do you want me to do that?" He wanted to know what people were saying about him. I then asked him "how long have you been here?" To which he replied, a year or so. With the straightest face I could muster, I told him it was not my job to Google him and after a year, no one was still talking about him. You need a sense of humor—and take good notes. When you retire, you may have enough material for a really good book.

News Librarian
Misty Harris

What I Do

Being a news librarian is getting paid to be a detective or, as some say, a nosy professional. When a breaking news story happens, you have to start getting as much information to guide reporters or back up claims from sources. This can be anything from finding court records or police records, finding sources for reporters to question, and verifying personal information such as names, ages, home addresses, and phone numbers. For longer projects, it entails various tasks such as pulling together data, requesting documents such as filings in court cases, digging through our archives to fact check information, or pulling several papers together to analyze a pattern. Oftentimes you will unearth information no one else in the newsroom has found.

Part of my job as a news researcher at the *San Antonio Express-News* (EN) also entailed being the keeper of the archives, which may sound boring, but is actually a very important job. I had to keep tabs on San Antonio history and the history of the EN, fact-check articles, and help the public locate past issues of the EN. Additionally, I also preserved history for future generations by making sure the paper was correctly formatted for archiving, and by protecting the microfilm, photos, and other items relevant to San Antonio history. I also did copyright work for those seeking to reprint *Express-News* items such as articles, photos, or PDFs of the paper, both newly printed items and items from our archives.

One of the most important pieces of the job (and one of my absolute favorites) was teaching classes to reporters, both experienced and new to the profession, about how to conduct their own research. I enjoyed seeing reporters grasping concepts I'd taught them to help them in their jobs. I'm often told people still hang on to a tip sheet with resources and other helpful information I used in my classes, and some even use it daily.

My Favorite Things

The highlight of the job was definitely all the wonderful people I met every day, from the seasoned reporters to reporters just starting their journeys to sources, editors, photographers, fellow librarians, and historians. I was constantly learning, and every day brought a new challenge. Knowing I helped tell an important story was priceless—oftentimes I was told there would not have been a story if I hadn't persisted in my research. I also loved the feeling of satisfaction when our reporters achieved something or made an impact with a story they wrote. Sometimes it was politicians and government officials reviewing policies and making changes; often it was just a reader reaching out to say they enjoyed a piece.

Challenges

This job isn't for everyone; you have to think on your feet and strive for perfection. It often requires long hours, answering questions by email or phone after hours. Due to the nature of some of the stories, the job can also be challenging, stressful, and incredibly emotional. There will be days when reporters are extremely thankful, readers write in to thank the paper, and you feel as if you've made a difference in getting someone's story told. On the flip side, sometimes reporters forget to thank you, the facts aren't what they seem, you are digging for information but cannot find it, or readers call or email to say what a terrible, stupid, unacceptable story is in the paper this morning. And when you are wrong, you are wrong, and you have to admit it publicly with a correction. There will be days you will say "I can't do this," but it is all worth it when you see your research put to good use.

My Career Path

I got my undergraduate degree in journalism and worked for several years as a community newspaper reporter and editor. It was proving very stressful, so I took what I thought would be a year or two break from the field. I wound up getting a library job at Trinity University in San Antonio. I fell in love with working in a library and kicked myself, as a big reader and writer, for never considering this career path. Many of my coworkers encouraged me to pursue my MLS. I searched for an academic librarian position for almost a year after earning my master's, while continuing to work my staff position at Trinity. Then I saw a job posting on a listserv that intrigued me. The *San Antonio Express-News* was looking for a news researcher and they specifically wanted someone with an MLS. I thought this was perfect: I could use both of my degrees. I stepped into my second home when I walked into the newsroom for the first time. Best of all, I really used both degrees every single day. I still use a lot of skills I learned in the newsroom, unrelated to librarianship. All my skills from school and my newsroom experience such as quick thinking, creativity, thinking outside normal research methods, and the joy of collaboration prepared me to try new jobs.

Advice

If you love deadlines, working with talented people, and breathing the news, this will be your dream job. It is tough to break into the news industry, as it is shrinking and constantly changing to meet the demands of the readers. But don't lose hope: there are still a lot of good jobs in news librarianship out there. Most of these jobs are at national publications like the *Wall Street Journal*, *Washington Post*, or *New York Times*. You will sometimes see major metropolitan papers such as the *Dallas Morning News* or newer news outlets such as ProPublica and the Texas Tribune that have librarians on staff, so keep your eyes open. The best way to get your foot in the door is to first reach out to someone who is employed in one of these roles (usually found via LinkedIn) and ask if you can set up a brief informational session. It doesn't need to be in person; it's easy to meet on Zoom, chat via text, or message through other services. Ask the employee if you can shadow them at work or if they know if their company has an internship program willing to accept someone interested in news research. In this field, on the job experience is the best trainer.

Anything Else?

One of my greatest triumphs was helping tell the story of a migrant family from Guatemala that tragically died crossing into the border of the United States. Reporter Silvia Foster-Frau, now of the *Washington Post*, approached me one day saying a source gave her the names and ages of three small children who, along with their mothers, died in South Texas. She asked me if I thought it would be possible to locate family members, as she really wanted to piece together what happened and tell their story. I told her it would be near impossible, as they were minors with few records, and the fact that they weren't US citizens might make it even more difficult. But I told her I would try my best, as I knew their story needed to be told.

I started by using my old friend Google but was having absolutely zero luck. I started thinking maybe their names were written down wrong or somehow transposed, so I started purposely misspelling the names given to me. Finally, I landed on a news article from Guatemala detailing this family's tragic journey. I looked up both the author and photographer and learned that the photographer was a freelance photographer based in Florida. I contacted him via Twitter and connected him with Silvia. From there, Silvia was able to start working the phones, finding family members in both the small Guatemalan village this family was from, and the family in the United States they were traveling to meet. The newspaper ultimately sent a reporter and photographer to Guatemala to interview the family, and Silvia interviewed the family in the United States. Together the *Express-News* was able to tell this important story. (You can read the story at https://www.expressnews.com/news/local/article/No-other-solution-With-children-in-tow-a-14088409.php and listen to our in-depth podcast about how the story came together at https://www.expressnews.com/news/local/article/Podcast-With-children-in-tow-mothers-journey-14099790.php.)

Prison Librarian
Margaret Lirones

What I Do

As senior librarian at a state prison, I currently run three libraries within my institution. Each library runs one day per week. We provide library and information services to an underserved population. We provide access to the court by providing reference services and access to a database of legal books and cases. We provide court forms, paper, photocopying service, and envelopes for mailing. In addition, we have a popular reading collection with books and magazines incarcerated persons can borrow and return. Since we are part of the education department, we provide some materials and support to teachers. On the days I am not running the library, I answer grievances from incarcerated persons, fill requests from people who cannot come to the library, update our reference material, tabulate data for reports, log periodicals arriving in the mail, pick up and deliver materials, update offline computers, and attend meetings and training.

My Favorite Things

I like knowing that I am providing a valuable service to people who need it. Going into the institution each day is a privilege reserved for staff and volunteers. Corrections is a big part of the state budget and is frequently in the news. I have an inside view of this big operation and our emphasis on rehabilitation. Many library users are very appreciative of the service we provide. I also like collaborating with multiple staff across job classifications.

Challenges

One challenge is familiar to school librarians everywhere: being the only librarian among staff and having supervisors who are not always sure what we do. Some of our clientele tend to be self-centered, sometimes controlling, with little regard for rules—and there are a lot of rules. Our biggest challenge is the lack of library staff. At present we have two staff and four vacant positions. It is frustrating to be providing only the most minimal, basic service when there is so much we could do if we had the staff.

My Career Path

I originally started working in a public library part time while I was a graduate student in another field. I liked the work and advanced in the six years I was there. After taking time out to raise my children, I worked as a paraprofessional in school libraries for twelve years. My time in a junior high library had some similarities to my current job. When I was free to relocate and was ready to increase my income, I earned my MLIS while working in an elementary school library. I was intrigued by prison librarianship, but also had many questions and concerns. The reality was that was where the jobs were, and I wanted a full-time job. I worked three years as a prison librarian, learning on-the-job from the senior librarian. I then applied and was hired as senior librarian at a neighboring institution.

One thing that surprised me when I first walked into prison was the variety of hairstyles and accessories incarcerated persons wear. I expected more regimentation. It was also surprising to see how compassionate and helpful some incarcerated persons can be with each other. Some spend a great deal of time and care creating art from found materials. If you are fortunate, some of this artwork will find its way into your library for all to enjoy.

Advice

The more library experience you have, the better! When you arrive in this job, you are the expert. Library staff statewide are in touch via email and a monthly online meeting. You can ask questions, but it is very helpful to know how a library circulation system works and how to do copy cataloging and book processing. It helps to have some computer maintenance skills, enough to have an idea what is going on with computers when something isn't working. If you know a little American Sign Language, Spanish, Vietnamese, or any other language predominant in your area, people who primarily speak those languages will appreciate it and will teach you a little more. It is helpful to have some understanding of the ways trauma and addiction affect the brain. I recommend reading *The Librarian's Guide to Homelessness* by Ryan Dowd for an introduction to these topics. Every skill you have ever gained applies in some way to this job. It helps to be a creative, motivated self-starter, and be willing to learn. You will learn something new every day and have continuous opportunities for professional development.

Anything Else?

The way library services are provided in institutions varies by state and locality. Federal prisons have their own library system. In some states, prison library services are provided by the state library. In some states prison libraries are decentralized with the library in each institution operating fairly independently. Other states have centralized leadership and training. In county jails, library services are sometimes provided by the public library or a contractor. Some libraries provide only legal resources, others provide only reading materials, and some provide both.

Two more books I find helpful are *Just Mercy* by Bryan Stevenson and *Tattoos on the Heart* by Gregory Boyle.

Research Institution Medical Librarian
Kelly Stormking

What I Do

When people find out that I work in the library at St. Jude Children's Research Hospital, they immediately ask about working with patients and families. Although St. Jude does have a wonderful library dedicated exclusively to patients, the biomedical library focuses on supporting the landmark research, education, and clinical informational needs of all St. Jude employees. Imagine an extensive mix of scientists, clinicians, researchers, doctors, nurses, administrators, and more all working toward eradicating the catastrophic childhood diseases of the world: this is the community I support as a medical librarian.

Most of my job is hidden behind the scenes. So much of what I do goes unnoticed and is thus unacknowledged, but at the same time, my goal is for our users to have such a seamless experience locating resources that they forget there was ever an intermediary. In my role within the Biomedical Library, I manage our print and electronic collections. I maintain our online catalog while also running our library websites and research guides. We do not have access to an integrated library system (ILS) and instead use a combined content management platform and discovery tool. This means we do not have access to a complex system with helpful features for streamlining workflows. However, our multitool approach is far cheaper and, due to our small library size, is currently more practical. Our online collection is made up of close to 40,000 journals and databases, with our print collection close to 1,500 items. As our institution continues to grow rapidly, change—the familiar friend to every library—will inevitably appear again and guide us toward new platforms. To ensure we are always offering the most efficient and accessible platforms, I am responsible for continuously reviewing our approach to ensure the best user experience possible.

After collection management, and closely related in scope, is collection assessment, which I lead as my second largest job responsibility. This is broad, to include developing library collection policies, generating communication plans, conducting surveys, and organizing usage statistics. Outreach and communication across campus always require copious amounts of attention, as we strive to connect incoming employees to our offerings and share updates with regular users. Each month we table in multiple locations across St. Jude, collaborate with employee resource groups, develop content for the daily newsletter, and participate in several campus events. Connecting feedback to the data from usage and synthesizing information each year in an online deliverable is essential to reflecting on all we do.

When needed I provide reference support by answering questions via email or in person. Occasionally there are requests for technological assistance with our printers, computers, fax, and copiers in our library space. I also collaborate with our interlibrary loan (ILL) librarian to support our program by processing daily requests and updating our holdings in DOCLINE, the National Library of Medicine's ILL system for sharing resources across medical libraries. With our small size, we must be knowledgeable and flexible in numerous areas of the library to step in and cover for vacations, sick days, and times when one person has far too much on their plate.

My Favorite Things

I enjoy the regular technical troubleshooting and investigation required for solving tricky problems in electronic resource management. This includes fixing broken links, restructuring websites for easier navigation, or restoring access to journals that are suddenly showing paywalls. Solving problems that have bothered our users is immensely satisfying. Combined with regular outreach and synthesizing user feedback, the opportunity to implement requested changes within the library to improve the workplace experience is extremely gratifying. Knowing that the work we do can have a direct impact on the historic research underway at St. Jude is why I love working in the Biomedical Library.

The part of my job that I was least prepared for has also grown to become one of my favorites. Although I do not lead research consultations, I regularly work with our scholars who have received grants from the National Institutes for Health (NIH). I lead our support service for the NIH Public Access Policy and the various National Center for Biotechnology Information (MyNCBI) tools required for grants management. My interest in open access has exponentially grown upon learning that the NIH requires all peer-reviewed publications stemming from taxpayer-funded grant research to be deposited into a free, public repository known as PubMed Central (PMC). Learning more about scholarly publications and even the innerworkings of ILL has formed an interest in expanding public global access to research.

Challenges

In comparison, the biggest challenges are not necessarily unique to my role as a medical librarian or unique to medical libraries. There is never enough time and never enough staff to offer the support that is requested. While there are many Biomedical Library fans across St. Jude who are our champions, there are still individuals who do not see the need for a library, and others who think we only offer print books that provide little institutional benefit. Feedback from our annual survey has revealed a wide spectrum of opinions, from resounding enthusiasm for our work to apathy from people who say they do not need the library because they can access articles easily online (without realizing that the library is the reason they can do so). Advocacy and communication remain ongoing priorities.

My Career Path

I stumbled into the medical librarianship field by accident, after spending months looking for a library job that would work well with my graduate school schedule. For most of my schooling, I envisioned working in a botanical or horticultural library leading children's programming. From years as a preschool teacher, I was drawn to librarianship due to the integral value of information access for all within the profession as well as the opportunity for greater community collaboration. The happy accident of applying for a job in the university's medical library that was specifically looking for a student, and was open to hiring someone with limited experience, allowed me to step into the health sciences. From there I was able to gain experience working with doctors by assisting with introductory reference questions. Offering these introductory workplace opportunities to students is essential and is what led to my transition into medical librarianship.

Simply accepting the job was not enough to get me to where I am today. As a solo librarian in my first health sciences institution, I spent hours training myself in various skills. I studied online guides on reference management tools like EndNote and Zotero, read manuals on our ILS Koha, and participated in far more webinars from the National Library of Medicine than I can count. In school I pivoted to studying library systems and nurtured a growing interest in the hidden tools of librarianship. Paired with the training and reference experience in medical databases like PubMed, I was naturally guided toward a career in the health sciences libraries.

Advice

What ultimately benefited me the most outside of mentorship, and greatly assisted me in securing my current job, was all the additional training I sought out independently—in particular, focusing on learning skills for navigating medical databases. For those interested in medical librarianship, the National Library of Medicine (NLM) and the National Network of Medical Libraries (NNLM) offer a wide variety of classes to learn more about PubMed.

This includes courses on the basics to more in-depth discussions of Medical Subject Headings (MeSH) and other PubMed features. Most of these classes are available for free and are available online to view on your schedule. Along with NNLM courses, the Medical Library Association (MLA) offers an extensive collection of training programs and educational opportunities. They offer numerous programs for those new to the field, including the fantastic Research Training Institute for medical librarians who have never conducted research but are interested in leading their own project. This is but one offering I have participated in and could not recommend it more. For those interested in health sciences, the community for librarians is vast and rich with opportunity.

Research Medical Library Director

Clara S. Fowler

What I Do

As a library director, my job is to strategically position the Research Medical Library to have the greatest positive impact on patient care, education, and research at the University of Texas MD Anderson Cancer Center. I am responsible for the budget of the library and for making sure that our resources meet the needs of our institution and community while being a good steward of the allocated funds. I oversee all hiring of staff, and I am responsible for making sure that my staff are productive and trained for the jobs they must do now as well as preparing them for future work.

However, I do none of these duties alone. I have a team of experienced library leaders who manage the budget, collections acquisitions, materials access, and all the services that we offer in our library. My day-to-day work involves making sure these leaders and their staff and teams have the resources they need to run their services and do their jobs. I work to create a culture of collaboration by sharing important data and institutional initiatives that impact the library and encouraging staff to work together on shared goals and projects. I spend a lot of time in meetings with my leadership team or with division leadership, in institution management meetings, and meeting with library directors at the local and state level. I also informally meet with leaders throughout the institution to listen to their concerns and to position the library to be a resource in future projects and plans.

My Favorite Things

I have always wanted to be a leader in libraries, and this position has fulfilled a career-long goal. I love the challenge and responsibility of being a director. I enjoy that it is a space where I am expected to continuously learn and retool my skills. Passing those expectations on to the library staff and supporting their learning is invigorating.

We define what our future looks like as we work amidst tremendous changes in higher education and in healthcare and libraries. Being at the nexus of that change sometimes feels like jumping off into the unknown. You have no idea what the next year will bring, but you set your goals and know that the work you do is making a difference in the work lives of our educators, researchers, and clinicians and ultimately benefitting the patients that seek care at MD Anderson.

I would recommend being a library director at an academic health center to those who want to be a part of something that is bigger than themselves. Leading successfully in this environment requires knowledge of health sciences, library management practices, and higher education leadership. Experience with managing budgets, project management, and improvement science is also important to be able to lead effectively. It is a position that requires dedication and self-confidence.

I am happiest when the library makes a significant difference in the work lives of the people who work to research, treat, and cure cancer. Knowing that our work makes people feel more connected to the mission of the institution is inspiring. Seeing 200-plus people attend one of our library education sessions to learn about a new tool or resource makes my day. Connecting two researchers across the institution who will help each other with the methodology on a project makes me very happy. I get to see the impact and value that my staff bring to the institution, and my job is to make that value known and amplify it for a greater impact.

As library director, I can prioritize ambitious projects like a new institutional repository, a new system for interlibrary loan, an oral history project, or a data services initiative. Being able to direct and lead big changes that involve many people is very exciting, especially when we see that our work can have a global reach.

Challenges

Leading with purpose can be the most fulfilling job, especially when the mission of your institution is one in which your library team wholeheartedly believes. At MD Anderson, our mission is to eliminate cancer and this purpose drives everyone in my organization. I recommend finding an organization where you can feel connected to the mission, as it will help you embrace the inevitable challenges. That said, when leading in a very large organization that is also a state institution, there are rules and regulations we must follow, and it does require patience and adaptability. Reorganizations and shifts in leadership outside of the library create instability, and communicating the library's role to new leadership is important. During the forming stage of new leadership teams, it can be very stressful to regain a seat at the table and form connections with new leaders.

My Career Path

My first professional librarian job was at the University of Texas at Austin undergraduate library where I was hired as the electronic instruction librarian in the digital information literacy office. I was a member of the development team for TILT: the Texas Information Literacy Tutorial, which was one of the first online library tutorials. The four years I spent at UT Austin were amazing and it was difficult to leave, but I wanted to live in the same city as my husband, who was working at the *Houston Chronicle*. I landed at the University of Houston Libraries, running their undergraduate instruction programs, and I started to develop leadership skills by growing and leading a small team of librarians. I became active in our state library association and the Association of College and Research Libraries (ACRL), taking on more responsibility for leading committees and task forces. Through my work with professional organizations, I gained the confidence to lead large groups to consensus. I found I had a talent for running meetings and managing organizations.

After a year-long stint at the CUNY Hunter College of Health Professions in New York City, I was excited about the overlap between evidence-based practice and information literacy. When I returned to Houston, I was hired by the University of Texas MD Anderson Cancer Center to lead library instruction services for their new undergraduate school. What I found at MD Anderson was an environment rich in opportunities to teach undergraduates to postdoctoral students. I quickly realized that to teach the highly specialized information-seeking skills my students needed, I'd need to ramp up my knowledge. I spent my first three years at MD Anderson in night courses learning medical terminology, anatomy, statistics, and health care management. I started a path of constant learning that continues today.

I jumped at every opportunity to attend leadership development seminars, institutes, and institutional trainings. One workshop that was pivotal to my development was the Women's Leadership Institute run by the Association of College Unions International. It brought together women administrative leaders from across the academy, and I learned so much about the functions of a university and how to collaborate with others outside of the librarians, faculty, and students whom I'd focused on up to that point in my career. This became an important skill set when I became a library director, as my peers are people in these administrative job functions.

Advice

For those interested in becoming a library director, it is important to find good mentors and to become an observer of leadership in those around you. Volunteer to serve in professional organizations, as they provide opportunities to develop leadership skills and network with others who will be important in your career. Librarianship is a very small universe, and the professional relationships you cultivate and the reputation you build will carry with you throughout your career. Take formal training in leadership through workshops and classes. Create a reflexive practice to reinforce your strengths and successes, as well as identify gaps and opportunities to improve. Create a sounding board of people you trust who have a different perspective on your organization and will willingly give their opinions on your leadership and help you broaden your view.

Anything Else?

Should you pursue a doctoral degree to be a director or dean at an academic or medical library? In pursuit of increasing levels of leadership in academic and medical libraries, there is a point where you may question whether you will need a PhD or and EdD to get a job as a dean or director. When I was hired as the director at my current library, I realized that I was the only one in my organization at my level without that terminal degree. Other directors of student services, education support, and faculty training programs all had EdDs, PhDs, or MDs, and sometimes more than one of those. This gap was never called out by anyone at my organization, but I noticed, and I have heard similar stories from other library deans and directors at other institutions. As a dean or director in an academic or medical library, not having a EdD or PhD is not necessarily a barrier, but having it gives you power to extend your reach and level the field with other institutional leaders.

I'm currently working on my EdD, and I have found the coursework to be highly relevant to my work as a director and feel it is making me a more confident and well-rounded leader. My fellow students in the EdD program have created a network of scholar-educators who support, encourage, and provide a sounding board for each other. Our commitment as librarians to be lifelong learners is part of our culture. The EdD program provides a framework to do that successfully and make a real impact on the quality of education at our institutions. Ideally, we should see more librarians rise above the library dean and director level to leading colleges and universities. Our position in the academy gives us a unique perspective on our institutions, and having more librarians with doctoral degrees is one step towards helping us achieve that goal.

Science Librarian, Department of Defense
Gloria Miller

What I Do

I'm currently the command librarian of the Army Futures Command (AFC), which means I run a program office. I have policy oversight of six research and development (R&D) libraries in the Army but have no direct supervision of them. My work mostly involves working on joint purchases and planning for the future. I'm also the first point of contact for AFC staff at our headquarters as well as for other offices within AFC that are less focused on direct R&D and therefore don't have a library.

All the command librarians are also members of the Army Libraries Steering Committee, chaired by the Librarian of the Army. In that capacity, I lead a working group focused on training and career development for library staff.

My Favorite Things

I still enjoy being able to help customers directly, although that doesn't happen as much now as when I was in a library. I still remember special research projects I've done for some of the scientists. I also like being able to see a bigger picture of how the libraries fit together. An added perk is not having to work evenings or weekends.

Challenges

For the first thirty-plus years of my career, the biggest stressor was government shutdowns when Congress didn't pass a budget. Now that we are guaranteed back pay, it's less of a concern. Many people don't realize that most government funding comes as "annual appropriations"—you can't start spending money until appropriations are passed into law, and you can only spend it during that fiscal year. Any leftover funding disappears. I'm now in a newly created position that started with no budget and no program, so my biggest challenge is building a program in such a way that the people with money are willing to fund it.

Adaptability is an essential skill in a military library. When running story time in a morale, welfare, and recreation (MWR) library, librarians stay aware that some parents may be gone for months at a time due to deployments. We continually adapted library policies to fit the needs of our customers. For example, a military member had to spend several months away while working on a degree; we let him take books for as long as needed. It was okay that the books came back with sand inside.

My Career Path

I discovered the special libraries career field before I started college. It was the perfect match for my science interests and my high school library volunteer work. Throughout my career, I've worked in eight different libraries within the Department of Defense (DOD). I started out working for the Air Force in a base library. These are also called post libraries, general libraries, or MWR libraries. Think of it like a public library set on a military installation. But for most of my career, I've worked in science and technology libraries, for the Air Force, Navy, and now Army. I have a BS degree in the sciences, which has helped but is not required.

When I started, OCLC was only available as a hardwired terminal. I got my first work computer in my third position; my first work email came in the next one. The technology we use has changed, but the principles of library science have stayed the same. Customer service is still the most important element.

Advice

My BS degree helped me get into my first science and technology library, but my adaptability and willingness to learn became more important for landing subsequent jobs. It's important to network with others in your field and join an association. Personally, I've been very involved with the Military Libraries Community (formerly Division) of SLA. Many MWR librarians are members of ALA's Federal & Armed Forces Libraries Round Table (FAFLRT).

I like to say that the military members have to move, but civilians get to move. I've often moved because I took on a new position, usually a promotion. Working for the federal government can be a wonderful career. Every special library type that exists is probably available in the government as well. Someone with no military experience can come into a DOD library at the early or midcareer level, with only a small learning curve.

Don't be reluctant to apply and be willing to relocate. Most positions are advertised on USAJobs. A federal resume is structured differently than most others; use the USAJobs resume builder to be sure you include everything. Use the same key words as in the position advertisement; your resume will be screened by someone from personnel who won't know, for example, that "deacquisitioning" is the same thing as "weeding."

Seminary Librarian

Rebecca A. Givens

What I Do

Seminary librarians have the same jobs that exist in any graduate level academic library, with a special focus on the subjects of theology and pastoral training. I am the technical services librarian, and I catalog both print and electronic resources. I do more original cataloging and record enhancements than the typical cataloger, because we specialize in a subject area that the average cataloger knows very little about. I also oversee book processing and repair. Our public services librarian manages circulation, reference and instruction, and social media. Our library director oversees everything in the library and represents the library in faculty and school administrative meetings. He also does library instruction and reference for all our Doctor of Ministry (DMin) and Master of Divinity (MDiv) students who are writing dissertations.

We are a small library, so our daily duties tend to overlap. On any given day, I might be original or copy cataloging print or e-books, checking our package subscriptions, answering reference questions, checking out books to students or faculty, supervising staff and student workers, attending committee meetings for the library or our consortium or a professional library organization, learning how to use or testing Folio for our upcoming system migration, helping prepare our self-study report for accreditation, interviewing and hiring new employees, working on a special project, or whatever else needs to be done.

My Favorite Things

I love the study of theology, which makes a seminary library a great place to work. I even get to take classes, making me a sort of covert embedded librarian. My seminary is the official seminary for my denomination, so it really is a perfect fit for me since work in a special library requires a solid knowledge base of the subject. I also love the variety of things I do; I am not stuck at my desk doing one boring repetitive or stressful task.

As a technical services librarian, I find my job in the seminary especially rewarding. Cataloging is often seen as a job that can be replaced by using vendor records or copy cataloging from OCLC, but a special library needs catalogers who are experienced in their subject area. I love picking up a book that has never been cataloged, figuring out what it is about and finding the perfect subject headings to describe it, and assigning the call number so it sits in just the right place on the shelf. I enjoy creating name authority records in the Name Authority Cooperative Program (NACO), a much-needed service for all other libraries, as there are very few religious cataloging specialists creating name records. I have also enjoyed my work within our consortium and professional organizations, which my institution encourages.

Challenges

I love my job, but every job has challenges. Here are a few I have experienced:

A specialty library requires specialty subject knowledge. You will likely need to have or acquire a second degree, which can be stressful if you are juggling family or other responsibilities. Our director has an MDiv as well as an MLIS. Our new reference librarian has an MDiv and is working toward his MLIS. As cataloger I have a theological studies certificate and an MLIS, and I regularly audit seminary classes.

Even just within my specialty of cataloging, I must continually learn new systems, standards, and skills; and it's not just cataloging. Because we are a small institution, I am often asked to do things I do not know how to do. This can be a stressful or exciting challenge, depending on the task and my current frame of mind. But asking for clarification or help, and balancing learning something new with doing the familiar parts of my job that I enjoy, gets me through.

In my years here, I have found that budget cuts and staff turnover are the most stressful part of my job. Administrative issues such as this affect all of us in the library, especially the director.

My Career Path

Librarianship is my third or fourth career. My undergraduate degree was aviation technology, and I spent a few years as a flight instructor and mechanic. When I had children, I chose to be an at-home mom and homeschooled them. As they got older, I held several part-time jobs, including employment and tenant screening research manager, martial arts instructor, and clerk in a used bookstore. As my children began to head off to college, I found myself needing a career to support myself. While I loved working with books at the bookstore, I did not want to go into retail management, and I realized that librarian was the career I never knew that I had always wanted. I went back to school in my early fifties and was pleased to see that I was not the oldest student in class, and that library students come from a wide variety of backgrounds.

During class orientation, it occurred to me that seminaries had to have libraries … and how cool would it be to work in a seminary? I had an assignment during my first semester related to the kinds of jobs librarians do. I was not finding the answers to my questions in the job ads I saw, so I emailed as many seminary library directors as I could find addresses for. The first person to respond was the library director of my denomination's seminary. That led to a conversation that lasted five years, through several library school assignments, an in-person meeting at a conference, a library visit when I was in the area, and eventually an interview and job offer. I accepted the job and moved halfway across the country. That director has since retired, but I am still the technical services librarian here.

Advice

If you want to become a theological librarian, while you are a student, you should join one or more of the librarian organizations that support librarians in religious studies. Atla is a broad religious studies library association. They offer significant discounts for student memberships, and generous scholarships to attend their yearly conference. You should also research to see if there is a library group specific to your faith. I am also a member of the Association of Christian Librarians and have found it to be a very supportive group. They also offer student membership discounts and annual conference scholarships. Two others that I am aware of are the Association of Jewish Libraries and the Catholic Library Association. I am sure there are many others representing different faith groups. These kinds of associations typically have a job board, offer annual conferences and professional development opportunities, and provide an opportunity to connect with employers and colleagues. These are great places to find librarians currently working in the field you are interested in, and to ask questions or find a mentor.

I also recommend that you take the Atla online theological librarianship class through the University of Illinois School of Information Sciences LEEP program. I took it during my last semester and had the credit transferred to my library school as an elective. I found this course to be very helpful in learning how librarianship works in the more specific field of theological librarianship.

State Librarian
Jamie Markus

What I Do

The Wyoming state librarian is the director of a special library that houses government information and provides a variety of services and resources to state agencies, libraries, library staff, and residents of the state; manages federal funds provided to the State of Wyoming from the Institute of Museum and Library Services (IMLS); and collaborates with a variety of library-related stakeholders and influential organizations on long-range planning and to promote the importance of libraries.

As the director of a federally recognized State Library Administrative Agency (SLAA), the Wyoming state librarian manages the annual Library Services and Technology Act (LSTA) grant awarded to Wyoming from the IMLS. LSTA allotments are allocated to SLAAs using a population-based formula and must be spent using federally designed cost principles on activities found within an IMLS-approved five-year plan that is evaluated on a regular basis. While this may sound rather bureaucratic and report heavy, it is simply a federal grant with a fair amount of paperwork and forethought attached. The state librarian has the full authority and obligation to write the five-year plan to meet the current and future needs of the Wyoming library community and to adapt, as needed, to meet unexpected challenges. In Wyoming, the majority of the funds were spent to supply research, early literacy, and recreational resources to libraries and patrons, and to support the WYLD Network, a statewide integrated library system used by over 100 libraries, including all public and community college libraries as well as a handful of school and special libraries. One-time projects, including targeted training and marketing efforts, were also part of the annual budget.

Cultivating positive, long-term relationships with stakeholders is a major portion of the state librarian's job. The state librarian coordinates meetings with public, academic, school, and special library directors on a regular basis. Additionally, the state librarian sits on the executive and governing boards of the Wyoming Library Association and WYLD Network of Libraries. These efforts give the state librarian insight into the current and future issues facing the library community and give an opportunity for feedback on state library plans and efforts. Additionally, the state librarian conducts outreach to library and non-library related stakeholders in an effort to support the library community and promote library services and partnership opportunities. From literacy groups to local government entities and even groups with anti-library charters, the state librarian is willing to meet with nearly anyone to explain how libraries operate, how the library community collaborates, and to attempt to clear up confusion or misinformation about local library services and policies.

Last, but certainly not least, the state librarian coordinates or participates in many efforts aimed at building a stronger library community. These actions take many forms, but often center on making sure that someone or some group is actively monitoring situations that may impact a local library or the statewide library ecosystem. Some of these activities focus on budgets and regulatory changes, such as state and national legislation concerning libraries or helping local government officials fill a library board or director vacancy, while others focus on building future capacity, such as working on strategic plans for support organizations or writing/coordinating grant applications for anticipated needs.

My Favorite Things

Being a state librarian is truly an amazing adventure. The opportunities to influence and impact local library services are only limited by imagination (and administrative rules).

I enjoyed the opportunity to create and direct innovative programs that would be implemented in local libraries, to use state and federal grants to fund new and interesting ideas and projects that had the ability to push the profession in new directions, to supply resources for all libraries and residents, and to oversee the policies and processes used to expand library access and services to underserved communities.

I also loved the monthly opportunity to visit libraries and talk to library staff about what they do, how they do it, and who they serve. Libraries do amazing things every day, and very few have the time and ability to regularly tell their own story.

Challenges

Politics

State librarians work at state libraries that in one way or another eventually report to statewide elected officials. They must also follow state statutes and policies; there is not a lot of wiggle room.

Dealing with the politics of the position is not necessarily difficult, or even a hardship. However, being so close to statewide policy makers does impact and influence state library decisions as well as the ability to offer (and the requirements found within) statewide grants, services, and programs. State libraries are often forced to respond to state or national questions and concerns about library services, resources, and programs, even if those issues are not relevant to the state library's mission or even offered or promoted by local libraries across the state.

My Career Path

I held several interesting and markedly different positions at the Wyoming State Library (WSL) over eighteen years. I was originally hired to work with and support library services at the thirteen Wyoming state institutions, which included all prisons and correctional facilities as well as a handful of retirement centers, two schools, and the Wyoming State Hospital. My role was soon expanded to oversee and coordinate continuing education opportunities for all libraries and library staff in Wyoming and the LSTA funds used to support those activities. After several years supervising individual and medium-scale projects, I took on the role of library development manager and directed all aspects of the WSL's library development and outreach program. Six years later, I was named state librarian.

As my state library career advanced and my role expanded, I was forced to shift my perspective and focus. In my first position, I concerned myself with individual programs and resources for specific facilities. The further up the administrative ladder I moved, the more I needed to concentrate on the big picture and prepare for the ripple effect that local issues could have on the library community as a whole. By the end of my tenure, I focused on the significance and effectiveness of statewide programs, while thinking about how singular projects could be turned into large-scale services that could potentially be used in over 100 libraries on any given day.

The biggest surprise to me over the years has been how creative local libraries can be when taking a broad statewide initiative or project and adapting it to suit the particular needs and patrons in their communities. Many libraries can take off-the-shelf plans and tweak them to make the result truly amazing. These instances constantly reminded me that state library staff, or anyone tasked with implementing a large-scale project, does not need to know or control every aspect of any program. Allowing and promoting local control over projects often leads to better, more impactful results. Plus, seeing the different iterations of similar projects inspires new grant ideas and thoughts on how to best roll out the next initiative.

Advice

State libraries are incredible places to work if you want to have a broad impact on library users and services. State libraries may not be the best choice if you want to work face to face with the public or need to see how your day-to-day actions will have a direct impact on your local community.

Big picture, long-term strategic thinkers are needed to dream up, plan for, and manage projects that may take months or years to see the light of day. The ability to oversee intricate multifaceted, multiyear budgets, as well as complex grant funds and reports, is required. Potential state librarians need to be aware that bureaucracy is built into the system, as are the mounds of paperwork needed to accomplish anything worthwhile. Nearly every new state librarian finds themselves responsible for a legacy project, grant program, or manual of procedures that cannot be updated without legislative approval or public meetings. Patience and a good sense of humor is needed, as is the ability to think and act quickly while keeping the long-term goals and health of the organization and library community in mind.

Anything Else?

At some point everyone will need to manage a budget. Programs, projects, and materials all require money and someone to make sure the paperwork is done correctly and on time. Learn how fiscal cycles work for your library and the libraries you work with. An amazing, fully funded project can fail simply because it was started too late in the year.

Money pays for things, but people do the work. Do not forget that the best idea in the world cannot get off the ground or impact library patrons if no staff member has adequate time to implement it and help it grow.

5 Beyond the Library

Archival Consultant
Dominique Luster

What I Do

As the CEO of The Luster Company, my responsibilities encompass a diverse array of tasks that extend beyond conventional archival duties. It's an exciting blend of business administration and preserving history. My work encompasses everything from managing client relationships and strategic planning to handling finances and marketing. But at its core, my job is to protect and support the historical records of our clients while protecting and supporting the financial solvency of this company. The client work can involve helping them through digitization projects, developing preservation plans, or providing project and strategic support to projects they may be working on. Like all archival work, this requires meticulous attention to detail, a passion for history, and a talent for problem solving.

As the owner of a small business, it is imperative for me to constantly innovate and evolve the services we provide to remain competitive in the market. For example, two years ago as of this writing, we started offering private archival services for individuals interested in preserving their families' materials not included in traditional archives. And while we still provide personal archival services, we now work with organizations within and outside of conventional archives to expand the scope of whose histories get included in the first place and to stretch the limits of history-making as a practice.

My Favorite Things

I love the variety that comes with being an entrepreneur, whether in the library and information science field or anywhere else. On any given day, I could be working on a project for a client, strategizing ways to grow and expand my business, or both! This keeps me on my toes and prevents monotony from setting in. Additionally, making decisions and seeing them implemented is incredibly rewarding. In a traditional job, you may have to wait for approval from higher-ups or navigate bureaucratic processes, but as an entrepreneur, you are in charge and can move at your own pace. More than anything, I enjoy the flexibility and the freedom of time. I believe that money can come and go, but the *time* we have at the dinner table with our family, the *time* with friends at that concert, or the *time* away on that romantic ski trip is a finite resource. While I may work long hours at times, I have the freedom to set my own schedule and prioritize my personal life when needed. It's a balance I cherish and one of the main reasons that drew me to this path. The price (the responsibility, the stress, the fear) can be high, but for me, the freedom of time has been worth it.

Challenges

My biggest challenge has been balancing the administrative tasks with the actual archival work. As an entrepreneur, I am responsible for all aspects of my business, from handling finances to managing contracts and marketing. Juggling these responsibilities while meeting client deadlines can be overwhelming at times. In truth, this can become stressful because there is no safety net. Everything is on your shoulders, and no one is coming to save you. There is no backup. There is no annual review or performance plan. And while there is always margin and grace in life, your ability to stay out of the margin directly impacts your ability to take care of your financial responsibilities and your family. You have to be self-motivated, organized, and able to handle high degrees of responsibility.

My Career Path

I left my supported, secure, full-time employment in the middle of a global pandemic to break out on my own and chart my own path, having no idea what I was doing or what the next six months would look like. Full stop. I gave up my health insurance, my retirement plan, and my sense of truly being an "archivist" to chase my dream. It was a considerable risk, and in hindsight, I will admit that this path isn't for the faint at heart. But I have been blessed beyond measure and was more determined than I could reasonably describe.

Before founding The Luster Company, I had the honor and privilege of serving as the Teenie Harris Archivist at the Carnegie Museum of Art and working in the archives at the University of Pittsburgh, the Smithsonian Archives of American Art, and the University of Kentucky. These roles allowed me to gain a wealth of experience and expertise in the archival field. However, as time went on, I began to crave more autonomy and control over my work and life. I wanted to create something that was truly mine while being in the service of others. That's when the idea for The Luster Company was born. Starting my own business has been challenging and sometimes terrifying, but altogether, I feel more alignment than ever before. I have been able to create a company that reflects my values and utilizes my skills and expertise in ways I never thought possible.

Advice

The advice I would give to someone interested in starting their own business is to just start. Too often, we get caught up in perfecting our plans and ideas before taking the first step. No, you don't need to perfect that website. No, you don't need the perfect logo. In entrepreneurship, there is a crucial mindset game that requires both incisiveness and decisiveness. Make a plan, yes, please do! But then start, and be willing to adjust that plan as you gain more experience and knowledge. Start, even if you don't have every detail figured out. You will learn more from starting than you ever will from planning.

The real-life experiences I had working with communities on their archives day in and day out provided the education I needed the most. The hands-on interaction with the materials, the problem-solving experience, and the communication skills developed by giving tours and teaching classes have been foundational to my work. Of course, the formal MLIS education gave me the theoretical knowledge and conceptual background necessary to understand archival principles. Still, it was the practical application in real-world settings that truly honed my skills and shaped my approach to the kind of archival work I do now. It taught me how to adapt to different situations, work with diverse communities, and handle a variety of materials. As for what I wish someone had told me when I was a student? Every experience, whether it seems significant at the moment or not, contributes to your growth and development in this field. So don't discount anything and just let each moment flow through you.

Association Director
Jenifer Grady

What I Do

My whole career has been characterized as weird because it was hard for me to describe what I was doing and harder for others to relate it to something with which they were familiar. For many years, friends said I was head of all libraries in the nation (*never* was Librarian of Congress a dream job).

After library school I was a National Library of Medicine (NLM) Associate, a one-year program where we met with staff from throughout the library and worked on projects. If you can imagine, one project I designed was a directory of all websites about HIV/AIDS. This was when the internet was text only, and to my surprise the list of potential sites grew by ten to hundred sites *daily*! That was a great introduction to what the internet would become.

Next, I helped medical professionals form queries to run on Medline, in the dial-up days when every second cost money. You had to be precise. There was no such thing as "just Google it." After that, I was the information specialist for an international nonprofit that wrote millions of dollars in grants annually. I created an intranet so staff could repurpose the content and secured a vendor for a more interactive website.

I worked between two medical libraries as an informatics apprentice. The two schools formed a partnership and I was the first product of the collaboration. I learned informatics at one institution and implemented practices at the other. It was fascinating to go between them, experiencing different demographics and funding. I was also a clinical librarian teaching clinicians to try to answer at least one of the average of three unanswered questions they had per patient. We also prepared research summaries for departmental Grand Rounds. I actually facilitated placement of the first computer on a floor in a hospital. My, how things have changed.

I went to business school after this because I wanted to earn more money and thought that an MBA was the accomplishment that would cause this to happen without any effort. When I saw the job ad for the director of the American Library Association-Allied Professional Association, I took this as a sign. I could train others to advocate for themselves and stop saying, "I'm not doing this for the money." We all need to be compensated fairly. I encouraged and fortified library workers so they had the tools to ask, simply ask. I helped develop and launch the Public Library Administrator and Library Support Staff Certifications. Being at ALA (the mothership), working with state librarians, brilliant staff, and passionate leadership, introduced me to my next industry, association management.

Librarianship and association management united in library consortia. I directed a state, mixed library type consortia where I negotiated group discounts with vendors for lower database and e-book prices, and managed an interlibrary loan service for public and academic libraries. When I wasn't negotiating and billing, I planned an annual conference.

You can probably understand why no one in my circle could envision me as a librarian, based on their experience. It was liberating for me, though. I realized that every job I had before I went to business school was connected to the National Library of Medicine (NLM) Associate Program. That is a major lesson: *Networking can be a real, tangible benefit.*

My Favorite Things

I was often the first to hold many of the positions I held, which was not intentional, though I have an entrepreneurial streak. I like to start and build with a regular paycheck, which is why I am not a full entrepreneur. I also served in nontraditional roles and libraries. This also was an unconscious choice that appealed to my love of a challenge. I often say that one day I would like to succeed someone so that I would have a blueprint and some low-hanging fruit to pick, instead of starting from scratch.

The choices I made were adventurous for the times; what is considered nontraditional depends on the opportunities available and taken. You determine what it means to be a fulfilled librarian. You may have to live in places you didn't expect, earn more or less initially (but please minimize the less), hear no and find ways around it, and craft a career that grows with you.

Challenges

People, policies and budgets are generally the stressors. I recommend taking personality and behavioral assessments like DiSC (https://www.discprofile.com/) and StrengthsFinder (https://www.gallup.com/cliftonstrengths/) to know yourself, how you communicate, how you prefer to be communicated with, and how you react to those who differ from you. We are all complex, so self-assessments can help you be more self-aware and prepared for broader variations of work styles. Pay attention and document situations that made you uncomfortable and those where you excelled. Note the personalities and leadership styles that bring out your best and worst. Culture is an umbrella term for acceptable behaviors and interactions in the workplace, which may be set by the institution and/or the leadership and/or strong personalities. Be aware of the impact of culture as well on your sense of belonging, on being heard, and on professional growth. Review employee manuals and policies and procedures before or soon after being hired. Ask about anything you do not understand.

Budgets—well, they are what they are. Learn about your employer's spending priorities. Find out if the budget changes from year to year. Find out if there is room for you to help expand the offerings. Ask to go over the budget with someone from the leadership. Admittedly, it may make some uneasy, but it will be impressive to others that you care enough to be acquainted with one of the decision-making influences (and influencers).

My Career Path

When I was a preteen, my local librarian noticed that I was reading dozens of teen novels between visits. She allowed me to check out books from the adult section. That was an eye opener for me in many ways. I later became a page at that library. In college I was going to be a guidance counselor. I experienced equity in the library and saw other high school students experience discrimination from guidance counselors. Both career choices were driven by a desire to treat everyone with respect.

Due to a misreading of the library school catalog, I chose the librarianship route. I didn't read carefully, which is what we often say about each other, right? I didn't notice that I had to conduct research for a thesis to graduate; it worked out fine. I ran away from being "in charge" for most of my library career, and in fact went to business school to find another way to command a higher salary other than becoming a director (again, no magic).

Advice

Know your worth. I have always saved performance reviews and documented scenarios and outcomes for future performance reviews and interviews. I thought worth would be tied to my salary or a title, but it is a mindset. Do what it takes to develop this mindset if it is a struggle for you to know and describe what you offer.

Learn to negotiate for yourself, and practice. No's will hurt less and less, and you might just get a yes.

Take a chance and apply for scholarships, internships, fellowships, and offbeat positions. Ask if your skillset or idea is needed. Talk to people who are doing what you want to do, even if it has absolutely nothing to do with librarianship. Tell others your dreams. You never know if those conversations will become opportunities in the future.

What you do in your lifetime does not have to make sense to anyone but you.

Author
Chrissie Anderson Peters

What I Do

I'm a writer. I get up every morning around 6:30, go across the hall to my office, and join my 7:00 a.m. Zoom writing group. This group gets my creative juices flowing by writing to a random prompt, helping me think outside the box, in case I was stuck on something or even finished writing a piece the day before. We only write for thirty minutes, then everyone in the group can share our writing. It's also good because it gives me a social outlet. Writing can be a very solitary occupation. Finding a group you're comfortable with and creating some sort of community to be part of, whether in person or online, can serve lots of useful purposes, both socially and structurally (critique groups and more).

After the Zoom session ends, the real work begins. Right now, I'm working on a fiction collection that I hope to shop around to would-be publishing houses.

I typically write nonfiction, so this is a change for me. I have twenty-four pieces in this collection, and, if my average word count holds steady, I will need at least eighteen more to hit the minimum word count. Writing the stories is just the beginning. After that comes numerous revisions, preparing for working with an editor who will likely suggest even more revisions, and maybe even striking part of the stories from the collection before presenting it to a publisher. Then we will need to find a publisher who likes the collection enough to publish it. I will submit it to small independent presses, which is different from shopping it around to major publishing houses. The publishers I will submit to will likely all be regional since my writing tends to be Appalachian-based. Someday, that may not be the case, but that is the process for the manuscript I'm currently working on. There's also no guarantee that I will find a publisher who will want to publish the collection once it is finished. If that is the case, I will need to decide whether to rework the pieces in the manuscript and try again, or whether to self-publish it, which is a viable option. (My first three books have been self-published and are all collections of fiction, nonfiction, and poetry.)

In addition to the writing part of my job, I attend writing conferences and workshops throughout the year. Some workshops require a writing sample and participants are selected based on competition against other applicants. Others are simply contingent on paying the workshop fees. I also take as many classes as possible (mostly via Zoom) to learn more about writing. Two of my favorite instructors are Darnell Arnoult and Diane Zinna (Google them and check out their excellent online classes). I belong to various local and regional writing groups and associations, too, which allow for that important community-building that I spoke about earlier.

I also submit work regularly to magazines, journals, and contests. Sometimes there are fees; sometimes submission is free. I find out about many of the opportunities through sources like ChillSubs.com, Submittable, and Duotrope, as well as through the organizations I belong to. Each year, I try to have fifty rejections—with the idea that so many rejections means that I'm hustling to get my work out there and some acceptances will come along, too.

I have a website where I post blogs monthly, and from which people can order my books. When someone orders from my website, I ship books via USPS. My books are available via Amazon, too. As a self-published, independent author, however, most of my sales are made in person, which involves paying for spaces at book festivals and craft fairs. Most of these events cost $25 and authors must provide their own table. Some events are better advertised than others, which means higher attendance and more opportunities to sell. An "elevator pitch"—a summary of what your books are about—is imperative, because you have a limited amount of time to grab people's attention as they browse your titles. Sometimes a title or book cover will draw them in. Being willing to talk and smiling are requirements; an outgoing demeanor sells more books than sitting in a chair waiting for people to come to you. Prices must be competitive; I typically offer a discount for in-person events.

My Favorite Things

Being a writer is what I dreamed of doing my whole life. For someone who loves building worlds with words and creating characters whose lives matter as much as their own, it's a wonderful career choice. I'm still doing it part-time while working towards my ultimate goals within the profession.

Challenges

I'm fortunate that my career is supplemental to our household's income. It is tough to make it as a full-time writer; very few people make it to that status without at least teaching writing on some level. For now, though, I'm happy doing what I do, where I do it, and working my way up. There are some paying gigs to be found in submitting pieces or being included in some anthologies. These opportunities are just harder to identify and are usually highly competitive. Another challenge is that it can be rather solitary work day-to-day. Unless I'm at a conference, workshop, or in an online class, I sit at a desk working alone and have no one to interact with except my cats when I leave my office for a break.

My Career Path

I received my BA in English/Education. Unable to find a teaching job, I immediately started working in libraries (public and academic). Several years later, I started the MSIS program at the University of Tennessee and then worked in a community college for about twelve years. I left to write part-time and to learn to enjoy life again, which I've been doing for ten years. Thus far, all my books have been self-published, which has required learning many new skills (fortunately early on I discovered Peggy DeKay's book, *Self-Publishing for Virgins*).

There are numerous transferable skills from librarianship. I do many reference interviews and perform a lot of research. I constantly learn new things about myself and my abilities. Ten years ago, I would never have imagined trying to prepare a 70,000–120,000-word short story collection to shop around to publishers. I was perfectly content to self-publish for the rest of my life—and there's nothing wrong with that. I have grown as a writer, though, and have become ready for new adventures.

Advice

More than anything, my life experiences have helped my writing. I mostly write about real life. More than a few library-related incidents have made their way into stories over the years, though. Book-related classes from my grad school program have proved immensely useful, such as classes about book production and literature. I was never good at the "techy" aspects of librarianship, which probably explains part of the reason I left the field. Not to say that there aren't technological aspects to writing (especially self-publishing and print on demand); technology continues to evolve and there's always something new to learn, much like in librarianship.

Community and User Research Manager
Jamie Lin

What I Do

I call myself a librarian's librarian. I work on behalf of librarians to ensure our field is preparing for the future, that we have plentiful and relevant opportunities to learn new skills and supportive communities to draw upon and lean on when needed.

For now, this means I find myself working on the peripheries of our field. The company I work for is a tech startup focused on libraries, so by nature it exists as a library vendor as well as a precarious startup environment where no one knows what will happen next on any given day.

As head of community and user research, I'm helping to shift the platform from its original format as a database of skills and training opportunities for librarians into something more searchable, social, and interactive. My goal is to create a structure that lets our members find and connect with others who have similar jobs, who live near each other, who work for similar institutions, or who have the same interests.

My Favorite Things

My position asks me to look into the future of our profession and consider what we need to know to adequately face that future. While this involves technical skills as well as change management in the sense of rethinking our organizations' existing structures and bureaucracies, my favorite aspect of my job is connecting people with each other. Librarianship is strongly tied to collaboration and partnership, and I firmly believe we all need an expansive network to thrive—meaningful relationships built on trust, transcending place of employment and even geographic location. Twenty-first-century society is online and interconnected, and our careers are strongest when they reflect that, too.

Challenges

As I do not work in traditional library spaces, I sometimes feel out of touch with what many of my professional colleagues do and with the challenges they face, aside from what is relayed to me anecdotally from those in my network. My work is shielded from the worst of budget cuts, leadership issues, or book challenges, and there are librarians who do not consider me a librarian because of where I work and what I do. I was motivated to join this profession for many of the same cultural values and ethics that prompt others to do the same—access, education, intellectual freedom, and social responsibility—and I'm often checking in with myself to determine whether my work is still in alignment with these values and ethics. Some days the response is murky, and I feel like I am wearing beautiful shoes that don't fit quite right and are giving me blisters. Luckily, at this point in my career, I have the experience and the network to be able to transition to other sectors of librarianship if desired.

This brings me to another detail about myself. I'm open to change, I can respond quickly, and I don't mind instability as far as employment goes. Through my various positions I've learned to be more extroverted, which is a performance skill that is much needed in our profession. My path is not for everyone, especially those who want something more quiet, predictable, structured, and stable. However, large bureaucracies can stifle your growth and are not for everyone. Strict hierarchies in academic structures can also feel uncomfortable to certain personalities. It's important to know yourself well and to determine what environment you would work best in.

Keep in mind that what has been stable, tried, and true for the last 100 years is probably not going to remain that way for long, based on how quickly our society is changing. There are very few positions in libraries that will not be affected by all the new technologies changing the way our society communicates and works.

My Career Path

Upon nearing graduation for my MLIS degree, I considered my options carefully. My experience working at a public library had prompted me to pursue graduate school in information science, and I had been focusing on an academic track in my class choices. However, both public and academic systems required that I already have completed my degree before even applying to these positions. As a thirty-something entering the field after pivoting from my first career in film sound design, I wanted employment, and I wanted it immediately. I had met some very smart and interesting folks at the Qualcomm library through local library events. Through my networking efforts, I was able to begin working at Qualcomm while finishing my last semester of graduate school. The starting salary was also higher than a starting salary in a more traditional sector of the field.

Joining Qualcomm immediately put me on a special library track. As a corporate researcher, I had access to expensive databases full of company and financial information, and I developed an interest in new technologies and how they would change our society. I like to describe my time there as "corporate spy work." It was a great introduction to my professional life in information, but I kept thinking that if I was going to work for a mobile tech company, I should have gone for an MBA—I'd at least be paid more! After a corporate layoff, I took a position that motivated me to teach myself more about instructional design, multimedia tutorial development, and user experience. This was a wonderful position for my own education and growth, in an area of expertise that is needed in libraries but not formally taught in library school. I wanted to share more about these skills with librarians and began presenting on topics like online accessibility at conferences. When the next layoff occurred (layoffs are expected in the corporate sector, and always lead to growth and new skill development) I decided to move a little closer to libraries; I joined Atla, a member association for librarians working in the area of religious studies and theology. My focus was on creating continuing education and professional development opportunities for Atla members and working with member committees to develop new programs bringing theological library education to a global audience. I also played a key role in organizing the annual conference each year. During the pandemic I launched the first online conference to great success, then transitioned the event to a fully hybrid conference with multiple tracks streaming live at the same time. My role at Atla allowed me a lot of autonomy in determining my day-to-day and longer-term goals, and I thoroughly enjoyed working there, but I eventually moved to a different organization because my goal was still to work on behalf of all librarians, or at least a larger subset of librarians.

Advice

Librarianship is full of introverts, which is often apparent in my remote working environment of silent and awkward Zoom meetings. How do you stand out from this crowd? It's not hard, but you have to make the first move. If you're really shy, please remember that the majority of us are also very shy, and we gravitate towards those who give us an opening, who take the lead, and who carry a conversation and listen well. Be that person, and see what happens.

Introduce yourself to others, join associations, volunteer for said associations and practice leadership through those roles, build a network of people you like, who understand you, and who will support you. For the most part, we're not a profession that cares about hierarchy. Don't let titles intimidate you when meeting people. Definitely talk to people after their conference presentations and tell them why you enjoyed their talk. Connect on social media (even if you don't often use it) and start creating a core group of colleagues whom you can turn to for advice, or just to vent. You'll need that space to vent! Our profession is transitioning like everything else, with generational and philosophical differences that are often misaligned based on differing experiences and understanding of the changing world. Find your people and find your strength.

As a student, any practical experience in which you interact with and meet other librarians is ideal, whether that's an internship or a volunteer role. Tell others about yourself and your interests and what kind of role you're hoping to find. Ask them about their work and find where you align and where you don't. Ask them to introduce you to others in their networks. Librarians love to help; that's what we do!

Anything Else?

The best opportunities for career growth and job diversity are found in nontraditional library spaces, and the potential for new areas of librarianship centered around human-machine interaction will be in high demand sooner than we think.

I encounter a lot of students interested in archives. There are a limited number of positions in archives, though digital archives is a growing area. What is it about archives (or whatever area you are interested in) that is so interesting to you? How might that translate to other work?

What kind of environment will you thrive in? Take some time to understand yourself, what motivates you, what drains you, what is important to you, and what you want to learn. We don't always know the answer to this question until we find out through experience, so if you find yourself in an environment that causes you stress and pain, don't try and squeeze yourself into it; find your way out of it. Nothing is a failure. Experience is a process of learning; it's a practice of living.

Competitive Intelligence Director
Chad Eng

What I Do

I do a type of corporate research called competitive intelligence. I track what my company's competitors are doing, and report back to my business leaders with recommendations about how my own company could respond. Often, it's maintaining up-to-date competitor profiles and other times, it's comparing our company's products to others in the market. I work with a lot of senior business leaders to determine what their highest priorities and big bets are, and balance that with the salespeople in the field who are asking about competitors that keep taking business away from us. The people out in the field also have information on some of those small players, so it's my job to extract that information from those teams and figure out a way to use that information that no one else has access to. I spend a *lot* of time reading news articles—thankfully there is technology and automation that help me with this—and making sure no important competitor movements slip through the cracks. I also get to use social media to find out what competitors are promoting or when they're doing something that our company might have to respond to.

But one of the most unusual parts of my job is going to industry events, trade shows, and conferences and having face-to-face conversations with my competitors. Even after I tell them who I work for, they are still willing to have a conversation with me, and since they don't know what kind of information I'm looking for, they often tell me things that are of interest to the people I work with. Here's a relatively clear example of what I do: my employer sends me to a trade show and I'm supposed to find out where our competitors buy tires for their machines. I go to the exhibit floor and ask a couple of people at my competitor's booth where they buy tires (I don't ask directly, but I guide the conversation around to the point where they tell me where they buy tires from, and often where some of my other competitors buy tires from). I take that information back to the strategy team at my company and a couple of months later, we acquire that tire manufacturer. Now, our competitors either have to buy tires from my company or find a new tire supplier. Fun, right?

My Favorite Things

I get to do deep research and turn a hundred pieces of information into a story (insights or intelligence) and then convince someone they need to act. I get to travel to trade shows and talk to our competitors and guide the conversation to get the answers I'm looking for that they didn't mean to tell me—it's a very fun game. I work at a very large company that places an incredible amount of value on intelligence from the field, which means they fund access to an impressive suite of electronic resources that I get to leverage every day. Working internationally has been an added perk that is extremely eye-opening, as it demands that you get creative with who you talk to while also factoring in different business cultures and buying behaviors of different populations. All of these pieces of information can be seen through different lenses, and how you turn them into a story is the real value to the intelligence you're providing.

Challenges

Like most librarians, convincing people I'm not a human Google is always a challenge. Convincing people I'm not a corporate spy or doing reputation-crippling espionage is even more difficult, but thankfully all my research is ethical and won't get my company in legal trouble.

Another huge challenge is the memory capacity of my own brain—it's really difficult to remember every detail of every conversation you've had, while you're being flooded with news/reports and simultaneously trying to recall what might be important from weeks or months ago, especially when you are working on ten projects at the same time. Documentation is vitally important, but comprehension and remembering details is critical.

Finally, there is a surprising amount of negative sentiment coming from fellow MLIS librarians in the public and academic setting—I get called a "sell out" more times than I care to recall. Working for a for-profit entity and getting paid well for my unique and advanced skill set is seen as less of a higher calling than working for a nonprofit or educational institution for a smaller salary.

My Career Path

I worked in a public library as a shelver in college and someone suggested I look into library school. I got my MLIS at the University of Illinois Urbana-Champaign and became head of reference at a public library. I had an interest in corporate libraries, and someone at a Fortune 500 company gave me a chance and taught me how to do competitive intelligence (wildly different than public library work). I worked with a lot of smart people who convinced me to add an MBA to my skillset to get smarter at adding business insights to my research. Having the MBA on my resume opened a lot of doors for me in the corporate world and honestly added some credibility to my recommendations when I could "speak the same language" as the people running the company.

The combination of degrees and experience allowed me to work my way into customer insights roles, international competitive intelligence, and knowledge management from there. I've worked in the same research department of my company for more than thirteen years, but I've spent time supporting the research needs of multiple areas. This has given me experience across my company and also connected me with a large number of people that I lean on for brainstorming, education, or networking in multiple areas. That company diversity has helped me gain a reputation for quality and collaboration across a broad set of employees.

Advice

You don't *need* an MBA and an MLIS degree to do competitive intelligence, but it does help immensely in determining what competitor moves might be important for your company to be aware of. Competitive intelligence is also not just about sitting behind a computer and snooping on the internet; if you can have conversations with your own company employees or have conversations with people at a trade show, it will allow you to find things out that would never be published anywhere. If you can help people in multiple areas of the company you work for, this can be career-boosting. If you can find out how each department consumes information (and there is a surprising array of ways people leverage your work), you'll get smarter and build up your own skillset *and* your value to the company. Finally, find people with "competitive intelligence" in their LinkedIn or resume and see if they'll give you thirty to ninety minutes of their time.

It's a fascinating field that I wasn't taught anything about in library school and there are a lot of applications for this type of work. Informational interviews are extremely valuable, even if you think your public or academic library experience isn't transferable. Being able to dig into research is pretty universal in my field, so there isn't a hidden skill set that will unlock this career path; just have some conversations.

Three pieces of advice I've been given and always provide to other interested parties:

1. Don't get stuck in a rut—successful senior leaders work in many departments and sometimes many companies.
2. If you can draw the connection between what you do and what your company sells, your work will seem a lot more meaningful.
3. Never turn down a happy hour invite.

Consortium Executive Director
Nancy S. Kirkpatrick

What I Do

I am the dean of University Libraries at Florida International University, having started a few months ago; right now, my priority is getting to know the people, acclimating to the administrivia, and navigating campus and state politics. Prior to this, I was the executive director and CEO of OhioNet, a multi-type state library consortium representing members across Ohio and adjoining states. While my role at OhioNet was administrative in nature, I was much more active in a variety of activities because of the small size of the organization. So, one day I might be meeting with the board and setting the vision and mission for the organization, and another day I could be facilitating a workshop for a member library, or attending a State Library of Ohio board meeting to keep up to date on the work our partners were doing. I also spent a fair amount of time on administrative work, as is the nature of many director roles. I appreciated the ability to get out of the office and actively support and participate in the work in which our member libraries were engaged.

My Favorite Things

I would recommend consortium work for a variety of reasons. First, it seems an area that is often overlooked. I didn't learn about the existence of consortium while getting my master's degree, though that may just be an indicator of my course load. However, librarians are really the powerhouse behind many consortia and can fill traditional librarian roles as well as others. Like to catalog? Great, there are consortia who need catalogers. Like to negotiate contracts and licenses? Work on websites? We need those skills, too. Are you great at instruction? How about marketing? Whether you have a technical services background, public services, or something totally unrelated—there is probably a consortium that needs your skills.

I enjoyed my consortium work because of the variety, and because I was actively involved with our library members and their work. Being involved kept me in touch with what was happening in the library world because I was out there experiencing it for myself. And it's a great way to get to know many different aspects of the field of librarianship.

Challenges

The biggest struggle of consortium work had nothing to do with the job itself, but with the benefits. Because we were a small organization, each year I had to work with our insurance company to try to find affordable healthcare alternatives for our small group of fifteen. This was a challenge because healthcare in the United States is often tied to employment status, so the size of your organization determines the affordability of the available options.

As for the stressors or struggles of the job, it can be easy to feel disconnected from the field, depending on your role and the type of office environment in which you work. Many consortium opportunities are remote, so if you enjoy being in a bustling office, that might be a negative factor for you.

My Career Path

My career path looks like spaghetti junction in Atlanta, for those who are familiar with that area. My first career was as an attorney. I graduated from law school, passed the bar, and worked first as a contract attorney and then for a nonprofit for about two years. I had two children during that time, and our family decided that my staying home with them was a higher priority; we were basically losing money after the costs of daycare, dry cleaning, parking, and so on.

When my former law school library dean called to talk to me about getting my MLS, I was initially uninterested. However, I knew that eventually I wanted to go back to work. A year later, I called him back and he put me on the path to librarianship. It was the best career decision I ever made, and it totally changed the trajectory of my life in positive ways I hadn't anticipated. And having that terminal degree was a huge help in fast-tracking me to library administration and executive leadership, where I've stayed and found success.

Advice

Be open to the nontraditional possibilities; they might surprise you and be the space where you can find your niche and make your mark. Also? Almost every skill and experience is transferable in librarianship.

Consultants
Cindy Fesemyer and Amanda Standerfer

What We Do

When libraries and library support organizations need answers to questions, they come to us to help them find answers in order to better serve their communities or members. We spend the majority of our time—and earn the majority of our incomes—working on strategic planning and other planning projects. We offer planning processes that include board and staff members from start to finish and are very community oriented. We collect lots of data from stakeholders, from quantitative community surveys to qualitative focus groups. We firmly believe that libraries are among the last bastions of democracy and strive to offer planning processes that honor democracy, diversity, and community.

In addition to strategic planning, we offer, both independently and together, training for library staff and trustees on a wide variety of topics, mainly related to capacity building. We offer these sessions in person and/or virtually for library systems, state libraries, state library associations, individual libraries, and more. Though this is a smaller income stream for each of our businesses, it's something we both enjoy immensely.

This means, at the core of things, we're both small business owners who happen to also be librarians. There's a lot that goes on behind the scenes that our clients won't see when we work with them. We are doing bookkeeping, paying taxes, writing proposals for new work, booking flights, scheduling meetings, and in Amanda's case guiding a small staff.

Our Favorite Things

We both wholeheartedly recommend consulting! But there are some caveats to that endorsement. To consult, you need to have an area of expertise. In Cindy's case, it's community engagement. In Amanda's case, it's strategic thinking. It took us decades, two different career tracks, and many different jobs before we felt we knew enough to hang our consulting shingles.

Before making that leap, we volunteered for our state library associations and for the American Library Association and Public Library Association. It was through this statewide and national work that we expanded our professional networks enough to have a base of potential clients across the country.

To be a successful independent consultant, you also need to assess your personal needs in relation to your work. Personally, we both like working on our own from home. We love the flexibility it affords when melding personal and professional schedules. We are both comfortable with the ambiguous future of a consultant who may not know who they'll be working for six months down the road. We've learned to trust that the work will come. And it does.

Neither of us set out to be library consultants. We simply sought out training that led to paid positions that expanded our knowledge bases and volunteered to help organizations we loved. In short, we did the work of librarians because we loved it.

Challenges

Working for yourself as a library consultant has its downsides. No matter how hard we try, neither of us seems to know the right formula that informs how much work we should accept at any given time. To line up work, we typically submit three to four proposals for every job we're offered. When we get more jobs than we thought we would, we are suddenly slammed with work for months to come and earning more income than we thought. When we get fewer accepted proposals than we'd planned, we're left twiddling our thumbs and earning less money than we'd hoped. So, how many proposals should we submit at any given time? We truly don't know; sometimes we get it right and sometimes we just don't.

Another challenge we each face in slightly different ways is how to handle the isolation of working alone, traveling alone, and generally being professionally alone. Amanda's actually very introverted (though you may not notice that when working with her) and prefers to work alone, but she has built a close-knit team to support her work and they frequently spend time on process improvement and generally thinking about how to offer more to libraries. Amanda also travels a lot, meeting with clients many times each month. Cindy is more of an extroverted introvert. She's happy to work on her own and to travel just a couple of times each month, with recharge time in between client visits.

Our Career Paths

Both Cindy and Amanda have experience in the nonprofit sector, which greatly informs their library consulting work. Cindy spent many years in nonprofits before turning to libraries as a second career. Amanda left libraries (twice!) to work in the philanthropy sector but was drawn back to libraries both times. Through this nonprofit work, we gained skills in project management, fundraising, human resources, and more. As librarians we both worked as library directors and in various public library support roles. Independent of each other we took on smaller consulting work throughout our library careers. Eventually, we each gave up our day jobs to pursue library consultancy full-time. Besides the direct work we do with clients, we also spend time on our own business development and strategic planning. We always look for new ways to help libraries improve their capacity to serve their communities or members.

Advice

Start small! And start with consulting as a side hustle to your regular employment. If you have an area of expertise, look for a way to share that as a consultant. You can do this either on your own, or as part of a team on a larger project. As an example, Cindy started consulting by saying *yes* to people who asked her to lend some expertise via paid webinars and library staff training. If it fell into her lap, she was all in. These smaller, intermittent gigs led her to seek out opportunities to earn a little extra cash to supplement her day job. Those smaller intentional jobs helped build the confidence needed to seek out bigger clients and to partner with existing consulting firms. Amanda's path was similar, and she credits a high-quality facilitation training that she attended early in her career as the foundation for her consulting work.

Consulting started as a very small snowball at the top of a snowy hill. With time, it grew.

As library school students neither of us had consultancy on our radars. We wanted to provide direct service to the patrons who needed us. And so we did, for many years. It took all of those years in nonprofits and in libraries to build the confidence, professional relationships, and knowledge base required to even consider making such a bold move. It was a big, scary leap to eventually quit our day jobs, but we're so glad we took it.

Content and Workflow Strategy Consultant
Pam Matthews

What I Do

I am a content and workflow strategy consultant (CWSC) at Proquest (part of Clarivate), which really is quite a mouthful. Informally I refer to myself as a "tame librarian" or an "ad hoc librarian." I work closely with product sales managers (PSMs) to sell books—both print and electronic—to libraries. My colleagues like to quip that the PSMs sell stuff and the CWSCs make the stuff actually work for the libraries they sell it to.

Because yup, in addition to working closely with PSMs, I also work very closely with customers. I help them set up and maintain automated ordering plans, I get them customized product lists (any size, any subject, any format), and I train them on using our various types of ordering software.

I also educate librarians on the various ways to set up automated ordering. This can include everything from demand-driven acquisition, where a bunch of book records are added into a catalog/discovery layer so that a title gets ordered automatically if a library user chooses one; to approval slips plans or title alerts, where librarians are notified of new titles that match their given criteria; to full on approval or selection plans, where any title matching the criteria a library wants is automatically ordered.

Since I'm officially part of the sales team, I do a lot of outreach to customers as well. I do check-ins with customers to see what's up at their libraries and to gauge whether we have any products that might be useful to them. I review their automated ordering plans with customers to see if the plans are working as desired, or if maybe tweaking them a bit might be useful.

My Favorite Things

Most of my interactions with customers are either by email or virtual meeting, but one of my favorite things is getting to travel to meet customers face to face. I travel about every six weeks or so, and I can't overstate what a difference it makes to meet people in person. Virtual meetings are incredibly useful, but face-to-face meetings yield a whole new level of engagement.

Another one of my favorite parts about this job is there are always new puzzles to solve, new people to talk to, new things to learn. With three different ordering systems, each with its own idiosyncrasies, there are a slew of never-ending challenges (in a good way!). We also have to be familiar with the back end of our systems, the librarian-facing parts of the systems, and even the library-user parts of the systems. It's a lot! But it's never boring.

Having many different kinds of customers also keeps things interesting. Although almost all my customers are academic librarians, they run the gamut from teeny-tiny seminaries with fifty students to massive universities serving over 68,000 students. Their needs are different, the right solutions are different, and the approaches needed are different. I enjoy talking with them to find out what their needs are, what approaches work best for them, and what kinds of solutions make the most sense.

I also love working with a team of passionate, dedicated librarians. All my fellow CWSCs and even one of the PSMs are librarians, and the other PSMs have worked so long with librarians that librarianship has rubbed off on them! No one is ever too busy to help out a fellow team member, and information sharing is a way of life. Even though we are all remote, we are definitely a cohesive team.

Challenges

Of course, as with any job, there are some downsides. Remember those challenges I mentioned? All the different systems, all the different customers? The vast majority of the time "challenges" are fantastic—at least, if like me, you'd prefer to be puzzling out solutions rather than being bored. But then there are the days (or sometimes weeks!) when everything hits at once and it can be ... a lot. Even with a supportive boss and a supportive team, it can get stressful, trying to juggle priorities and deadlines while new emails with new problems keep coming in.

Working remotely is not a problem for me but was for one of my colleagues. They ended up going back to libraryland because they missed their daily in-person interaction with coworkers and library users. Remote work really isn't for everyone. Most of our positions are on-site or hybrid, but some current CWSC positions are remote. I personally am happy with messaging and emails and video calls on the regular, with face-to-face meetings as occasional "treats," but not everyone likes working in relative isolation.

My Career Path

One of the very best things about this position is that it pulls together so much of my past experience. I started working in libraries as an undergraduate student. I worked in acquisitions and one of my jobs was to sort actual, physical, approval slips—how could I possibly have realized I would be working on the same thing, but in electronic format and from the other direction, almost forty years later?

My career has encompassed both public and academic libraries. I've mainly worked in acquisitions and collection management but also rocked the occasional reference or cataloging gig. I've worked for other library vendors as well, doing mostly collection development and marketing. Knowing the ins and outs of acquisitions and collection management—and having experienced them in a wide array of settings—has been invaluable in my current position. I understand exactly what customers are asking for and dealing with, and I understand how solutions that are perfect in one institution would be absolutely ineffective in another.

Working in marketing honed my communication and networking skills—skills I use every day as I work with customers.

Advice

Shop around. Try different jobs. Talk to different people. Be open to new experiences. Knowledge gained is never wasted; it might get transmuted, but it doesn't go away.

Maybe even try "going to the dark side" and working for a vendor. I can unequivocally say that working for vendors has made me a better librarian, because it made me more open to working *with* vendors. I realized that vendors often have expertise that can be leveraged for the good and convenience of libraries, and that the relationship can be collaborative instead of adversarial, benefiting both sides.

I would be remiss not to mention another perk of working well with your vendors: it might even launch you into a new career. My last two jobs have come about because of relationships I had with vendors as a librarian.

Which leaves me with my last bit of advice: never stop networking. Not in a sleazy, used car salesman kind of way, but in a don't-burn-bridges, don't-hesitate-to-check-in-on-former-or-current-colleagues kind of way. Networking keeps you on the pulse of the profession and can alert you to all sorts of wonderful opportunities.

Continuing Medical Education Coordinator
Karen Burton

What I Do

As with most people straight out of library school, my first job was with whoever would hire me. So, I worked as a continuing medical education

(CME) coordinator for the University of South Carolina School of Medicine Greenville. All doctors must earn a certain number of CME credit hours every year to maintain their licenses, and these educational opportunities must be offered by a program accredited by the Accreditation Council for Continuing Medical Education (ACCME). Our program was considered large because we served both the medical school and the hospital system next door, and I was responsible for coordinating about half of the CME activities.

My overall responsibilities were running the learning management system (LMS) and managing data, but the reality was that I wore many hats. I worked with three main systems: the LMS where we tracked attendance at CME sessions and awarded credit; Smartsheet, where we managed the logistics of each session; and the ACCME's Program and Activity Reporting System (PARS), where we reported learner data. On the LMS side, I was responsible for creating CME events; maintaining and updating every CME session page; updating user accounts; and using analytics to retrieve data. On the PARS side, every single CME activity had to be created in PARS every year and the total number of learners for the year reported. We ran on an academic year schedule, so every June we had to report the learner numbers from the previous year and create a new series in the LMS. This sounds easy, but with about 110 activities with up to fifty-two sessions each it was very time-consuming.

We had about 100 CME activities that met regularly at weekly, monthly, or quarterly intervals. One of the most vital ACCME accreditation requirements is that accredited CME be free from commercial influence, which meant that every single CME activity speaker for every single CME activity had to sign a required disclosure form where they disclosed any financial relationships with "ineligible companies" as defined by the ACCME. If they did have financial relationships, I had to follow a mitigation protocol and their slides had to go through peer review before they could speak. If they didn't sign the form before the session started, we could not offer CME credit, which led to unhappy doctors. Now imagine 100 CME activities, most with weekly sessions, and often with a different speaker each session: accidentally becoming noncompliant was a real risk. We used Smartsheet to automate the process of tracking and managing speaker disclosures and session information. Smartsheet is a web-based program that was first described to me as a "spreadsheet on steroids." Each activity had a Smartsheet that contained all the data we had to track for accreditation and was programmed with automations to notify the appropriate people if information was not filled in or if disclosures were not signed prior to the session. We also created a report that showed the data for all upcoming CME sessions sorted by date, which allowed us to quickly identify and resolve any missing information.

My Favorite Things

This CME coordinator job was an excellent fit for the skills I learned in library school. I used knowledge from my metadata class to improve our usage of the data analytics in the LMS and used reference interview techniques to effectively communicate with doctors, hospital administrators, learners, and guest speakers. I created a variety of instructional materials in written and video tutorial forms and regularly led training sessions for new employees. My favorite project I initiated was standardizing vocabulary terms from multiple sources to create a controlled vocabulary for the LMS that described every CME session, then creating a taxonomy for CME activities and implementing a content tagging system. This allowed us to use the LMS analytics to pull reports in five minutes that used to take hours of manual labor.

Learning to use Smartsheet has been incredibly useful both in the CME coordinator job and beyond. It is an amazing tool for project and data management that allows you to automate workflows and reminders. I have taken that knowledge and applied it to many different projects in subsequent jobs such as benchmarking projects, weeding projects, and data analytics. I also enjoyed the culture of continuously looking for ways to improve processes and workflows.

Challenges

Sometimes there wasn't a good process in place or someone who knew how to do a specific task or project, so I had to figure it out myself. For example, the LMS had an analytics system, but no one knew how to use it because it was new. We needed to be able to see how many CME sessions occurred per department for a given time without taking hours to look it up manually. There were numerous metadata fields throughout the LMS, but no data dictionary or documentation on how they mapped to which fields in the analytics dashboard. Through trial and error, I learned where the metadata fields mapped and used that knowledge to drastically decrease the time needed to create reports.

My Career Path

My career path has been a long and winding road. My undergraduate degree is in entomology, and my early jobs included counting pests on crops, raising beetles, and teaching violin. One of my favorite jobs, and the one that I left to go to library school, was tutoring student athletes at Clemson University. The athletics culture valued education, and that was reflected in the actions of my students. During my four years in that job, I unwittingly learned library skills such as how to conduct a reference interview, refer students to resources, guide them in creating study materials, and help them research topics I knew nothing about. As much as I enjoyed that job, the hours were impractical and the compensation too low for me to continue. I wanted to go back for a master's degree and decided on the goal of working as an academic librarian because I enjoyed working with college students, and I lived within commuting distance of several academic libraries. While I enjoyed the CME coordinator job, I only stayed there one year before I took a job as science librarian at Clemson that was much closer to home and was exactly what I wanted to do long-term. However, I learned many skills and developed relationships that I have taken with me and applied to my new job, and I will forever be grateful I had the experience of working as a CME coordinator.

Advice

Think about what you learned in library school and how you can frame those skills in a more general way. For example, reference interview skills are customer service skills. Also, don't be afraid to look at careers that use a similar set of skills that are not in a library. I know librarians who work in electronic health records, digital asset management, streaming media, user experience, private investigating, development and fundraising, and project management. The Librarian Linkover podcast broadcasts interviews with people who successfully took their library skills outside the library and is a great resource for getting ideas about potential nontraditional careers.

Cybersecurity Analyst
Tracy Z. Maleeff

What I Do

I turn data into intelligence. I monitor the publicly available resources and private outlets for news, information, and data that could negatively impact the company where I work and package all that into easy-to-understand alerts and briefings. I follow a five-step process called the "intelligence cycle," which consists of direction and planning, collection, processing and analysis, dissemination, and review. There are daily, weekly, and monthly briefings to prepare, so it's a cycle of report building and articulating awareness of a situation. In the plainest way possible, I help provide the decision-makers with the information they need to make determinations about risk management in a corporate environment. It can be hectic and frightening at times, but it can also be exhilarating. It requires great research and analytic skills, along with a good foundation of technical knowledge to understand how an event you see in the news translates into my world as a risk that needs to be mitigated.

My Favorite Things

I love the research aspect. I love finding things. I love being the first to find something. It's almost like solving puzzles all day. I like interacting with our stakeholders, whether it be a member of the C-suite or another department within the company. I like connecting people with information that they can value and use. It's great to present a solution to a problem in a way that no one has thought of before. That's what comes from being in a technical industry with a liberal arts and library science education: I think differently in a way that compliments the technical-minded folks. I highly recommend a role like this to an LIS student who is good with research, ethics, communication, and who enjoys a fast-paced environment. (The pace can be the exciting part!)

Challenges

Perhaps the biggest downside of a position in cybersecurity threat intelligence is constant terrible news. You rarely deal with good news. Ransomware. Data breaches. Identity theft. Risk, security, and privacy are always at the top of your mind. The pace can be very fast, and because criminals operate on weekends and holidays, you won't necessarily have a traditional nine-to-five kind of job. Those demands will vary a lot by industry and company, so ask questions about a position to see if there are on-call components and to learn what you are expected to keep track of.

Another challenge can be the human aspects of the job. I teach "empathy as a service" when I speak at industry conferences as one method to improve communications. Your work can be difficult when people don't follow the proper security measures or when you encounter resistance from territorial departments in the company. You need to be mission-focused and keep going despite the challenges.

My Career Path

Although I loved being a librarian, I became concerned about ten years ago that the role of the law firm librarian was in jeopardy. All around me law firm libraries were downsized or closed; sometimes the entire law firm itself would close. Plus, at that time I felt as though I had reached the pinnacle of my librarian career. I wasn't interested in being a library director, but I also wasn't content with doing the same job until retirement. I thought a lot about what else interested me and realized that I liked technology and computers. I started a journey of discovery and quickly learned that the technology industry wasn't a good fit. As I learned more about cybersecurity, I really fell in love with it. I made learning about cybersecurity my quirky hobby: I took workshops, studied, and immersed myself in information security. I asked the law firm's chief information officer if I could help with the firm's cybersecurity awareness month campaign, and I ran a successful program. Six months later I was on a plane to San Francisco because I had quit my library job and created my own company to freelance as I skilled up to enter the cybersecurity field. About a year later, I landed my first security operations center job, and my new career was off and running.

Advice

I found it extremely helpful to have hands-on technical experience in a security operations center before I eventually pivoted into threat intelligence. I wasn't exceptional at computers, but I picked skills up because I was willing to learn. You must have a curiosity that *drives* you. You need to *want* to learn.

Communication skills will go a long way toward your success. Being able to explain something complicated in a noncomplicated way, without being condescending, is how you get things done. I took one computer science class as an undergraduate but wish I had taken more. Almost any role in the information security industry is great for someone with library science training. There are endless amounts of data to be organized, playbooks to be written, classification of information to be streamlined. Professional colleagues often ask me how I can help get more librarians involved in information security. They need our skill set, whether they realize it or not.

Anything Else?

Know your transferable skills and how to clearly articulate them. This is useful when interviewing for a job, especially if you lack experience. Worked in a fast-food restaurant? You excel in a fast-paced environment, you are an efficient multitasker, you communicate effectively with the general public, and so on. Babysitting is taking on the responsibility for another human life. I'm not saying to lie or exaggerate, but capture the essence of skills you have and be able to describe them to show you can learn and adapt.

Get better at professional networking. Having a large network and knowing how to properly maintain it can be enriching and helpful. You can learn from new people and help each other get jobs. Which is why, by the way, it's important that your network is diverse. Rethink how you define the word diversity. In addition to the commonly thought-of aspects, diversity should also include different perspectives that come along with age (connect with close-to-retirement persons and new college graduates); education (befriend someone with a GED and someone with a PhD.); industries (get to know people in petroleum and in fashion). Don't look at people just as Pokémon in your collection, but as reciprocal instruments you can all use to support each other with personal and professional enrichment.

Development and Alumni Relations Administrator
Selma Permenter

What I Do

As the assistant vice president for development services and administration at a large, public research university, I'm responsible for leading a team of sixteen professionals who support the institution's fundraising efforts. My team is part of the development and alumni relations division and has a variety of responsibilities that can be divided into five distinct groups: talent and business operations, development data and technologies, gift administration, endowment services, and prospect development and research. Depending on the day, my work can focus on any or all of these areas.

The talent and business operations team is responsible for hiring, engaging, and retaining development and alumni relations professionals and ensuring that the development and alumni relations division runs smoothly. This includes managing a nearly $10 million budget and creating and supporting professional development opportunities for the development and alumni relations team of more than sixty employees.

The development data and technologies team manages the data and technology that fuels the work of the university's fundraising and alumni engagement efforts. Most notably, team members manage the alumni and donor database of approximately 400,000 constituent records and field requests for lists and reports from across campus. They provide files used to send newsletters, invitations, solicitations, surveys, and a variety of other communications from the colleges and schools to our alumni and donors.

The gift administration team records and receipts all gifts to the university and works to keep the alumni and donor database updated with the most current contact and biographical data on our constituents. The team also reviews and drafts gift agreements and ensures that IRS rules and regulations related to philanthropic giving are followed closely.

The endowment services team works closely with the frontline fundraisers on all matters involving endowment creation. The team also carefully monitors endowment spending to ensure endowment distributions are used in accordance with the endowment agreements and reports back to donors each year regarding the use and performance of their endowments.

The prospect development and research team identifies and researches prospective major gift donors and develops confidential research profiles using information from our alumni and donor database and paid sources like LexisNexis, ResearchPoint, LinkedIn Sales Navigator, and iWave. In addition, the team records and tracks major gift proposals, develops prospect lists for various fundraising campaigns, and produces a variety of reports and dashboards to measure fundraising productivity and frontline fundraiser performance.

My Favorite Things

A career in development can be very rewarding. When I reflect on the work I do and how it ultimately leads to more dollars being raised for the institution, I think about the impact of our donors' generosity on the lives of our students, and I feel proud to have played a small role in that.

But when it comes to my daily work, I find that I'm happiest when I get away from the day-to-day administrative responsibilities and do what I have always loved. For me, that means digging into the data. Whether I'm helping one of our prospect researchers connect the dots on a particularly hard project, focusing on data management tasks like improving our data quality, or developing a report that highlights our fundraising success, working with data is where I would spend most of my time if given the opportunity.

And while administrative tasks, and even managing a team, are not my favorite aspects of the job, working with my team members is a tremendous privilege. Development professionals are great people. They are incredibly hard-working, and they care about raising money not just because it's their job, but because of the tremendous impact it makes on our donors and on the mission of our institutions. Being surrounded by people with this mindset is good for the soul.

And finally, development professionals are compensated well for the work they do. Highly skilled and experienced development professionals are very much in demand. And those who are on the frontlines soliciting gifts are even more in demand. If you go into this field and thrive, you can expect to be actively recruited and offered competitive salaries.

Challenges

While development work is very rewarding, it also comes with certain challenges. First, development is a results-oriented profession. Typically, the fundraising goal increases every year, and each member of the team plays a vital role in trying to achieve it. When the year is successful, the development team will celebrate together. But during a more difficult year, everyone feels the pressure to raise more money.

Second, it seems like the team is never large enough to complete all the work. There are always more prospective donors to research, more data to analyze, and more solicitation lists to develop. Managing your workload can be difficult, so it's important to prioritize and manage expectations.

But perhaps the biggest challenge for those in development is hiring and retaining talent. Because development professionals are so in demand, they can often leave after a year or two and make more money elsewhere. High staff turnover, coupled with the difficulty in recruiting talent, impacts the entire operation. As a result, development programs are putting a stronger emphasis on building a culture where people want to stay.

My Career Path

My mom worked in a school library, and I worked my way through college by working in the university library while attending undergraduate school. After receiving my BA degree in English, I earned a master's in information science (MIS) and learned that my love for libraries ran much deeper than just a passion for books. I loved the organization of information.

I found myself working in the development office for my undergraduate institution while pursuing my MIS. I was lucky that this time in my life coincided with the emergence of prospect research in development programs. My first professional job out of library school was as the first prospect researcher for the development program at my institution. I served in this role for four years before broadening my experience with stints in annual giving and major giving, eventually finding my way back to development services in a leadership role.

I quickly learned how reliant strong development programs are on data. Data drives strategy, informs success, and feeds the work we do to solicit philanthropic gifts. My MIS education laid the groundwork for how I work with data today.

Advice

For MIS graduates, the most obvious point of entry into the development field is as a prospect researcher. This is where I first developed my love for fundraising and an appreciation for data and the story it can tell. As you serve in your first development job, keep a few things in mind. First, strong data management is fundamental to fundraising success. Good data doesn't just happen; you must work for it every day. Develop a plan for how you will improve the quality of the data and work that plan. Second, it's important to prove your worth. Measure your work and tie it back to dollars raised. Tell that story in your self-evaluations and any other opportunity you get. Third, don't be afraid to step out of your comfort zone. Good work leads to greater opportunities. Be open to the right ones and learn from them. Fourth, take every opportunity you can to hone your management skills. Whether it's managing projects or a team, you need strong management skills to advance in development. And finally, before you accept a development job, make sure you believe in the organization's cause. Development work requires passion and dedication, and it's impossible to do your job well if you don't believe in the mission of the organization.

Digital Asset Manager
Lisa Grimm

What I Do

I've been fortunate to have a wide variety of roles in digital asset management (DAM) and taxonomy since leaving more traditional library and archive spaces. Each of those experiences helped lead me to my current position as an executive consultant at ICP, a global consultancy and managed services organization in the content orchestration space. I also teach in the Rutgers DAM certificate program, so I have the opportunity to work with people at every career stage, from a senior executive to those just beginning their work lives in this field.

My Favorite Things

Although I have "consultant" in my title, working with clients is only one part of my role, and no two days are alike, which is ideal for me. I may be on a Teams call to work through a tricky taxonomy problem or perhaps I'm putting together a proposal for a potential new client. I do a lot of thought leadership in the DAM space as well, and that may come in the form of writing a white paper, presenting at a conference, moderating a webinar, or filming a video snippet. Although I primarily work from home, I take the opportunity to travel to the office in London every six or so weeks, and am also happy to visit a client on site when that's helpful—each engagement is different.

DAM is a field where you can go both broad and deep in terms of specialization. I have worked with some fantastic taxonomists who built and maintained incredibly complex data models; generalist digital librarians who span across many different verticals; and consultants and product managers with niche expertise in life sciences, museums, nonprofits, and fast-moving consumer goods (FMCG) content. There is no single path, and expertise gained in other roles is often quite relevant.

Challenges

There's always pressure to bring in new business and to produce relevant content that continually drives that sales pipeline. A high level of comfort with ambiguity is also a must, as things like job titles and roles and responsibilities can change frequently if you're on the more strategic end of the business, while things can be (but are not necessarily) slower on the execution side. There are absolutely roles out there for people who simply want to work behind the scenes, building taxonomies and tagging content, but for most senior-level positions, there's a lot of "peopling" involved, for both individual contributors and those in people management. And that is perhaps one of the biggest challenges: there is very little formal training or broader institutional understanding for many roles in DAM. While there are now more options in terms of continuing professional education, even some degree programs, it is a constant challenge to educate businesses on the value of DAM. While the conversation can include return on investment (ROI), painting the bigger picture for senior leaders who don't work directly with DAM is a key element of strategic leadership.

My Career Path

But the great thing about DAM is that it is filled with librarians; the importance of a solid taxonomy and governance model for any solution is well understood. There is no one way in, and my own path illustrates that. Although I began my career in technology somewhat accidentally, by getting a part-time job building websites during my MA in Archaeology, this is not at all unusual—so many have ended up in this field because of an unexpected opportunity. I became disillusioned with the technology industry and went back to library school; my goal was to become an archivist or rare books librarian, and I achieved both. However, the pay cut I had to take was not sustainable in the long term. The real irony was that I'd been doing many of the same tasks before, without knowing there was an existing framework, for a much larger paycheck. Indeed, much of my education work now is convincing people that they already have the skills and experience to succeed; it's about framing it up on their CVs or in interviews.

But had it not been for several digitization projects, I would not have become so specialized in DAM, working with some amazing collections that have led directly to where I am today. Along the way, I've worked for huge multinationals (GSK, Amazon, Novartis), small vendors, and nearly everything in between, and I've been lucky enough to have my whole family, cats included, moved twice (including, permanently, to Ireland) at my employer's expense. This is a very portable career that can grant you access to things like work permits and generous relocation packages. I've had a wide range of job titles in DAM: content librarian, product manager, technical program manager, taxonomist, director, global director, and even VP DAM evangelist, but in each case, that foundational knowledge of the principles of librarianship and knowledge organization let me build up the rest as I've learned new skills on subsequent jobs.

Advice

That said, it would have been preferable to do a bit less on-the-job learning in some key aspects of product and people management, budgets and reporting, or navigation of giving and receiving critical feedback. I've had some supportive workplaces where this was handled well, and others that were absolutely toxic, so having a baseline knowledge of some of those more critical business leadership skills would have been beneficial. As mentioned, more programs now exist to address those gaps, but there isn't always the opportunity to access them, whether because of cost, time, or other factors.

But all told, my library degree, my love of writing and presenting, and my ability to identify and build helpful partnerships are what have powered my career in DAM, and I've loved the ride. This is an ideal field for the always curious, with many different possible directions across product, program, and delivery.

Anything Else?

So many people are already "doing DAM" without realizing it, whether they are digitizing images, tagging assets, or managing digital rights for their organization. By pulling these diverse skills together, they can transition into a career that can take them all over the world.

Roles in DAM range from incredibly detail-oriented and technical to very high-level and strategic, with nearly everything in between. Experience gained in one area is incredibly valuable in others; cross-pollination, continuous improvement, and sharing of best practices are all actively encouraged. While the foundation is all about information management, the possible career paths offer a wide diversity of options.

Digital Content Librarian
Maria Fesz

What I Do

Although I'm team lead for public library collection development at OverDrive, I'm also a digital content librarian for library partners. Because this is what most of my team does, I think the best place to start is with "a day in the life" of a digital content librarian (DCL). Ten out of the twelve members of our team work directly with OverDrive's public library customers, whom we call partners. Partners in the United States and Canada are split up into territories. Each territory has its own digital content librarian along with an account manager and product support specialist.

Our days consist of working on our own tasks, communicating with partners via email and Zoom, and collaborating with our territory team on Slack or in meetings. We also collaborate with internal teams at OverDrive.

The first stop of the day is to Slack to check in with the digital content librarians and territory team. Then it's off to email. Our priority is always our library partners, so if any of them have sent anything, that's what I'm handling first. Messages of course come in throughout the day as well.

Many of our regularly scheduled tasks are for partners. Partner tasks range from recurring weekly/monthly/quarterly tasks to one-off requests. Most of our tasks are carts and curation (curation is what we call merchandized lists of already-owned content that displays on the Libby site), but some administrative tasks come up for us as well, such as special sale requests for book clubs/community reads. Some common task examples are:

- Weekly carts: *New York Times* unowned bestsellers and preorder fiction with a publication date six months out

- Biweekly carts: high holds and new/popular unowned content carts, split up by audience level
- Monthly curation: Thematic and seasonal curated display lists on main page (Libby landing page) and catalog guides (kids, teens, job/career and business, etc.)

Every public library DCL also makes recommended lists. These are lists of content in OverDrive's Marketplace that can be shopped from or used as a starting place for curation. Some of these lists are one-offs that we think will be fun and often tie into our area of expertise, trending topics, or a suggestion from a team member or partner. We also make lists for our marketing team to feature in emails or advertisements in Marketplace.

Other ways that the DCLs get to flex their content expertise is by writing blogs for both our library partners and Libby users. We also work with our training team to present content webinars for library partners to feature forthcoming titles we are excited about and under-the-radar titles that we hope will help partners build balanced and diverse collections. We keep up with content by attending publisher presentations, reading book news, and attending webinars from NoveList, Library Journal, and the like.

Every month each DCL has a variety of partner calls. Most of these are monthly check-ins to let partners know about important updates and answer questions. Upon request, the DCL will lead OverDrive's diversity, equity, and inclusion (DEI) audit report. Sometimes, we also do ad-hoc training sessions with partners, usually on shopping tips, curation, or metered access content management.

When time allows, we also work on our own team projects. We collaborate with other teams as needed; most of these teams are directly related to content, like metadata and publisher services. We give product feedback to the development teams behind Marketplace and Libby as we work in Marketplace every day and can express the issues our library partners are having with helpful context.

My Favorite Things

I currently work with libraries in several states in the Midwest. I love that I've been able to make lasting partnerships with these librarians. Every territory

I've worked with has had wonderful partners that I enjoyed communicating with, meeting at conferences, and generally trying to make their life easier while also getting patrons the content they want to read. Having this connection to libraries and being able to help them make the most of their OverDrive collection, assure them their concerns are valid, and ultimately make their patrons happy is one of the best parts of the job. I also get to work with an amazing team of fellow digital content librarians, which doesn't hurt either.

Challenges

When it comes down to it, I work for a technology company. This comes with its own unique challenges that I hadn't faced as much in other library work. Being an in-between for librarians and our other internal, non-partner-facing teams can be challenging in both directions. Internal team members, many of whom have never worked in a library, sometimes struggle to understand why our partners' priorities in the digital library space are what they are. Part of my job, especially being team lead (which puts me into more collaborative internal meetings than other members of my team), is to effectively convey the context of libraries' biggest concerns and needs. This can sometimes be exhausting. On the other hand, it has certainly been eye opening to see how much development work goes into changing even the smallest aspect of one of our products. Managing libraries' expectations so that we don't overwhelm our development teams, metadata teams, and other internal teams is crucial to the company.

My Career Path

My career path has been a winding one. I entered undergraduate school with a plan to major in literature, minor in music, and then go to library school. After a month of music and English classes, I knew without a doubt that music was what I wanted to study for the next four years. I earned my master's degree in music performance, and my library use during that program replanted the seed of interest in pursuing librarianship as a career.

When I started my second master's at Pitt, I kept my MLIS area of specialty open so I could explore options in the library world. I immediately became interested in academic libraries. I interned and worked part time at Duquesne

University and landed my first full-time library job at a community college right after graduation. I worked in community colleges for several years in various roles including instruction, collection development, and research support. I decided to move back home to Ohio and took a job in public libraries as an adult services librarian. About two years into my tenure there, the library decided to centralize collection development, and I felt without that aspect of my job, I wouldn't enjoy it enough to stay. That's when I applied to OverDrive.

Every type of skill I've acquired from different jobs over the years has contributed to the skills I've had to use as a librarian, and specifically as a digital content librarian. Being able to combine problem solving, collection development, readers' advisory, and customer service into one job has been rewarding, but I wouldn't have been as confident about my skills if I hadn't held jobs in multiple types of libraries. This gave me a unique perspective and a willingness to be flexible in various work situations.

Advice

The most helpful thing I did for myself was to take classes in and get real-life experience in all aspects of librarianship. I didn't realize how many options there were until I started the program, and I don't think I would have found the path that worked for me if I hadn't branched out and discovered what I liked best through trial and error. It never hurts to try a new type of library job. You can move between different arenas if you keep an open mind, have a solid work ethic, and make yourself a valuable colleague.

Anything Else?

I've been lucky enough to interview most of the existing DCL team at OverDrive, and I see a difference between applicants who just want to get out of libraries and those who seem genuinely interested and confident that they'd enjoy the job. Librarian burnout is very real, but burnout happens in any job; it's wise to weigh the most rewarding parts of your job with its biggest stressors before venturing out into another professional area.

Freelance Editor
Priscilla K. Shontz

What I Do

Freelance writing or editing can be a fun side gig that allows you to explore your own interests, build your expertise, and share your findings with others. It's a great way to network, collaborate, and expand your community. In my case, editing kept me connected and active in the field while I was an at-home parent, which then helped me ease back into the workplace when my children entered college. There are various book publishing roles such as writing, volume editing, copy editing, proofreading, and so on. Because I've learned that I love editing essay collections like this one, I'll describe how that process works for me.

Brainstorm ideas. What do you like to read or discuss? Choose a topic you love, as you'll be immersing yourself in it. What do you wish you could find in the literature? Research to see what's already been written on topics that interest you.

Send queries. Email acquisitions editors, briefly describing your ideas, to ask if they have any interest.

Write a proposal. If an acquisitions editor likes your idea, they'll ask you to submit a proposal (don't worry, they'll give you guidelines). If the publisher accepts your proposal, they'll eventually offer you a contract. Your acquisition editor will guide you through this process but don't hesitate to ask questions. As you're waiting for that official contract, flesh out your outline and create an elevator pitch to use in author invitations, calls for contributors, and other publicity.

Solicit authors. Search your network, their networks, social media, networking sites, search engines, publications, discussion lists, professional organizations, and so on. Email people and post calls for contributors, summarizing the project, deadline, and word count, to give potential authors a sense of what would be involved.

Assign tasks and deadlines. Send clear directions to your contributors. Perhaps send them a writing sample, questionnaire, or guidelines to help them understand what you have in mind. You might want to ask for a rough draft early in the process. Remind them of deadlines and follow up if they need extensions.

Edit and format. You'll exchange revisions with each contributor until you're both happy with the draft. Then you'll reread everything as you format the manuscript according to the publisher's guidelines. After you submit the manuscript, it will typically go through peer reviewing, copy editing, typesetting, and proofreading. Acquisitions and copy editors will guide you through these stages.

My Favorite Things

Although I'm fairly introverted, I love meeting people and learning what makes them tick. I'm fascinated by personalities and by life stories—I love hearing why you like what you like, how you got where you are, what you've discovered along the way. Editing connects me with people I'd otherwise never meet. Meeting a diverse array of people broadens my perspective beyond my own personal experiences and local networks. And particularly during my at-home parenting years, editing kept me connected to the professional community.

Editing is mentally stimulating. I love gathering ideas from others, organizing them, and presenting them to potential readers; it's a lot like reference librarianship. I also enjoy feeling like I'm helping others by packaging and sharing real-world, practical career information.

Challenges

Editing a collection, especially a large one, means you work with many other people, asynchronously, online, for a long period of time. You're not always in control of your own timeline. Communicating by email, waiting for submissions, reminding authors about or extending deadlines, filling gaps when authors withdraw—you'll need all your project management skills and a lot of patience, understanding, and flexibility. As with any long-term project, you're likely to hit a slump about two-thirds of the way along, wondering why you started this project in the first place; lean on your determination and encouraging friends to power through this phase. The print publishing process is slow, often taking a couple years from query to book release.

My Career Path

While earning an undergraduate journalism degree, I worked as a circulation student assistant, then moved into staff positions while earning my MLS. I worked in academic, medical, and public libraries before opting to stay home with my children. During those years I did part-time gigs–editor, private school librarian, office assistant, photographer–and I'm now back in academic librarianship.

My freelance writing and editing began in one of my early jobs, a tenure-track university position where we were expected to publish. We were also expected to participate in professional organizations, which prompted me to join the ALA New Members Round Table (NMRT), probably one of the most influential steps in my career path. Through NMRT I made lifelong connections, developed leadership skills, and discovered an interest in career topics. I started small, writing for newsletters and such, and my supervisor encouraged me to follow my interests and keep writing about career management issues.

After I left that tenure-track position, I stayed interested in writing. I became intrigued with writing a book that would share practical career advice from experienced professionals. As a new-ish librarian, I didn't have the wisdom or experience to give advice of my own, but I felt that interviewing others would allow me to learn while gathering advice to share. Over time I've realized that my journalism and library science interests incline me to research, interview, organize information, and report. I've discovered that my personal style—in publishing, photography, and everyday life—is to be practical and candid. And after trying both writing and editing, I've learned that I prefer editing.

When my children were young, I used editing to stay involved in librarianship. As time went by, I drifted further from the field but maintained contact with library friends. To my surprise, returning to academic librarianship revived my interest in writing. I emailed Bloomsbury Libraries Unlimited, asking if there was any interest in updating my book *A Day in the Life: Career Options in Library and Information Science*, and here we are.

Advice

Don't be afraid to try. Bounce ideas off trusted friends. Send queries; it never hurts to ask.

Flex your project management skills. Be organized but stay flexible. Plan for everything to take more time and effort than you'd anticipated. Set deadlines for yourself and your contributors well in advance of your publisher's deadline to allow for delays. Have contingency plans.

Communicate regularly with your contributors, collaborators, editors, and so on. Be honest and communicative with all the people you're working with. Send clear guidelines and keep them updated on the process. Don't be afraid to ask your editors questions.

Network. Use your research skills to find potential collaborators via every method you can think of. Ask your contacts to help you widen your search if needed. After your project is finished, stay in touch with your expanding community. These are your people; you'll often find that you collaborate again, help one another with career moves, and, if you're as lucky as I've been, become treasured friends.

Independent Information Professional
Kearin Reid

What I Do

I provide information or library services on a contract or one-time basis. While there are many different types of independent information professionals, I work within the areas of research, training, and consulting. I specialize in systematic reviews and clinical (medical) guideline development, and most of my clients are nonprofit associations or research groups. When working by contract, I often have agreed-upon deliverables, a specified budget for hourly charges, or a set timeline for each step of a project. Each contract is negotiable and tailored to the client's needs as well as my own. For example, I always specify coauthorship or acknowledgment in my systematic review contracts so that I know that I will be given credit for the work I do on a publication. Sometimes I even provide a list of available add-on services if the client wishes to extend the contract. On the other side, the client often specifies a maximum budget and due date if I am charging an hourly fee for my services. The deliverables I provide can range from the results of a literature search to a PRISMA chart, a written methods section, or a written report. I also provide one-time services for a set fee when consulting on methodology for guideline development, consulting on project development, or providing training in any of those areas.

Independent information professionals are sometimes called "infopreneurs" because they often start their own businesses for liability and legal protections. Being an independent business owner or self-employed comes with additional responsibilities and job requirements. About half of my time is devoted to tasks that do not translate into immediate income, such as marketing and advertising, professional development, or business management. In terms of marketing, I maintain a website with descriptions of my services, my credentials, and ways to contact me or schedule a meeting. The rest of my marketing is dependent on professional networking, word of mouth, and job listings. Professional networking and professional development require involvement in relevant associations and courses to maintain skills. Even the business management side of my work takes continued education and training. It is possible to pay others to help with the management responsibilities, but there is still the need to keep track of finances, business insurance, and other legalities.

My Favorite Things

Despite the difficulties of business ownership, my favorite aspects of the position are the freedom and control of being my own boss. I decide when I work and which jobs I take. While I try to work "normal" business hours, I am not held to them, and I can easily modify my schedule depending on my needs. As long as I meet client expectations, it doesn't matter when or where I get the work done. I also appreciate the ability to negotiate with a client and set terms that work for everyone involved. By choosing clients and projects, I get to focus on the aspects of librarianship that I am passionate about and excel in. While I do take jobs because of business needs—it's not always a passion project—it is always a choice that I have made and a project that I have accepted. I like the ability to choose which tasks I do and which ones I outsource. This allows me the opportunity for personal and professional growth where I can challenge myself to grow in areas that interest me versus meeting a larger organization's needs.

Challenges

The biggest challenges of my position also come from business ownership and working as a solo librarian. Starting your own business can be a little intimidating, and while there is freedom, there is also responsibility and no one else to shoulder the burden of your choices. From selecting and pricing your services to marketing or managing your accounts, there are a lot of decisions to make and new skills to learn. There is the worry about where your next client will come from and how to maintain a steady income and workflow. The finances, marketing, and legalities of a small business are not an area in which I had a lot of experience as a librarian. This can be a steep learning curve and a lot to manage.

My Career Path

This is not a job that I ever envisioned for myself or set out to achieve, but rather an opportunity that evolved. Some information professionals dream of owning their own business and spend their personal time developing a business plan while working part-time or full-time jobs. Others take time off work, for whatever reason, and decide to go independent based on contacts developed over time and a dream of doing something different. In my case, I needed to take time off work and decided to apply for a short-term contract job doing systematic reviews. This was just supposed to keep me afloat financially and connected to the profession in the interim, and I fully intended to return to academic librarianship. However, once I started to look around, more opportunities presented themselves and I realized that I had something very niche to offer. I think that is what surprised me the most; I didn't plan on a career change, but it naturally evolved as I took advantage of opportunities. I was also surprised at the support and community that I have found from other information professionals and associations. I am essentially a solo librarian, but I have been able to find connections that I need to succeed.

Advice

Becoming an independent information professional means diving into business ownership or, at minimum, self-employment. There's no right way and no single path. However, starting any new business takes persistence, self-motivation, initiative, and a financial cushion. There are questions you should ask yourself to assess where you are in your professional and personal life. For example, do you have the credibility, track record, and qualifications to attract clients and persuade them to hire you? Given your skills, background, experience, and specialized knowledge, what challenges can you help potential clients address? Success is not just about you, it's about the client's perception of their needs and problems and their willingness to invest in your services. The field of information services is broad and it's difficult to market to potential clients when you can't pinpoint what you do and what value your services add. You need to define your potential services and clients and know that they are willing and able to pay for what you offer. Having that vision and definition clears the path for your services to be in demand.

Anything Else?

While many independent information professionals are librarians, you do not have to be a librarian to work in this field. Information professionals manage information for clients, guide clients who are navigating technology choices and changes, and may function as information managers, knowledge management consultants, information architects, taxonomy specialists, project managers, technology specialists, and more. The five main areas of work for independent information specialists are information management and technology; marketing and communications; research; training and consulting; and writing and editing. Many librarians develop skills over time that lead to branching out or specializing in any one of these areas and may find themselves transitioning to a new career.

Independent Librarian
Jessamyn West

What I Do

I do a variety of library-oriented and library-adjacent jobs, ranging from writing and speaking about librarianship and library issues to working in rural public libraries helping people with technology questions and tasks. Some of this writing and speaking is for organizations outside of librarianship—technology or civic organizations, mainly—and some of it is for library professional organizations such as state or national library associations.

Part of being good at this aspect of my job(s) is also keeping up with current topics in library and technology worlds, so I do a fair amount of reading and interacting with people online in places where discussions of library, technology, and civic engagement are happening. This can be on social media or, quite often, over email.

My Favorite Things

This sort of job works for me but I'm not sure it would work for other people. I really enjoy working with people in the public library but it's very part-time work and the pay is terrible. Public speaking is more lucrative, but I have to hustle up my own jobs and do a lot of admin for it. Writing about librarianship is perhaps my favorite task, but the pay can range anywhere from zero to decent. Having a combination of jobs helps me experience the good parts of many of these jobs but also mitigates the tougher parts.

I know it's a bit of a trope, but I really love helping people. I grew up with one very service-oriented parent, and one parent who was a technologist, so this work feels natural to me. I like not having to buy or sell things as a main part of my job. I like trying to serve everyone; I enjoy working on accessibility and inclusion issues like it's a muscle that needs constant flexing.

Above all, I like that librarianship is a sharing profession, not just with our patrons but also with each other. I don't feel that I am in competition with other library workers. I feel like the work I do supports them and vice versa.

Challenges

Having a lot of little jobs means that if multiple jobs suddenly require more effort or attention at the same time, you can be stretched pretty thin. When Covid-19 started in the United States, I suddenly had a lot of jobs that required 50 percent more effort and that didn't scale well.

Also, technology work means that things are always changing. This is the good news—never a dull moment—but also the bad news. People I work with often find the pace of technological change frustrating, and sometimes part of helping them is listening to gripes about that. I find that the most challenging part of what I do.

People often don't understand what I do. I live in a rural area where having jobs "on the internet" is still a little novel. My most recent work is doing online community management for the Flickr Foundation, and every part of that job description needs explaining!

I like the work but I don't always feel that I have peers who do the same things as I do, so while I am very collegial with other library workers, I don't always have people who are sympatico with the way I live my life.

My Career Path

I went to an alternative college in New England and then spent a few years doing miscellaneous office-type work in Seattle. My undergraduate degree, linguistics, didn't really lend itself to a specific job so I decided to go to graduate school. My first choice was law school; I felt that would be a good way to help people. I didn't get into the local state school, which would have been affordable, so I started looking at what other local opportunities I might like.

When I was in college I'd always looked up to the librarians. They seemed like they could do neat things with computers and had a constant curiosity. I enrolled in the local library school, which was at that point inside the old funky library. It's now a nifty iSchool in an entirely different part of the campus.

I didn't really know until I got to library school how much the values of the profession—intellectual freedom, rights for young people, access for everyone, LGBTQIA+ friendliness—aligned with my own values. The school I went to was also very technologically forward-thinking, so I got access not only to technology but also to people who understood it and enjoyed it.

I took a year off between the first and second years of library school to live in Transylvania with my husband at the time. I got a job teaching internet skills to Romanian journalists for the Freedom Foundation. This was when "internet skills" meant things like Gopher and Lynx and email. I really enjoyed it, so during my second year of library school I focused more on bibliographic instruction and on becoming someone who could explain technology. My first job out of library school was for VISTA, helping set up a basic internet skills program for Seattle Public Library, something not that different from the "drop-in time" I do at my local library now.

I have a lot of skills that aren't usually found together—public speaking, writing, technology education, service orientation, love of travel—and I think this makes me good and somewhat unique at what I do.

The most important part of what I do is being "up for it." While I am not someone who craves novelty, I do enjoy having varied tasks within the generalized routine of my days. I keep good records. I understand math and taxes. I don't lock up my content into proprietary silos without at least making a copy. Being willing and okay with doing the parts of these jobs that support the main human interactions is a part of being able to do this well.

Advice

Recognize that you have something to learn from everyone you interact with. Always send thank you notes or emails. Understand privilege power dynamics and how they affect not just your life and the way you interact with people—it will be different for different folks—but also how it affects the worlds of libraries, technology, commerce, and online interactions.

Above all, do your best to manage your debt, particularly when choosing a library school, as this will give you significantly more options and flexibility. As former ALA president Emily Drabinski said, we are stronger together. Take advantage of the fact that we're a worldwide profession and make change happen.

Anything Else?

Ideally, there would be lots of people in the world who do what I do. As I've gotten more climate conscious and become more of a homebody, I've been traveling significantly less. I believe that local areas can and should be cultivating local talent, particularly in technological directions. I think libraries' focus on sustainability, honestly thinking about how the entire library ecosystem runs, is a very positive trend.

Libraries are uniquely situated for the weird times we find ourselves in. People have questions about what is real, how we can verify facts—deep epistemological questions. People doing knowledge work are trusted, and we can help.

Information and Content Strategist
G. Kim Dority

What I Do

I combine my research, writing, and strategic thinking skills to create content that helps organizations meet their goals by using information as a strategic asset. That content could be an article, a book, information resources for a website, a monthly newsletter for a specific audience, a list of authoritative statistics for a press release, a strategic plan for community-sourced articles, an analysis of internal information resources that could be repurposed as marketing assets, a directory of resources with value to members (e.g., a list of MLIS scholarships most students are unaware of), and similar types of materials.

I describe myself as an information and/or content strategist because the type of work I've done and continue to do generally involves understanding an audience's information needs and creating the resources to meet those needs. So, for example, I have led the team that created the first online academic library, working with subject-specialist academic librarians across the country; ghost-written books for a CEO; led content development for a website focused on resources helping those with disabilities lead their most independent lives; and written books on alternative LIS careers, among other projects. I've mostly worked with corporate and nonprofit clients until recently, when, although still somewhat client-centered, my career became more focused on MLIS students through both teaching and career advising.

What all my work has had in common, in addition to combining research and writing, is the goal of using information to improve people's lives, and happily, I find that both LIS teaching and career advising, in addition to my client projects, allow me to continue that focus.

My Favorite Things

In my Dority & Associates work, I thrive on the exhilaration of a challenging new project, especially if I get to learn new skills or familiarize myself with new knowledge areas as part of my work. I enjoy learning about my client's goals for the work we're going to do together and using my information strategy skills to determine the best way to achieve those goals. And working with MLIS students is simply the most rewarding thing I've ever done.

Since I enjoy both research and writing (or what I would describe as turning information into actionable insights, whether for an underserved community or the president of an environmental start-up), I'm always energized by the challenge of figuring out how to make that connection between "information" and "information that can improve lives/careers/communities/organizations."

I'd recommend this type of project-driven career to anyone who enjoys professional independence (and doesn't mind the occasionally scanty revenue stream), likes to take on new challenges, and is comfortable jumping into a situation even when they "don't know what they don't know." But this type of work can also be done as an employee for an organization— job title is usually some variation of "content strategist"—if a steady paycheck is preferable.

Challenges

The challenges of working as an independent are similar to those faced by anyone who's self-employed (a great resource is Mary Ellen Bates's *Building & Running a Successful Research Business: A Guide for the Independent Information Professional*). How will you find clients? How will you market your services? How do you manage client expectations? What will you charge? Can you manage multiple clients and projects at the same time? (And its corollary, how many all-nighters can you pull off if needed?)

In addition, how do you keep up with rapidly moving technological changes that impact how you work, and equally important, how your clients work? (Every client I'm currently working with has a different internal communications platform—and yes, I often want to cry.) How do you quickly master a new knowledge base, such as green construction or micro-lending, and its relevant information resources to apply your research quickly and efficiently? This is especially challenging when your client is in a new discipline or area of growth; they'll be relying on you to figure it out, because this is why they hired you!

My Career Path

I've often described my career trajectory as sort of "falling over backward" into unforeseen opportunities that turned out to be amazing in themselves but then, because of connections I'd made, led to other equally interesting projects. I didn't set out with a specific career path in mind, but I did tend to look for situations where information skills could be an asset, even if it meant selling myself as the person who *was* that asset.

Also, I'm an introvert who really enjoys people (in small doses) and I ended up establishing long-term relationships with colleagues everywhere I worked. Because I was the only "information person" most of them knew, they reached out to me when they moved to new organizations that needed my skills. At the time I appreciated my good fortune in having work come to me, but later I realized that my extremely wide range of professional relationships, which I had simply enjoyed for the wonderful people involved, was in fact the key to my career opportunities.

Advice

I encourage LIS students and professionals to consider a concept called "professional equity," comprising:

- your domain knowledge (what you know/know how to do)
- your professional network (who you know/your community of colleagues)
- your professional reputation and visibility (who knows about you, how many people know about you, and what do they know)

Doing independent work is much easier if you know a lot of people who are aware of your amazing information skills (whatever they may be) and you keep those skills current and marketable. It's easier to do that if, at the start of your career, you first work for an organization that enables you to build your professional reputation, your skills, and your relationships, both within and outside of your employer. Think of this phase of your career as building the launch platform that will enable you to pivot in multiple career directions, including eventually going independent if you'd like.

And if you're still in graduate school, start building your professional equity while you're working on those assignments. Look for interesting projects to work on or create your own; volunteer with the student chapter of LIS associations and use that connection to reach out to practitioners who are also members; find ways to apply your domain skills to real-life projects that demonstrate your mastery, even if on a volunteer basis. Identify or create opportunities to become professionally visible—present at conferences, blog, write guest articles, create online information resources on a topic you care about, and engage in strategic volunteering, which helps you meet people you'd like to know (and impress with your expertise).

Bottom line: developing a career as any type of independent information professional takes effort, patience, and a willingness to invest in relationships, but for those who thrive on the challenge of a project-based career, it's incredibly rewarding.

Information Specialist and Micropreneur

Sue Easun

What I Do

I run two businesses: Second Hand Knowledge (SHK), devoted to editorial projects within LIS, and First Things First (FTF), for everything else. Affiliated with them are SHK Book Production & Distribution and FTF Book Production & Distribution, respectively, should any of my clients wish to self-publish.

My Favorite Things

First, I love setting my own priorities. Nobody harping on what I can and cannot do or insisting I conform to the status quo. Instead, my clients and I agree on what they want and what's required of me, which keeps me focused on the task at hand, not split between it and the possibility of third-party interference. Plus any workarounds are mine to deal with as I see fit.

In case you haven't guessed, I'm not keen on being told what to do or how to do it. And it's gotten worse as I've aged. Apparently, there's a word for it: unmanageable. Not something you should aspire to unless it's a foundational element of your personality as well. If so, read on.

A close second is the ability to work in solitude: fewer interruptions and, equally important, fewer opportunities for the aforementioned interference. So I not only get to decide what to do but when. However, this is not the same as being unable/unwilling to collaborate. I can, still do, and am quite good at it. But as with priorities, the more control I have over how often and with whom I'm collaborating, the better I focus.

When I went solo, my mental health improved practically overnight (as did, I'm sure, my old bosses'). So did, in time, my physical health. If I'm being fair, this unexpected perk should be number one.

Challenges

Finding work that pays and being paid for it. Which of course is what one must do in lieu of a salary to stay above the poverty line. Otherwise, it's an expensive hobby.

In the early days, I hoped (in vain, as it turned out) that former colleagues and clients would be lined up outside the proverbial door. Which is when I came up against a hard truth about freelancing: people don't like paying other people unless it's something they really don't want to do. This explains why plumbers command higher fees than editors: most of us are happy to avoid getting up close and personal with our toilets, while all I do is make things sound better (far from an easy sell if the client thinks their writing is already good enough). Now add to that a genetic aversion to sales, including self-promotion. The result? Growth in both businesses has been serendipitous, organic, and glacial. That's on me.

As for the act of receiving payment: Let's just say not everyone abides by their contract. And I am meticulous about issuing contacts. But when even my lawyer confesses he gets stiffed, what chance do I have? Deadbeats abound. Some ghost you; some keep forgetting, hoping you'll ghost them; some decide you didn't honor your part of the agreement (once they have enough of your work in hand). For all my talk of control, I'm never certain when a job will begin or how it will end. And while that's mostly on them, it still feels like it's on me.

Is it stressful? Of course. Financial concerns are wearing. Does that negate the health benefits I mentioned above? Not by a long shot. Though I can't say it has no effect. Rather, it's a constant simmer as opposed to a furious boil.

My Career Path

Mine is not an inspirational story. I didn't wake up one day with a burning desire to be my own boss. It didn't even dawn on me gradually. Instead, it was the only option left to me.

I started working in libraries when I entered high school and kept it up through university and beyond. It was all I knew; I never babysat, waitressed, or detasseled corn as my peers did. The game plan was to become a school librarian. Except I graduated at the height of teacher redundancy in Ontario, when the easiest way for a surplus teacher to avoid being let go was to run the library and earn their specialization through summer courses. Fortunately, a local book wholesaler was looking for someone with credentials in both library and education, which led to my first experience with the publishing industry.

The rest of my professional career has been full of similar ups and downs. With every new job, I was determined to stay until retirement. Never happened. Remember, I'm an unmanageable nonconformist! In those days, landing a job was as easy as submitting my resume. Each time, I would start out full of optimism and leave with reluctance. Then I'd pick myself up—how quickly depended on how painful the severance—and cast about for the next opportunity. While I don't hide my employment history, I don't revel in it either. The reasons for my comings and goings are complex and irrelevant to the topic at hand.

Eventually, freelancing was all that was left. (Turns out not only books have a shelf life!) The experts say that you should have a business plan before quitting your current job; they're right. When you don't, there's a considerable learning curve and corresponding lack of funds. I had the advantage of a dedicated home office, as my last job was as a telecommuter. But nothing has remained static except the physical space; there's always a need for more equipment and software and a constant investment in learning how to use/repair/debug them. While I'm nowhere near as optimistic as in my salad days, I make up for it with sheer doggedness.

Which brings us to the title "information specialist and micropreneur." It's not particularly descriptive, but it is the throughline of the services I offer.

Second Hand Knowledge is my firstborn and best beloved. Anything I can do to help the field and profession from which I hail falls under its rubric. Here, I have deep knowledge of both LIS and editing.

But it is of First Things First I wish to speak. I edit here as well, but for projects outside LIS. I've done a lot in psychology. I've even edited a novel. Which is partly why it's separate from SHK. When I work with clients in other disciplines, I have more to do more research, requiring significantly more queries for the author, resulting in longer time frames. In short, my expertise is solely editorial.

But there's another reason for FTF: I really take "information specialist and micropreneur" to the mat. For example, in addition to editing, I've become a professional organizer (even dealt with hoarders for a while!) and social media compliance expert. Both have strong information components and/or use skills and mindsets similar to those of the librarian I once was. Both were opportunities that came out of nowhere; I grabbed ahold, then figured out the courses I'd need to keep going. Even further afield is my government subcontract with the Ontario Ministry of the Attorney-General as an information and referral coordinator (IRC) with the Family Mediation Centre. IRCs are not librarians, though there are definite similarities. The "I" part of the job has more to do with listening to sad stories and explaining the mediation process than functioning as a resource center; and the "R" means I liaise with community service providers instead of making recommendations of my own. But, like the public library I cut my teeth on, whom and what I deal with during a given shift can be extemporaneous, varied, and keeps me on my toes.

You may be wondering: Is being split in so many directions really the way to go? Probably not. But for an unmanageable nonconformist, it appears to be the perfect match.

Advice

Entrepreneurism has a cool reputation. As more MLS holders go this route—whether as freelancers, contractors, or bona fide business folk—bear in mind that not everyone who finds themselves self-employed deliberately chose to be so. These are the people I hope will read my entry. Whether you're just starting out waiting for that first full-time job to reveal itself, are facing a stop gap in your career plans or, like me, are up against their best-before date, make sure you always have a skill or two in your back pocket that you can monetize. I came from a generation that didn't think this way, and I have had to scramble. Now that certificates, micro credentials, and webinars exist, there's little excuse for us to be caught unawares.

International Sales and Special Markets Manager

Ann Snoeyenbos

What I Do

I am a salesperson for a nonprofit aggregator. Project MUSE aggregates e-book and ejournal content from nonprofit publishers and sells that content to institutions, mainly libraries. My responsibilities include the creation and implementation of book and journal collection pricing models for libraries of all types (school, public, special, academic); communication with institutions, consortia, and government agencies related to pricing and licensing of Project MUSE e-books and ejournals; development and management of relationships with sales and marketing agents; creation of exhibit materials and management of exhibits. I have sales goals, but I do not earn commission or bonuses on sales. This allows me to work at the pace of my customers, and I feel it makes me more objective in the product recommendations I make.

My Favorite Things

My favorite aspects of the job are the sales agents and customers, the travel, and the cross-cultural experiences. I spend a lot of my day responding to emails about products and pricing. In many ways this is like library reference work; I answer questions as they come in. At certain times of the year (like journal renewal season in the fall), the volume of emails is high, and I have to work quickly to stay on top of all the questions. At other times of the year, I'm preparing for upcoming presentations (spring and fall are the conference seasons) or taking care of products/projects that are more long-term, like requests for proposals (RFPs) or negotiations for country-wide licenses.

I attend some large conferences, like ALA, UKSG, Frankfurt Book Fair, IFLA, or LASA where attendees are spread across multiple hotels and choose from multiple concurrent program options. I also attend some smaller conferences like ACURIL, AMICAL, or MELA where all the attendees stay in the same hotel and attend the same sessions each day. Those conferences often include a cultural night where the entire group enjoys a cultural event together. Those are my favorite types of conferences because publishers and librarians are enjoying something together, rather than being on opposite sides of a negotiation.

Challenges

My least favorite aspect of the job is video meetings. I enjoy engaging with my colleagues and customers face to face, but in video meetings I'm not able to read body language or process cultural cues and it is harder to understand and be understood. It's wonderful that video meetings allow me to stay in touch with librarians, consortium heads, and agents when travel is impossible, but I much prefer to engage face to face. Recently I chose not to apply for an internal promotion because it would have involved significantly more time in video meetings. Plus, I'm not keen to manage direct reports. I'm happy to take care of my piece of the business without directly supervising other employees.

Another big challenge is money. Project MUSE is a revenue share, which means a significant portion of the revenue we get from libraries is paid out to the publishers in the form of royalties. We are constantly trying to be library-friendly while supporting the work of our publishers, all of which are nonprofit. Libraries always ask for discounts, and our publishers always want more revenue. I often feel like I'm stuck between a rock and a hard place; there's no way to make both parties completely happy.

My Career Path

I completed an MA in West European studies before I went to library school. I was pursuing careers in government or in study abroad programs. My mother was a children's librarian when I was young, and I respected her librarian friends. I had worked in various departmental libraries in the university during my undergraduate years, and I finally gave in to the pull of a life in academic libraries. Right out of library school I landed my dream job: librarian for West European social science at New York University. I loved that job for many years, but once I was granted tenure, I felt that professional opportunities within the organization were being directed to the new hires, while the tenured librarians were kind of put out to pasture.

Project MUSE was hiring their first ever international salesperson, and they wanted somebody with language skills. I figured it was time for a big change and I jumped in. I am a good fit for this job because I have studied several foreign languages and have experience in cross-cultural communication; and I am a librarian so I speak library lingo, which is quite different from publishing lingo.

I think I have a good grasp of scholarly publishing and the structures that support the creation of books and journals. The financial side of nonprofit publishing is more complex, and sometimes more precarious, than most librarians realize. I work with all types of libraries and my product needs to fit the budgets of libraries worldwide, so I've learned a lot about library budgeting, procurement structures, usage patterns, negotiation skills, and about trusting your sales partners (subscription agents). I think the scholarly ecosystem is fascinating: how scholars work, how/where/when/why they publish their work, and how they are compensated (or not) for their intellectual work. Metadata has always been important for discovery on the journals side of things, but now that e-books are more common, I've come to realize that accurate, complete metadata is at the heart of every e-book sale and use.

In my job I need to be aware of the global economy and keep my eye on international currency exchange rates, and changes to value added tax (VAT) for digital products. Even when a library's budget is steady, the rise or fall of the US dollar makes a huge difference to their acquisitions budget, and then if the tax rate changes that can compound a difficult situation.

Advice

Twenty years ago when I left the library to work for a vendor, people asked me if I didn't like libraries anymore; they felt that I was moving over to "the dark side." I think vendor jobs are now more acceptable, and there seem to be a wider variety of vendors that want to hire librarians—for product development, for metadata creation and dissemination, and for work on standards related to electronic resources. I think there's a better understanding of the interdependence between libraries and service providers. This is probably the result of a reduction in librarian jobs, meaning that libraries must outsource more core activities to their vendors.

Many times in my career, I've felt like the only way to advance was to move into middle management with the aim of becoming a department head or library director, but I'm glad I resisted. I really don't want to manage other people, and that's okay. I love working on the frontlines with customers and users, and I'm good at it. I enjoy creative problem solving, and I enjoy the many individuals that I deal with around the world, each bringing their own flavor to the interaction.

I think it would be pretty easy for an e-resources librarian to move to a sales or customer service job like mine, or for a systems or cataloging librarian to move into a metadata job with an aggregator. The key element is to be familiar with a range of publishing platforms and demonstrate a broad understanding of many types and sizes of libraries. Standards keep us all working in the same direction, but each publisher brings specific strengths and weaknesses to the marketplace, and we love to compare and contrast functionalities.

Internet Research Specialist

Marj Atkinson

What I Do

I offer research services for businesses and authors and coach graduate students on research and writing. I spend most of my time working on client projects and educating myself through various resources. I also attend networking events and volunteer for professional associations. My primary responsibilities are keeping my business afloat, following up with clients, marketing, and reviewing my financial status. Fortunately, I belong to an accountability group with peers to keep myself on track.

My Favorite Things

I love the hunt. I also welcome the variety, autonomy, and schedule. I can set my own hours, unlike a corporate setting. I work from home and serve clients worldwide, so geography is not an issue. I rarely commute unless I need to meet a client locally.

I get to support authors working on fascinating projects with fact-checking, researching, and workshops. I enjoy working with businesses providing competitive intelligence and market research services, which keeps me apprised of trends and industries. I do grant searches for an organization that provides grant writing services. I love that I am impacting the community by helping fund nonprofits.

I particularly enjoy working with nontraditional graduate students. They have the unique challenge of returning to school, being unfamiliar with all the resources, and often juggling home and work responsibilities. Given that I was a nontraditional grad student, I can empathize with and support these students. Many schools are now outsourcing support services, so I am taking advantage of that opportunity to fill that gap.

Challenges

Owning a business is a huge learning curve and risky, so I have many mentors and business advisors. I continue to learn! You can start a business straight out of library school, regardless of age or career stage; it depends on your skills and experience and the type of business services you want to provide.

Setting my prices has been the biggest challenge. And now I'm in the process of expanding. Those grant search skills and being around grant writers have taught me to write grant proposals for my own business, and I have been awarded one grant thus far. I had been unaware of how many small business grants are available, especially for women and minorities.

Being a solopreneur can sometimes be overwhelming, trying to keep the business running, working on projects, gaining new clients, and finding people to support you. Fortunately, I can outsource certain services like accounting and tax preparation. I sometimes subcontract to colleagues when I have too much on my plate. I recommend building a good network and being involved in various professional associations. This way, you will have people to turn to for support.

My Career Path

I intended to go to library school after my undergraduate degree. But marriage, family, and finances paused that. (Plus, to be honest, I was tired of school.) I had a career in financial services and information technology (IT). When my daughter was young, I volunteered and worked in school libraries, which reignited my passion for librarianship. I worked for a company that provided tuition reimbursement, so I returned to school in my fifties to earn my MLS with a special library focus. I also worked at a community college, and after a series of layoffs, I decided to start a business coaching graduate students on research.

My client focus has evolved. My business clients are former vendors and colleagues, and they needed help. I had not initially intended to subcontract for businesses but seized the opportunity. Then, a couple of authors found me and asked if I could help research information for their books. I had worked with authors as a museum research library staff member, yet the idea of having authors as clients only occurred to me after I was approached. Perhaps it was because I was so focused on graduate students. I serve three different types of clients not only because I thrive on variety but also because while I am building my author and student client base, I need a steady income. The business clients continue to provide that, while also allowing me to learn about many industries.

Many business skills I learned throughout my career, such as marketing, sales, and relationship building, are helping me run this business. On the job, I have learned new skills like grant searching, and my IT background makes me proficient with technology and artificial intelligence. I have realized I've been entrepreneurial my whole career, but I was frustrated by many of the support roles I was in.

I have also learned that I like variety. That's not to say working in a traditional library or corporate setting lacks variety, but you often don't get to choose what tasks to do, what projects to work on, or who to work with or for. Even working as a reference and instruction librarian became mundane for me, although I enjoyed working with the community and student patrons.

I can't say I've followed a traditional path by any means. I love it, though.

Advice

Working in school libraries and growing up in libraries as a child helped foster my passion for the profession. Assisting students with research in school libraries launched my library career even before I enrolled in library school.

Being involved and serving on boards and committees in library associations has also helped, as there are so many people with all kinds of experience you can learn from. Professional involvement is a great way to build your network and get business. Associations are eager to help and educate you, especially if you are a student. Apart from being a graduate student SLA and ALA member, I wish I had been encouraged to become involved in associations and told the benefits.

Taking some entrepreneurial and business management classes would have also been great. Not all librarians work in office buildings or for organizations. There are plenty of solo librarians/information professionals. Although I love being called a librarian, people first think of someone who checks out books or works in a library building, so unfortunately I had to stop calling myself one in business groups and to prospective clients, as the term confuses them. I call myself a researcher and developed a catchy "research sage" title while working with a small business development center.

I also enjoy doing academic information literacy instruction. This was a big surprise to me; typically, I am not comfortable doing presentations because I am an introvert. In the corporate world, I was often required to present. Passion and expertise about a topic were vital to my becoming comfortable presenting material. I now present for various business and author groups on search techniques and finding resources and am working on developing a student research workshop series. So, as a student, find something you are very comfortable explaining, and you'll be surprised how easy it is to present that material. I wish we had presentation opportunities in library school (although I might not have felt as confident doing it then).

I had many supervisors and mentors who saw things in me that I didn't recognize in myself. So, take advantage of experienced leaders who may take an interest in you and foster your career. Do not be quick to dismiss an opportunity because you don't know much about it or lack confidence. I have often surprised myself with how much I have learned when challenging myself to learn new things and try roles I would never have considered.

Also, self-awareness is essential. Trying new things is great, and you may discover you enjoy a particular field or role. But also recognize when something is not a good fit. I did my practicum in a children's hospital. I learned a lot and enjoyed it. However, I realized I did not want to work as a medical librarian because it was not a good fit or good timing, and it had not been my focus in school. That is how I ended up in academia and I truly loved it.

Anything Else?

As a student, take whatever job or opportunity you can and try it out. When I worked at the community college, library students and recent graduates worked at the circulation desk and shadowed the reference librarians to learn how to do reference interviews.

Learn both primary classification systems. I was a Dewey gal for years, but at the college, I came to appreciate the Library of Congress (LC) system. Learn to weed materials if you are working in a physical library. Weeding is important in getting to know your collection and providing room for new materials. Help the collection development librarians if you can (although some libraries don't develop their own collections anymore, especially in K-12, which is unfortunate as each library and set of patrons is unique).

Also, explore areas you might not have considered. As a student, I volunteered in SLA's Competitive Intelligence (CI) division and learned from seasoned CI professionals. I also took a CI class. This was an area I would never have considered, but it is a fascinating way to learn about competitors, and I apply it to my business and for business clients.

Knowledge and Information Management Consultant
Elizabeth F. McLean

What I Do

I am a knowledge and information curator. My favorite way to say this is to say that I am a content gardener. My work provides users of enterprise knowledge systems with the best possible frameworks and tools for discovery, findability, and learning needed to succeed in work that they are doing. I'm first and foremost a knowledge management (KM) professional, so I apply my experiences in KM (people, culture, work processes, content/context, and technology) to grow collaborative learning and innovation for my clients. KM is a key enabler to ensure the continuity of business, knowledge, and collaboration for enterprise learning. I also describe myself here in the age of generative artificial intelligence (AI) and large language models (LLMs), as a knowledge management/information management (KM/IM) human-in-the-machine loop (https://blog.modernmt.com/human-in-the-loop/).

To do this work, I spend my time *learning* as much as I can about what the work is that project groups do and what they need to know to do it better. I *map* information and knowledge flows to find knowledge gaps and ways to improve info flow. Using stakeholder and focus groups, I *assess* primary business processes to determine how to *organize* and *describe* content collections within those contexts. Once I've identified these knowledge sources, uses, and flows, I *design* or revise controlled vocabularies and establish contextual relationships with these concepts so that content and taxonomy/ontology management tools can support and improve user discoverability and findability. I also use what I've learned in the assessments stage to tailor information architecture displays and tool features to improve ease of access to critical knowledge assets. I create user documentation and training and make recommendations about content and taxonomy governance and management. In all facets of my work, I place the user front and center in this picture, and I act as a primary user advocate during technology decisions and implementations.

If your superpowers involve distilling order from chaos, solving content classification and discoverability challenges, empathizing with user pain points of information access and knowledge flow, possess a comfort level with tech uncertainty and being in perpetual beta, and you have a sense of curiosity and empathy when you engage with your users, this work could be just the thing for you.

My Favorite Things

My grandmother and my mother were goddesses of information sharing. My grandmother read voraciously, especially newspapers, as my grandfather was a White House press correspondent. She was an expert at article clipping and mailing along with a cheery note. So was my mother! As a third-generation information sharer, it's second nature to me to come across ideas and quickly associate them with people who could most benefit from them. Creating frameworks to get the best information available to the people who need it when and how they need it just comes instinctively to me, and it makes me incredibly happy.

As an independent info professional, I thrive on the diversity of sectors and topics I have been fortunate enough to work on. A sizable portion of my work is associated with international development organizations and US government agencies.

Thanks to my Latin-scholar-English-major father, I developed a robust vocabulary early in life that far eclipsed my facility for things with numbers. We'll leave the numbers thing there! Controlled vocabularies are the underpinning of consistent discoverability and access, and the work I do affords me ample opportunities to delve deeper into meanings, associations, and context of collections and how they should be described.

Challenges

Initially I loved the technology that reduced early information-sharing obstacles, and I got really giddy about the problems I was solving with it. Later, my focus shifted completely to how people interacted (or didn't) with technology, and whether it was human-centric enough. I also grew more aware of and fascinated by the incredible importance of nurturing conversations and communities to bring tacit know-how out into the open and channel it to the right people. Today, my focus is "boomeranging" back to technology as I acquire ontology and knowledge graph skills.

I have had to learn to be comfortable with being in a state of perpetual beta and that can be daunting. To overcome that discomfort, I've realized that (after the initial broad learning) it is important to narrow my focus in large bodies of unchartered waters by seeking out solutions to specific obstacles that I'm trying to remove for my clients. This strategy streamlines my approach and helps me feel less like a fish out of water. The rest is figure-out-able. I know I will never know enough, but I also know who I can talk to who does.

Many participants involved in projects that I have been a part of do not fully understand what is meant by concepts of KM, taxonomy, governance, and the lot. When I speak with clients, I frame this work in their language and tie it specifically to their pain points and desired project outcomes. I have learned to *ask them what they mean* when they say "taxonomy" or "knowledge management." After I discover what the stakeholders mean, I work from there to guide, advise, and implement.

My Career Path

Prior to my MSLS, I worked as an executive assistant in C-suites and with general counsel in Washington, DC. I learned the vital importance of managing information flow. This work opened my eyes to how critical it is to understand and organize the lifeblood of how decisions are made and how they are captured. I worked for several multibillion-dollar start-ups in the satellite telecommunications sector, and at that time, the fax machine (wince!) was the main tool for information flow. When early portal technology emerged, I viewed it as a solution to information-sharing barriers, and I was an early adopter of extranets to bring geographically dispersed project teams into a shared network workspace hub. That sounds quite ho-hum today but was crazy talk then. Deploying a solution like that to international consortia of stakeholder companies, regulatory bodies, and subject matter experts who had no common networks at that time really changed everything.

When I began my MSLS, my goal was to obtain an academic credential with core knowledge for on-the-job KM/IM work that I had been doing. This degree has certainly taken me places I'd not be able to go without it. Core skills and philosophies of librarianship continue to inform me fundamentally, but it surprised me that there was not specific KM learning in my graduate curriculum. Learning began and continues today by doing, by sharing within knowledge communities, and by having an open and curious mindset. When deciding which graduate curriculum to pursue in the broader aspects of our fields, look closely at what is available to you—is the learning forward-thinking and diverse?

A state of perpetual learning is my comfort zone. As in, "I don't know enough about this yet!" I fight that voice every day to be the small- and medium-sized enterprise (SME) the client wants to see. It surprises me that this is still something I must reframe in my head, but it is getting easier.

Advice

Align your work with what sparks you. Do the most important research of your life. Spend the time to identify the work you are most passionate about doing. Understand your deepest impulse of effort. Know your superpower gifts *before* you choose your path, no matter what that path is (https://www.forbes.com/sites/rodgerdeanduncan/2021/09/28/are-you-sparked-find-the-work-that-fits-you-best/). Even if it takes you time to get to that place—it took me a long time—this essential discovery will help you to make better decisions to align your actions and work with what you're here to do.

Pay close attention to client or employer culture to avoid misfits. Use what you've learned about what sparks you to inform the kind of work culture you thrive best in, if that is important to you.

Be active in professional groups, such as the Association of Independent Information Professionals, that support your expertise as well as the development of you and your infopro business (if you choose to consult). Choose a community where you actively engage because lurking doesn't really teach you a ton. Whatever your community, cultivate conversations about what problems they solve and how they do that.

Regardless of your path, knowledge creation through experience and conversation in our communities is our mission.

For more information, I recommend Nick J. Milton and Patrick Lambe, *The Knowledge Manager's Handbook: A Step by Step Guide to Embedding Effective Knowledge Management in Your Organization* (2nd edition). See page 9 for a quick rundown of seven main components of KM to help you understand exactly what KM is.

Learning and Training Manager
Shanna Hollich

What I Do

I'm the learning and training manager at Creative Commons (CC). One of my primary responsibilities is to oversee our CC Certificates training program, an intensive online training that teaches librarians, educators, and other open culture professionals about Creative Commons licensing and our impact on open access, open education, and open culture. In addition to that,

I help run the open education platform of our global network, manage our community of 1,600-plus certificate alumni from almost seventy countries, and provide custom trainings of all sorts for a wide variety of clients including government officials; school faculty and administrators; independent artists and creators; researchers and scientists; and folks working in all aspects of libraries, galleries, archives, and museums. I also frequently present about our work or provide workshops at various conferences in the field of librarianship, education, and education technology. I work on various other projects, depending on my interests and availability, including helping to shape CC policy on issues like open culture and artificial intelligence (AI), working with folks at various institutions to advocate for open access and open education, and collaborating with other fabulous people in the open movement.

My Favorite Things

I came to librarianship through teaching. I got my MLIS at Rutgers because it was, at the time, considered to be the best school library program in the United States, and I wanted to be a school librarian. After doing that for a few years, I transitioned to several other types of libraries and library work, but throughout my career there was always a consistent focus on education. How can I use the skills I have to help people learn more and grow more and become their best selves? That's what librarianship is all about to me. Even after I became a library director, I spent much of my free time teaching online professional development courses through providers like the Midwest Collaborative for Library Services (MCLS) and Library Juice Academy.

So naturally, when I was recruited to make training my full-time job with Creative Commons, I jumped at the chance. I get to work with folks from all over the world who are doing all different types of work at different institutions, but we're all interested in the same principles of open access to information to benefit the public good. It's quite rewarding.

Challenges

This type of job varies from day to day; I would not recommend it to anyone who likes a strong sense of routine. I travel all over the world and meet new people all the time, but frequent travel can make it difficult to establish set routines, even outside of work. Sometimes training requests come in fairly last minute, and sometimes they're focused on a particular area that I may not know very much about yet, which means I have to learn new concepts very quickly, synthesize and understand those concepts well enough to teach them to others, and do it all in time to meet deadlines.

My Career Path

I have heard many librarians over the years talk about how difficult it is to transition from one type of library to another, or even from one type of library work to another. I have never found this to be the case. I began my career as a high school librarian, then a middle school librarian. I then transitioned into public libraries and cataloging, worked briefly for the United States federal government as a cataloger and government documents librarian, then became a "jack of all trades" at a small liberal arts college, where I eventually became the director. Next, I transitioned from academic libraries back to public libraries and spent a few years as a public library director before landing my current role. Librarianship is all about lifelong learning and making connections, and those skills are valuable in almost every type of job I could imagine.

I became a librarian because I wanted to help people, and I think the amount of human interaction is something that surprises a lot of non-librarians about this work. Folks assume that librarianship is a solitary job, but librarianship is all about people. If you don't like working with people, this is not the career for you.

Advice

Having an open mind and a willingness to dive in and learn new things are the skills I think have helped my career the most. If something needed to be done, and I had the time and capacity to do it, or to figure out how to do it, then I would jump in and do it. I never said, "That's someone else's job." If it needed to be done, why couldn't it be my job?

Interestingly, folks often assume I'm pretty outgoing or extroverted, especially as so much of my job involves dealing with people. However, I think all of librarianship is about dealing with people, even if you work in a back room and have little interaction with patrons. Everything we do is done with people in mind, and even though I'm quite introverted, I've been able to intuit what people need and how they might learn best.

If you're interested in something, give it a try. Your only limit is your imagination, and you can always make changes later in your career. Don't pigeonhole yourself, and don't place arbitrary limits on yourself and your goals.

MLIS Assistant Teaching Professor

Jason K. Alston

What I Do

The core component of my job is teaching MLIS students and preparing them for careers in libraries, but there is so much more than that. I teach six courses per academic year, in the areas of reference, academic libraries, business librarianship, intellectual freedom, cultural heritage, management, collection development, and basic library technology.

But teaching is not my only responsibility. In this role, I am also responsible for advising, recruiting, admissions, service, and scholarship/creative output. Advising is a neat part of the job because I get to learn a lot about my advisees as I help them plan out their program of study; this part of the job leads to pleasant conversations and a great chance to speak to budding professionals one-on-one.

Bear in mind that a non-tenure-track teaching faculty member (assistant teaching professor vs. assistant professor) may not have to publish and present as much as a tenure-track counterpart. If you want to focus primarily on teaching, this is the avenue for you.

My Favorite Things

Perhaps the most appealing aspect of any teaching faculty position at a university is the flexibility in schedule. I have to be "in place" for synchronized classes and meetings, but otherwise, I am able to do my work when I wish, and I do not need to be confined to the office to do it. The work is hard and plentiful, but I have some flexibility about when I do it, as long as it gets done.

I also enjoy caring for my students and having them look up to me. Because I teach graduate students, there are very few disciplinary issues. I am able to focus on teaching students about this profession and how to situate themselves within it without the pains of having to police unruly undergraduates. Library school students also tend to be interested in the subject matter because they are pursuing professional degrees, so there is not as much pressure to capture the attention of these students, as you likely already have it.

Challenges

This is said a lot in library and information science (LIS), but the biggest challenge for an LIS professor is handling the number of requests you get for your time and knowing when to say no. When you are in this role, you will be asked to collaborate with professional contacts on grants and research, help plan conferences, write recommendation letters, provide references for your former students, serve on university and other professional committees, guest lecture, sit on advisory boards, run for elected positions in library organizations, clarify assignments, share syllabi, answer questions that are best suited for other campus units/personnel, vote on faculty issues, and, of course, there will be endless requests from students for extensions, mediation with group work, grade challenges, and so on. Those of us in the caring professions are prone to wanting to help as many people as we can, but there are not many LIS professors in this country compared to other disciplines; therefore, we stay in demand. While it could be seen as an advantage that you will never be bored in this role, boredom is much less painful than overcommitment.

My Career Path

I always love to reassure people that if I made it to the professor ranks, they probably can too. I have never been seen as a particularly smart person. I am, however, a hard worker and someone who enjoys sharing wisdom with others, as well as mentoring others. After earning my MLS, my first professional librarian job was in a residency program. While serving as a resident librarian, I was asked to be a mentor to a cohort of LIS scholarship students at my university, as I had graduated from a similar scholarship program at a different university. Professors at this institution noticed my passion for mentoring, recommended that I pursue a PhD to become an LIS professor, and introduced me to the dean of a nearby program. From there, I was accepted into the PhD program and did a lot of work teaching, presenting, publishing, doing service work, and, most importantly, learning. I landed my professorship a year after earning my PhD.

Getting into the professor ranks is not about being the smartest person in the room. It is about contributing something to this field that most professionals within the field cannot contribute. It is about being unique and bringing something to the table that the field needs and that will move the field forward. If you offer something that few others do, have a solid research idea (that may later change), and have the time and support to enter a PhD program, you can do what I have done. And you can probably do it better.

I think one of the biggest reasons that some people who could successfully complete a PhD program never start one is self-doubt. Do not let that be you; you can do this.

What has surprised me the most about this job is how much students can differ from one university to another. I believe all aspiring professors should be aware of this. I currently teach in the Midwest, and my students are dramatically different than the students I had at the southern university where I earned my PhD. My teaching evaluations during my first year as a full-time professor were dreadful, but this taught me two valuable lessons: students are not the same everywhere you teach, and you have to understand who your students are and adapt to that.

Advice

The first piece of advice I give anyone who wishes to become a professor and wants to earn a PhD to get there is to enter a PhD program only if you are substantially funded. In this field, earning a PhD out of pocket is just not worth the cost. There are not many ALA-accredited LIS programs in this country, nor are there many universities that offer a PhD in our discipline. There is no guarantee that you will land a teaching professor job, nor is there a guarantee that a PhD program will ever admit you. If you do beat the odds and are admitted into a PhD program, it means they wanted you; and if they wanted you, they can prove that by funding you.

Also, if you want to become a teaching professor, find a mentor and see to it that this mentor is willing to mentor you after you are hired to teach. Hone your teaching skills by adjuncting; contact LIS programs to ask about being added to their adjunct pool. Many universities offer workshops and resources to help professors improve their teaching; take advantage of these opportunities as they really help.

And finally, do what our patrons do every day: ask questions about things you do not know!

MLIS Program Manager
Dee Winn

What I Do

Not to boast, but I think I have the best job ever. I mean, how many people get to work directly with incredibly talented students who are the next generation of library and information science (LIS) professionals in a city that is sunny 360 days a year? Most students are surprised when I tell them that I'm actually a librarian. Even though I work outside of a library (in an academic department), my official employer is University of California, Los Angeles (UCLA) Library.

My biggest responsibility is coordinating our internship program. One aspect of this work involves reaching out to potential internship sites and supervisors;

reviewing (and approving or denying) the applications that I receive from sites; advertising all available internships to students; and communicating regularly with all current site supervisors. Because the majority of students specialize in the archival or media archival studies tracks, I help a lot of students obtain internships at a number of world-renown organizations, including 20th Century Fox Archives, Academy of Motion Picture Arts and Sciences, American Film Institute, Getty Conservation Institute and Getty Research Institute, HBO Archives, Jet Propulsion Laboratory, Los Angeles Public Library, LACMA, NBCUniversal, UCLA Library, USC Archives and Special Collections and the Walt Disney Archives.

I also teach IS 498 (Internship), a class that students can take to earn credit while they are doing an internship. Each spring, I coordinate an Internship Fair so students can learn about LIS internship positions available to them across California. My job also includes lots of committee work and event planning.

My Favorite Things

If I had to state what I absolutely love most about my job in three words, it would be: helping students succeed. Our MLIS program is a two-year program, so in the first year, I primarily get to know students when they attend events that I organize for them. The real magic happens in the second year, when students are eligible to take internships. I can get to know students who take the internship course pretty well, and I view myself as one of their biggest champions because I am fully dedicated to their success. This means helping them secure internships that best meet their career aspirations and helping them prepare for their first professional LIS position. I love reviewing their cover letters, resumes, and CVs, and providing feedback. What I love even more is holding mock interviews and offering suggestions for how to polish their interview skills.

Another thing I love about my job is the professional development opportunities. Each year, I'm able to attend, and sometimes present at, conferences around the country. This goes hand in hand with research expectations because at my place of work, one of the areas librarians are evaluated on is our "research and other creative activity." I love participating in research projects and sharing the findings with others.

Challenges

Regardless of your particular field within academic librarianship (working in an affiliated department or center, archives, special collections, instruction, reference, e-resources, etc.) it can be extremely difficult to navigate without a mentor. Having a mentor is even more important for those who identify as Black, Indigenous, People of Color. To that end, I highly recommend joining a professional association and applying for a mentor. The American Library Association's ethnic affiliates is a good place to start. Those seeking community should check out We here and WOC+lib.

My Career Path

As with many in this field, librarianship is my second career. Because I had a strong teaching background, my transition into the field of academic librarianship was seamless. Also, I was a little bit lucky. At the beginning of my last semester in the MLIS program, the university where I had recently completed a full-time, eight-month-long internship hired me as their newest information literacy librarian. I loved my time there and gained a wealth of leadership and instructional experiences that would have been impossible at many libraries. I realized early on that I'd like to pursue management and/or administrative positions one day, so I decided to apply for jobs in large university systems because I thought they'd have more of these opportunities.

For my second librarian position, I accepted a job as a reference and instruction librarian in the education library at the University of British Columbia. My strategy paid off and within two years, I had the opportunity to serve as the acting head when the head went on sabbatical. I loved being the acting head and received quite a bit of positive feedback from my colleagues during this time.

I began looking for management positions and eventually accepted a position as the head of information services at Concordia University in Montréal. My time at Concordia was replete with library administrators making racial microaggressions and racist comments, and I decided I needed to relocate to the United States in order to experience less racism in the workplace.

Advice

If you're a current MLIS student interested in a job like mine, look for a job or an internship opportunity in an academic library. Depending on the institution, academic librarians may have some unique professional obligations and opportunities (e.g., research expectations, sabbatical) and it is important to understand the nuances in job postings (e.g., limited term contract vs. tenure track).

If you are already working in the LIS field, I encourage you to contact as many MLIS program managers as possible and ask them for informational interviews. This could provide you with a comprehensive overview of our responsibilities and how they may vary from one institution to another, as well as challenges that are specific to an institution.

Anything Else?

One piece of advice I have for early career LIS professionals is to get involved in a professional association. This can be a great way to build community, find a mentor, and collaborate on exciting projects outside of your workplace.

If you're interested in diversity, equity, and accessibility (DEI) issues, I strongly recommend attending the Inclusion, Diversity, Equity and Accessibility in Libraries conference. This was by far the best multiday conference I've ever attended. Kimberlé Crenshaw, the keynote speaker, set the tone for an incredible, enriching experience.

The best single-day conference I've ever attended is the People of Color in Library and Information Science Summit at Loyola Marymount University in Los Angeles. Registration for this incredible (and free!) event fills up quickly, so sign up for notifications at https://digitalcommons.lmu.edu/pocinlis/.

If you're in California and are interested in pursuing a leadership role one day, I would recommend applying for the California Libraries Learn Catalyst Leadership Development program. The program is designed to provide all levels of library staff the opportunity to build equity- and community-based leadership skills. It allows you to develop your leadership skills in a safe space and has the added benefit of encouraging you to build working relationships with other aspiring leaders. I was a cohort member (when the program was known as Developing Leaders in California Libraries), and it was an incredibly valuable experience.

Private Librarian and Curator
Christy Shannon Smirl

What I Do

I am a private librarian for homes. The work has many facets, but in a nutshell, I solve problems for book lovers around the world. Most of my projects involve curating a personalized collection and installing it in a residential library. Sometimes the work involves organizing, cataloging, or moving a large collection of books. Depending on the client, a project may involve new books, rare and antiquarian material, special editions, or a mix of those elements. Part of the job involves interior design: choosing a book for its appearance, styling bookshelves with art and objects, creating an aesthetic in a space.

Aside from the actual work with books and people, I also do my own bookkeeping, invoicing, shipping, contract writing, web work, social media, and technology troubleshooting. This is a luxury service, so much of the work is marketing, branding, connecting with clients, and retaining those relationships.

My Favorite Things

There is a creative aspect to this work that I enjoy, both intellectually and aesthetically. Everyone knows the feeling of coming upon a truly delightful book (whether for its content or how it looks and feels) or a book that would be the perfect gift for someone. I get to seek out books like that every day for all sorts of people. With every new project comes a unique focus and different priorities. I'm constantly learning something new, whether it's a subject I'm curating from scratch, a style of interior design that is new to me, or a type of rare book that I'm not familiar with.

I enjoyed the challenge of starting a business from the ground up so that it is entirely what I want it to be in terms of branding, values, and quality of service. I can't complain about working in luxury settings, often in interesting geographic locations. There are certain perks that come with working for a wealthy clientele. I mostly work alone, both in the office and in homes, which works well for my personality. I also love working for myself.

Challenges

Most of my favorite aspects of the job have a dark side. Working for yourself in a very niche field means worrying about when and if the next project will come. Most people don't realize this service exists, which makes it frustrating to market well. And while I love working alone, it can be lonely.

When I tell people what I do, the response is often "that's my dream job." I always wonder which part they are picturing. Surely the design, luxury, travel, and scouting for books? Those parts are real, but there are plenty of facets of the job that aren't dreamy at all. On any given day, I might be covered in dust, schlepping heavy boxes, checking what my insurance policy covers, or figuring out how a small business signs up to pay sales tax in Florida. There are work trips to fun places like New York or LA, but there are also projects in less glamorous locations (or with less interesting books).

Perhaps an obvious but key element of doing for-profit work with books is sales. If you want someone to pay you to do something, or to buy something from you, whether it's one special book or a room full of them, you need to be able to sell it to that person. That involves being the public face of the thing you are selling. It means networking, social media and digital marketing, and one-on-one conversation with a prospective client. Sales are perhaps my least favorite part of my job. They are also the key to success.

My Career Path

My first decade in library science took a traditional path: I went to library school at the University of Denver while interning in reference and collection development at a wonderful, forward-thinking public library in Douglas County, Colorado. Once I had my degree, I was hired to work in reference at

Teton County Library in Jackson, Wyoming, and was eventually promoted to management, where I supervised selectors, collection development operations, and policy.

When I trace the line from my public library work to Foxtail Books, I realize that I had several unusual opportunities along the way that were a key part of the equation. I don't recommend following in my exact footsteps; there is far too much serendipity and circumstantial privilege (right-place-at-the-right-time) to form a worn path. Take it only as a lesson in professional resourcefulness and creativity.

What do you do with 100,000 books when you remodel a public library? You phase the work and reconfigure the collection multiple times. Managing a project of that scale gave me confidence to do the same for residential spaces. It also taught me how people enjoy and access books in a room.

Jackson Hole is one of the wealthiest communities in the country. When I decided to leave the public library (and saw that the small town I lived in offered few other career options), I realized I was in a location where people with means put a high value on the intellectual and cultural content of their homes; they also tended to own homes in multiple locations. I knew I could do for individuals what I had done for the community at the public library: find a balance of books to suit their reading needs (and do it with style). As I looked at my own skills and the market around the country, a business plan emerged.

I started Foxtail Books & Library Services with quite a safety net: both savings and a supportive partner at home. I began in a home office to save overhead, did photo shoots of libraries at friends' homes, worked hard to make connections in my community, joined a nonprofit board, went to small business mixers, and invited acquaintances in adjacent industries to coffee. I quickly realized that I needed a better understanding of rare and antiquarian material, so I attended the Colorado Antiquarian Book Seminar, an invaluable experience. I earned little to nothing for the first few years.

In addition to my location, a few elements of my life that I couldn't have planned have helped enormously. I come from an entrepreneurial family. I have a good eye for interior design, graphic design, and photography. I am comfortable in luxury settings and am confident in conversation with a wide range of people.

Gradually my portfolio and reputation, through word of mouth, picked up. Eight years in, Foxtail Books has projects in most major metropolitan areas in the country, plus clients in Europe, Asia, the Middle East, and the Caribbean.

Advice

The skills that transferred directly from my public library work to this business include managing collection budgets, workflow, and staff. Public library work gave me experience with all manners of books, a wide variety of readers, and connection points between the two. Had I known I was headed toward private library work, it might have helped to gain experience, early on, in rare books, luxury services, and small business management.

I do not recommend going into private library work without living in (or having connections to) an extremely wealthy community. It's a small group of people who are interested in outsourcing the selection or organization of their books and have the means to do so.

If you are interested in working for yourself, take small steps, year by year, to approach your long-term goal. If you leave salaried work, start with a financial safety net, a side gig, and a backup plan.

Anything Else?

Remember that all the pieces of your path, even the ones that might seem silly, unprofessional, or pointless, make up who you are and how you show up professionally in the world. There are parts of my life that never wound up on a resume but nevertheless influence the work I do today—restaurant, administrative, and retail work—all of it taught me skills I use on the regular.

Take yourself seriously and other people will, too. Everyone started somewhere, and everyone has a dream.

Solicit feedback in your career and listen to those who might see you more clearly than you see yourself.

Move through your professional life with curiosity: if someone has a job you see yourself in some day, ask them to meet for coffee. Plan what questions to ask them ahead of time: what information do they have that would be useful to you, if they are willing to share?

Program Manager for Membership and Research

Christina Rodrigues

What I Do

I work as a senior program manager in the membership and research division of Online Computer Library Center (OCLC). The OCLC began in 1967 when a small number of Ohio academic libraries came together around shared cataloging. It has since grown into a global technology organization serving member libraries of all types and sizes around the world. Many people know OCLC because of the products and services that are used by libraries around the world, but there is so much more to the organization. Library workers can participate in the Community Center, an online community platform. OCLC Research is often at the forefront of library futures and trends research. OCLC WebJunction works closely with public library workers to scale library learning and training.

Much of my work revolves around member relations and engagement activities in support of the OCLC Global Council. This is a group of forty-eight library leaders, or delegates as we call them, from around the world who have been elected to serve as representatives of libraries in their geographic regions. They bring their perspectives and expertise to OCLC to help the organization continue innovating and serving the needs of libraries around the world. The OCLC Global Council is divided into three regional councils (Americas; Europe, Middle East, and Africa; and Asia Pacific). I love working with this group and learning not only about the different types of libraries that exist around the world, but also how each of them supports their communities. My experience working with Global Council has made me a true believer in just how valuable it is to come together to solve shared challenges and how much we can learn from one another.

Besides working with all the Global Council delegates, I am the liaison to the Americas Regional Council and oversee the work that this regional council does on behalf of the libraries throughout their region. Much of my work involves facilitating discussion among the delegates during regularly scheduled committee meetings and managing engagement activities such as global surveys or focus groups with other OCLC members and the larger library community. I often work closely with my colleagues in OCLC research who use their expertise to help guide these engagement efforts.

My Favorite Things

The best part of my job is working with and learning from library leaders around the world. I get to spend my time facilitating connections where people can learn from and share with one another. There are so many unique programs and services that libraries are involved in, and it is inspiring to hear the impact those offerings have on the communities they serve. Another part of my job that I love is the culture of OCLC itself. My coworkers believe in OCLC's mission. They are all dedicated library supporters, and many have library work experience or education themselves. It is this experience that helps in improving our products and services, and our research initiatives because staff really understand the needs of libraries.

While working at OCLC, I have had the opportunity to learn so much about libraries, about myself, and what I am passionate about. Being employed in a large organization requires strong communication and collaboration skills. I am consistently working across multiple departments such as research, marketing, information technology, and customer service and have developed strong program management skills and facilitation skills as a result.

Besides my day-to-day work, I have also been given the time and support to participate in professional library associations like ALA, building my network and working alongside colleagues with shared goals. I have learned so much by being involved in library organizations. I have met like-minded colleagues who have inspired and taught me, and who now serve as my mentors.

Challenges

Working in an organization as large as OCLC means being cognizant of multiple priorities and needs, which can mean being patient. Things don't always move as quickly as they do in smaller organizations. As a membership organization, we have a responsibility to be accountable and to make decisions that benefit the whole. Working behind the scenes to support libraries also means you may not get that instant gratification you would working as frontline staff in a library. I don't get to watch the joy of a child finding a new book, but I know that what I do every day helps libraries and library workers do their jobs, and that makes me happy.

My Career Path

Before coming to OCLC, I had a variety of jobs while I was working to complete my MLIS. I worked for a call center company routing inbound calls using telephony platforms. I then worked part time updating books in law libraries, before moving to a large urban public library system as a youth services specialist.

I didn't know very much about OCLC before I started working there. What I did know came from my cataloging class in library school. One day I saw a posting on my school's MLIS listserv about paid summer internships at OCLC. I was fortunate to get the internship and I worked both at the public library and OCLC.

How I got my job is actually a funny story: I was lucky enough to be attending my first conference while I was an intern, and when I was leaving a restroom, I saw a person with an OCLC badge on. I struck up a conversation and it turned out they were hiring for a full-time job. I'm thankful that I didn't shy away from introducing myself, from being bold and taking a risk. It's a lesson I remember to this day.

Advice

What has helped me the most in my career is my persistence and relationship building. I am always looking for opportunities to learn something new, to push myself. This might mean submitting proposals for presentations, writing articles, or serving on committees and boards. Try to approach every experience, good or bad, as a learning opportunity. Focusing on what you can learn from any given situation will help you to work towards a goal, stay positive in doing so, and grow in experience and expertise.

Networking is critical. Be open and willing to meet people everywhere you go. Get involved in professional associations and give back. There is so much value in connecting with likeminded people who are working towards common goals. I am a people person and networking has been a skill I have actively developed over the years. I love meeting new people, learning from each other, and finding out what makes each person unique. By building out my network I have a community to draw on when I need help or advice, and I can serve as a resource for others who need support.

Try to get as much hands-on experience as you can before deciding on a career path. Internships are so valuable in showing you what it's really like working at a particular library or library organization.

Public Health Analyst
Melody D. Parker

Disclaimer: The views expressed here do not necessarily represent the views of the agency or the United States.

What I Do

The heartbeat of the efforts of work that supports the public's health lies in the data we as an agency can collect and disseminate, both administrative and clinical. My job as a public health analyst at the Centers for Disease Control and Prevention (CDC) focuses on the data that move through immunization information systems. Immunization information systems (IIS) help providers, families, and public health officials by consolidating immunization information into one reliable source. The information can then be used to guide patient care, improve vaccination rates, and ultimately reduce vaccine-preventable diseases (https://www.cdc.gov/vaccines/programs/iis/index.html).

I serve as an information technology project manager overseeing a mass vaccine administration management system. In this role I lead a team of contractors in the development, implementation, and enhancement of the system. I provide guidance and technical direction, engage stakeholders, develop project plans, and work with my organization's acquisition and governance teams to ensure that my center provides a robust, stable product built on a modern, scalable platform to support not only public health emergency responses, but also other jurisdiction and partner needs. I lead efforts to ensure that my agency not only maintains emergency readiness with this mass vaccination tool, but also uses it during nonemergencies to ensure practice, meet multiple needs of stakeholders, and maximize the government's investment.

My Favorite Things

My first public health mentor once commented, "Melody works well in many environments, whether alone or in groups, her primary need being to work on things that *matter* in this world." If that strikes a chord for you, then I would recommend this type of position. The development and monitoring of data systems that contribute to the mission of protecting the public's health has the benefit of feeding both my intellectual needs and professional development.

Challenges

Working for the federal government is not for the faint of heart, especially during a global pandemic. Navigating the political landscape is fraught with opportunities for failure that you often can't see until after things go awry. My organization's tagline is "protecting the public's health, 24/7" and that can often be the literal case. The struggle to define what work-life balance looks like, let alone achieve it, is very real.

My Career Path

My origin story begins with temping into a job with a public health institution after a cross-country move. My plan for a terminal degree in another field fell through, and I was searching for something that would permit me to remain in this new field of public health that I'd found. My institution was in a situation where the library needed refreshing and developing, and that appealed to me greatly—plus, that was literally the first I'd heard of the MLS degree. Since then, in every professional pivot I've had to make, from public health to corporate libraries and legal research and back again, I have relied repeatedly on the foundations provided by my MLS degree work. I often say that I've ended up where I have because I speak geek, a skill that was enhanced by that work!

Advice

The skill that is most ideal for this work is the ability to be both a big picture and lost-in-the-minutia type of person—a skill that we also refer to as systems thinking. Predicting and understanding dependencies, intimate understanding of cause and effect, and application of system logic has been key to my success.

I wish I'd been told and encouraged more strongly that traditional librarianship wasn't my only path to professional success. My professors believed I'd be a rock star public librarian, an idea I balked at completely, but they were right about my ending up in government work, so make of that what you will!

Should you wish to follow such a path on a federal level, it's likely that you'd start your search at usajobs.gov, but first, develop your resume accordingly. You can't go into too much detail on a federal resume. Have a glance at one bullet point of your current resume. I can almost guarantee you it's not descriptive enough for a federal resume. For my agency, there is customarily a single statement outlining the minimum requirements for a posting. Review your experience and ensure that you can cite specifically where and when you've achieved those requirements. It's quite possible that you may discover skills and experience you didn't realize you had, as it may have never been described to you in this fashion. Either way, this is a useful exercise in resume building, especially for someone who may be mid-career, beyond the one-pager, or looking to build a document that's more like a CV than a traditional resume.

Rare Book Dealer
Patrick Olson

What I Do

I buy and sell rare books, with a focus on pre-1830 European printed material, mostly non-English. I sell primarily to special collections librarians and curators, which happens to be my own library background. In many ways, booksellers like me provide a first round of curation for libraries and private collectors. We identify items of potential interest from a rather overwhelming marketplace—more than I ever had time to monitor as a librarian—and try to connect them with our particular audiences. It's very much a relationship-based business.

I try to understand what my clients want, source appropriate material, and catalog it for sale. This cataloging work accounts for most of my time, and it generally goes far beyond standard library cataloging. Part of it is traditional bibliographical work—identifying the edition, collating the book for completion, providing a physical description. I typically provide a summary of the content, maybe pull some compelling or illuminating quotes, and frequently provide a little background on the author. A good deal of time often goes into contextualizing and interpreting the item. What's interesting about it? Why does that matter? What does it tell us about the past, or about the uses and users of books and print? In short, how might a given item fit the collecting criteria of a particular client? There are countless contexts and interpretations for any given item, of course, but the underlying goal is to help the potential collector, whether institutional or private, assess the suitability of that item for their own collection. When something sells, I cannot simply order another copy from the wholesaler. Everything is unique. So, the sourcing of new material is an endless task, and something that occupies a significant share of my time.

Together, cataloging and sourcing new material take up perhaps three quarters of my working hours. The remainder is spent on various other tasks: email, packing and shipping orders, bookkeeping, designing catalogs, traveling for conferences and book fairs, serving on professional committees, developing my reference collection, tidying up the office, troubleshooting technology, and anything else that needs doing.

My Favorite Things

I love the hands-on work with the books. I live for the research, and for the discoveries—sometimes large, sometimes small—that flow from this work. And I love that the work is so focused on building relationships. Far beyond email, attending conferences and book fairs keeps me in touch with librarians, collectors, and bookseller colleagues from around the world. If you enjoy working with rare materials, and if you enjoy sharing those materials with others—which I know describes many people in the special collections environment—then there's a good chance you would enjoy this work.

Challenges

For better or worse, bookselling is an entrepreneurial life, and entrepreneurship entails some degree of financial risk. Your paycheck really depends on working effectively. Time management is crucial. An ability to ignore distractions and stay on task will serve you well. Some may be turned off by the business aspects. You can certainly outsource your bookkeeping, but having a decent head for money and budgets is a big advantage. At the end of the day, this is a business, and the privilege of continuing to do the rewarding work depends on keeping that business profitable. And while the books themselves might be expensive, and large amounts of cash might sometimes change hands, do not expect to get rich doing it. If done well, it can provide a living comparable to that of a librarian, but you must be ready to work for it.

My Career Path

I was an English major in college. I wasn't entirely sure what to do with that degree, so I thought I might try indulging an interest in old books I developed in high school. While still in college, I simply approached a local rare book dealer and asked for a job. He hired me and I spent four years working there, learning the fundamentals of the work. In search of geographic flexibility, but wanting to stick with rare books, I decided to switch to librarianship.

I worked as a rare book cataloger, special collections librarian and curator, and eventually became head of special collections at a large university.

But life forced a move, as it sometimes does. In part to put an end to the professional leapfrog too often incumbent upon the dual career couple—my wife is in a similar line of work, but one with even scarcer prospects—I chose to go into business for myself and return to my roots in the trade. Fortunately, there's a good deal of overlap between the two career paths, selling rare books and working as a special collections librarian. Both require familiarity with the material, the ability to contextualize and interpret that material for a variety of audiences, and the ability to convey the importance of this work to others. I use library resources heavily in my work, and the work keeps me in regular contact with the special collections environment that was my professional home for ten years. And I get to do all of this without the added pressure of that tenure dossier.

Advice

The rare book trade is just that, a *trade*. There is no standard academic credential, no graduate program to serve as a springboard, no clearly established path to joining its ranks. If it interests you, set yourself to learning about it. Go to book fairs and talk to booksellers. There are some wonderful educational opportunities out there. The annual Antiquarian Books Seminar in Northfield, MN, will provide foundational skills for the aspiring bookseller. Rare Book School at the University of Virginia and California Rare Book School both offer a tremendous breadth of classes to introduce you to whatever kind of material interests you most.

Keep in mind that there are as many ways to be a bookseller as there are to be a librarian. We specialize in different material, buy and sell in different ways, and generally settle into our own methods. If there's a particular kind of material you love to handle, you can sell it. If there's a particular kind you hate, you get to avoid it. If the entrepreneurial plunge scares you, you needn't necessarily run your own business. Many rare book dealers do employ others, and seeking employment with one of them can be a great way to give it a try. If that isn't an option, take heart that booksellers are a very generous bunch of people and will gladly offer wisdom and advice if you decide to strike out on your own.

Go to rare book fairs, talk to the booksellers, get to know the people and the material. It's a great education and fantastic fun. I know it can seem intimidating, but trust me, everybody here just wants to gush over the cool stuff. And remember, this is a business built around the *physical stuff*. The most fundamental experience, however you get it, is to handle the physical material as much as you can. Curiosity, and the enthusiasm to share it, can take you far.

Records Specialist
Jeannine Berroteran

What I Do

As a records specialist through EPIQ Global, LLC, I am a part of the support staff divided into office services (i.e., mailroom and copy center) and records (or information governance). As a records specialist, I would describe my job as a cross between a records clerk and a records administrator, which involves the handling of physical records and the creation of digital records through scanning legal documents into the iManage software program. I also respond to requests for legal files that are either at the offsite storage facility or onsite and I process the release of physical legal files to be sent to another law firm or back to the client. On occasion, there will be a request to index estate planning vault files to the document level in the database so there is an accurate inventory list of the intrinsic documents. Detailed indexing is important, especially with both estate planning and corporate matters, so legal professionals can locate what they need, especially if there are several containers for one client/matter. Besides processing records requests and releases of physical files, I am also a technician monitoring the web help desk database where I respond to digital tickets and, when necessary, I route them to the appropriate department or across office locations.

I am also responsible for responding to inquiries from the legal staff concerning policies created by the headquarters office that would concern them, so it is important for me to remain up to date with any changes that the senior information governance staff members make. I see myself as either the bridge or the liaison between the legal administrative assistants who work for the attorneys and the information governance management who create policies related to file-level imaging, releasing physical records, and identifying intrinsic documents.

My Favorite Things

While my work involves direct service to the attorneys, legal administrative assistants, and paralegals, it is less front facing than my previous roles in librarianship, so it leaves me with more time to work on long-term projects that would not otherwise be possible. I can devote more time and focus on addressing those projects that require detailed attention, such as indexing, reviewing large client/matter files, and separating intrinsic documents from the rest of the client/matter file. Finally, I am also able to use both my intellectual curiosity and my previous educational and employment experiences to learn more about records retention and the different areas of law that are the specialties of this law firm.

Challenges

Handling legal records has helped me to satisfy my intellectual curiosity by learning about new subjects in law, but there are challenges as well. Because I am not a direct full-time employee with the law firm, my role is limited in several ways. First, I am in a service position to assist legal staff with any inquiries they may have, but sometimes I cannot answer these questions because I either do not have the level of access privileges that the legal staff have, or I do not always know how to answer due to the lack of access to certain software programs or lack of access to current policies and procedures created by management (which, sometimes, have not been updated in several years). A related challenge is that, because this law firm's headquarters office is out of state, the records retention policy is dependent upon the policies within the state where the headquarters office is located. EPIQ records specialists are required to listen to the information governance director, resulting in records specialists being placed in the middle, with the legal administrative assistants on one side doing their work based on state and federal laws while the information governance director, who represents the headquarters office, is following and enforcing policies laid out by senior management.

Another challenge is that, unlike librarianship, where there are universal guidelines and standards for organizing and classifying information, the private sector does not have universal guidelines and standards that are regularly reviewed and updated. Classification and labeling vary widely in the private sector according to the type of information the company or corporation retains. Law firms are no different than other private sector positions in corporate records. The database and software programs in use largely dictate processes such as fulfilling records requests and releases of legal information.

Finally, because guidelines and processes are always changing due to upgrades with the database and software programs, it is important that process documents are reviewed and updated in a timely manner. Unfortunately, it is all too common that they are either outdated or incorrect, causing delays or errors in identifying and organizing documentation. Offsite management is not always readily available to answer inquiries from records specialists, which makes it even more important for management to regularly update process documents and policies in a timely manner.

My Career Path

My original career plan was to become a foreign-language scholar with a specialty in French and Italian languages and literatures. Librarianship, at that time, was a way for me to make some money as a part-time employee working at both a small departmental library and the main library at a large research institution. Besides an income, these positions provided a convenient schedule to fit work hours in between classes. I enjoyed working in the different areas of information retrieval, circulation, materials maintenance, and preservation, serving both students and faculty. Librarianship became my educational path long after my undergraduate studies were completed, and I felt this would be the best fit to satisfy my educational and intellectual curiosity. I worked in several different specialties while I studied for my MLS, but opportunities for employment were unavailable to me. After several years of working mostly in contractor positions that were related to my skills acquired through librarianship, I was able to find a job in the private sector working for a multinational corporation in corporate records. Besides the skills acquired through librarianship, I was also able to make use of my foreign language skills when labeling both print and digital documents. I also assisted with creating a digital records system and a records retention database. After corporate restructuring, my position was eliminated and, three months later, I began working as an EPIQ records specialist.

Advice

EPIQ Global is a company that provides legal and business services to law firms, corporations, financial institutions, and government agencies, helping them streamline administrative and business operations. Because corporate restructuring is the foundation of EPIQ's operations, job insecurity is always present as clients regularly review and reduce overhead costs. One piece of advice is to seek out monetary support through the company and pursue educational opportunities for certification in the legal profession (e.g., legal administrative assistant). Another option is to seek out certification through the Association of Records Managers and Administrators (ARMA) to become a Certified Records Manager (CRM) or the Certified Information Governance Officers (CIGO) Association, focusing on information security and compliance. While the ARMA website features a job opportunities page, CIGO does not, so further inquiry is necessary to decide if it would be more beneficial to earn one or both credentials to improve your opportunities for employment in records management.

Anything Else?

Records management, retention, and information governance in the private sector have opened more opportunities for those with educational and employment background in librarianship. Those who have either burned out from librarianship or were downsized out of librarianship should remain open minded and look into employment opportunities in the private sector. Openness to learning new technologies and applying them to corporate records and compliance, along with skills in organizing and describing information, makes librarians a good fit for a career in organizing and managing corporate or legal records.

Research and Prospect Management Analyst
Laura Semrau

What I Do

As a research and prospect management (RPM) analyst I used my library research background to support the fundraising efforts of a large research hospital. In other words, I did background research on wealthy people! Previously, I had no idea such a role existed. Once I was immersed in it, however, I understood how development officers (i.e., fundraisers) can benefit greatly from the support of an RPM team.

The research component of this job means gleaning information about potential donors. In the context of working for a hospital, this need emerges when people who have been patients indicate they are open to the possibility of giving or have given a small gift. (Patient privacy is honored.) From a fundraising standpoint, the question arises: is this donor interested in giving again? If so, what is their capacity to give?

Prospect researchers use a combination of publicly available and licensed resources to determine a donor's wealth capacity and affinity to contribute to a nonprofit mission. A lot of financial information is free online: real estate holdings, nonprofit information, community involvement, and large donations to organizations. Tools such as Wealthengine, EDGAR (securities data), and GuideStar help researchers gather real estate, stock, and previous giving information. Our team gathered and summarized this information in software like Raiser's Edge or Affinaquest, which is designed for this purpose.

We offered different levels of research for different purposes. Some profiles (summaries of individuals) were brief and others more detailed. For instance, if a large fundraising event was coming up, we compiled in-depth profiles for prospects most likely to be most generous in their giving. This information provided the development officers with background on their prospects and gave them a sense of what level of gift was a reasonable request.

The "prospect management" part of the job meant maintaining data on portfolios (groups) of prospects so that development officers could make realistic predictions about the likelihood of incoming donations. We prepared Excel sheets according to certain specifications and met with our departments regularly to support them in these efforts.

My Favorite Things

Research and prospect management is an excellent job for someone who appreciates supporting a bigger cause. With my background as a librarian, I was thankful to use my skills to support important efforts such as cancer research and world-class medical care for children. I found the research part of the job fascinating and was thankful to contribute to a team that was united in their purpose.

Challenges

Even though I entered this job with two master's degrees, I struggled with the Excel skills required for the prospect management aspect of this role. I likely would have grown in this area, though, had I stayed in the job longer.

Most people in this role will probably face regular deadlines for meetings with development officers and for special events. Sometimes last-minute research requests might also arise, but generally the hours and deadlines for this job are predictable.

My Career Path

I discovered research prospect management work when at a life-turning point. I had recently moved to a new region of the United States and was looking for a job as an academic librarian. After several months of job hunting with no progress, I decided to expand the search past libraries, looking for job postings featuring skills relevant to my background. I was surprised when I was invited to interview for this position in research and prospect management. It turned out that another member of this RPM team had an MLIS, so the group knew that library training can be valuable to the role. In other words, the research and analytical skills I had developed as a librarian served me well in exploring this related field.

Advice

LIS students should learn about research and prospect management work to expand their career options. My LIS training in reference sources and reference interviews was especially applicable to this role. Research and prospect management is a good fit for librarians who are analytical, intellectually curious, and adept at data analysis.

I also discovered that professionals in this field often participate in their professional organization, Apra. Their website states that "members are the professionals who drive their institutions' philanthropic missions through work in prospect development and prospect research, data analytics and data management, annual giving, advancement, special gifts and more." Apra offers training, conferences, and network opportunities for researchers in advancement nationwide and is an excellent resource for both new and established prospect researchers.

If you are interested in a career in prospect research, consider the range of options available. Jobs in this field serve a wide range of organizations, so seek positions that align with your values. In addition, some roles are solo while others are team-based, so look for a position that suits your working style and life stage.

Anything Else?

Readers may wonder why I left this position after roughly one year. I was happy in my role and planned to continue in it, but when our first child was born, our family decided it would be best for me to stay home for a while. When I began exploring a return to wage-work years later, my former RPM supervisor helped me find freelance work that fit our family schedule.

About the Editor and Contributors

Louise Alcorn is the library technology coordinator at the West Des Moines (Iowa) Public Library. She presents widely at library conferences, focusing on implementing technology solutions in small- to mid-size public libraries. She has authored two books on library tech. Louise earned her MILS at the University of Michigan School of Information and a BA in American studies from Grinnell College. Louise writes and speaks about access to technology, library customer service, and how to help patrons print off their email without going mad. She hates muddle and loves to craft clear instructions. Her favorite soapbox is "don't reinvent the wheel."

Jason K. Alston is an assistant teaching professor at the University of Missouri in the School of Information Science and Learning Technologies. His research interests focus on diversity and libraries, information and emotion, and cultural heritage. Alston earned his PhD at the University of South Carolina, an MLS at North Carolina Central University, and a BA in English from the University of North Carolina at Wilmington.

Rick Anderson is the university librarian of Brigham Young University. He has worked previously for YBP, Inc., the University of North Carolina Greensboro, the University of Nevada, and the University of Utah. He is a regular contributor to the *Scholarly Kitchen* and has served as president of NASIG and of the Society for Scholarly Publishing. He is a recipient of the HARRASSOWITZ Leadership in Library Acquisitions Award. Rick is the author of three books, including *Scholarly Communication: What Everyone Needs to Know* (2018), which has been published in three languages.

Marj Atkinson is a certified internet research specialist passionate about research and fact-checking. She offers her expertise to authors, businesses, and college graduate students. Marj excels in scholarly literature research, citation, secondary research, and qualitative analysis. She's your go-to for meticulous fact-checking, efficient keyword searches, resource location, and grant searches. She also coaches graduate students on research, citing and writing. With experience spanning K-12 and academic institutions and backgrounds in finance, healthcare, IT, and nonprofits, Marj brings a diverse skill set to the table. If you still haven't found what you're looking for... Ask Marj at askmarj.com!

Glen J. Benedict (he/him) is the access services librarian at the University of the District of Columbia. He has been working in libraries for nine years. An avid advocate for freedom of speech and intellectual freedom, he has served on the American Library Association's Committees for Legislation and Intellectual Freedom, and has presented on book bans and challenges at diverse gatherings including ALA's LibLearnX and Annual Conferences, Awesome Con, Flame Con, Library 2.023 Mini Conference, and the Washington Research Library Consortium's Annual Meeting. In his free time, Glen can be found creating imaginary worlds and exploring our real one.

Jeannine Berroteran, MLS, independent scholar and records specialist, has over fifteen years of employment experience in several areas of academic librarianship and she has volunteered in public libraries in both Ohio and Minnesota. She has contributed chapters and articles for anthologies on volunteering in libraries and assessment in academic librarianship and maintains memberships in organizations devoted to academic librarianship and the social sciences and the humanities. She has also contributed to volume four in the *United States Holocaust Memorial Encyclopedia of Camps and Ghettos*, 1933–45 series (2022) and enjoys researching her family history.

Ashley M. Biggs is the marketing and outreach librarian for the Maryland State Library for the Blind and Print Disabled in Baltimore, MD. She focuses on community engagement, public relations, and the overall marketing of library services. Her full biography and a list of accomplishments can be found on her online portfolio: ashleymbiggs.com.

Elizabeth S. Blake is the 2022–5 Eugene Garfield resident for science librarianship at the University of Pennsylvania. Elizabeth holds an AS in psychology from Delaware County Community College, BS in psychology from Temple University, and MLS from Pennsylvania Western University.

Laura Blessing is the director of libraries human resources and employee engagement at North Carolina State University Libraries. She has an MLIS from the University of Texas at Austin and a BA in psychology from New Mexico State University. In addition to her librarian background, she is certified as a senior professional in human resources. Blessing's research interests include employee engagement-related topics, and she has written and presented previously on organizational communication, compensation, employee well-being, and new employee onboarding. Most recently, she wrote a chapter on employee engagement in *Emerging Human Resource Trends in Academic Libraries* (2020).

Kathleen Breitenbach is the teen librarian in the reference department at the Hamilton Township Public Library, NJ. They publish and present on issues of neurodiversity, book challenges, and LGBTQIA+ issues. Their first book is *LGBTQIA+ Books for Children and Teens, Second Edition*, with Liz Deskins (2023).

Morgan Brickey-Jones is the director of community engagement at UTA Libraries and the outreach director for ALA's New Members Round Table. After graduating from Florida State University with her MLIS, Morgan Brickey-Jones's first library job was at the Marion County Public Library System in Ocala, FL. After a few years in Ocala, Morgan moved to Texas and continued her career at the Arlington Public Library. As a children's librarian at APL, Morgan started a field trip program and specialized in STEAM programming for tweens. After six years at Arlington, Morgan was hired as the K-12 librarian at the University of Texas at Arlington Libraries.

Sarah Elizabeth Sheridan Bull is an early career librarian at East Tennessee State University. Her professional interests include the study of services, collection preservation, and patron engagement.

Megan Burdi is the national librarian for the United States Fish and Wildlife Service at the National Conservation Training Center. She connects conservationists to critical information through research services, training, and digital curation. She's held roles in libraries, archives, and museums, and brings an interdisciplinary approach to her work. She holds a master of science in library and information science from Simmons University, and a bachelor of arts in art history from West Virginia University.

Karen Burton is an assistant librarian at Clemson Libraries where she supports the College of Agriculture, Forestry, and Life Sciences and Clemson Extension. Karen graduated from Clemson with a BS in Entomology and received her master of library and information science from the University of South Carolina. Karen has worked in many different roles at Clemson over the years from raising beetles to providing academic support to student athletes. Before joining Clemson Libraries, she worked for the University of South

Carolina School of Medicine Greenville where she supported the Continuing Medical Education program for Prisma Health Upstate.

Monica Cammack graduated cum laude with her bachelor of science degree in interdisciplinary studies in May 2006 and worked in the education field for seven years. She earned her MLS degree from Texas Woman's University in May 2015. Since September 2015 she has worked as a librarian/professor at Lone Star College-Montgomery located in Conroe, Texas. She is also from a family of librarians who have all graduated from Texas Woman's University.

Lucy Campbell is an academic librarian focused on electronic resource management. She received her MLIS from University College London in 2011. Her areas of interest are technology as research, digital humanities in the design disciplines, library spaces, and emerging trends in discoverability. She is currently researching novel uses for facets in library discovery, DEI in e-journal publishing environments, and using applied research methods in collection assessment.

Kate McNally Carter is an open educational resources librarian at University of Houston (UH). Kate earned her master of science in library science from University of North Texas and her bachelor of arts in English literature from University of Houston. Prior to joining UH Libraries, she previously worked as a research and instruction librarian at University of Houston-Clear Lake. Her research interests include open pedagogy and the intersection of open educational practices and information literacy.

Marci Cohen was appointed the head of research services for instruction and consultation at Boston University Libraries after seven years as assistant head of the Music Library. She earned her MSLIS from the University of Illinois, Urbana-Champaign. She joined Stan Getz Library at Berklee College of Music while earning an MA in music at Tufts University. An active member of the Music Library Association, she has served on the board as fiscal officer, chaired the New England chapter, and held other roles. She is a frequent conference presenter and writes regularly on music topics for library audiences.

Delaney D. Daly is the branch manager of the Jacinto City Branch Library, one of twenty-six branches in the Harris County Public Library system. In December of 2020, she earned her master of library science degree from the Texas Woman's University School of Library & Information Studies. Prior to that, she earned a bachelor of arts in English literature from the University of Central Florida. She has experience working in city, county, and municipal libraries in Colorado, Florida, Idaho, and now Texas. Additionally, she is a published poet and essayist, avid traveler, and mom to Abby the Tabby, her beloved cat.

Eileen Davenport has worked in museums and corporate archives, and in public, academic, and corporate libraries. She currently works as a senior research librarian at William Blair.

Chad Deets is assistant librarian for metadata and specialized collections at Arizona State University. He has worked as an information professional for six years, with a focus on cataloging and metadata and government information. His current research focuses on how cataloging and metadata is used in providing reference services.

G. Kim Dority is the founder and president of Dority & Associates, Inc., a Colorado-based information strategy and content development consulting firm. In addition, her passion for all the amazing ways LIS skills can be deployed has led her to teach graduate courses on alternative LIS careers, write multiple books on this topic, including *Rethinking Information Work*, 2nd ed. (2016), and consult with several LIS graduate programs as a student and alumni career advisor. In addition to her client work, she also teaches online for the Kent State University School of Information program as an adjunct instructor.

Sue Easun, BA, MLS, BEd, PhD, is owner/editor of Second Hand Knowledge and First Things First. She has been a paraprofessional at the Chatham Public Library, a reference librarian at the Ontario Institute for Studies in Education and the University of Victoria, and an adult services librarian at the Toronto Public Library. She also worked for three years as a children's book buyer for the National Book Centre. More recently, Sue held a faculty position at the Faculty of Information Studies, University of Toronto for seven years, followed by stints as an inhouse acquisitions editor at Scarecrow Press and Libraries Unlimited.

Jill Egan received her MLIS from the University of Michigan and a post master's certificate from San Jose State University. She has worked as a school librarian in Maui Schools in Hawaii; Abqaiq School, Saudi Arabia; the International School of Stavanger, Norway; The American School of Dubai, UAE; Academia Cotopaxi, Ecuador; and the American Community School of Amman, Jordan. She currently lives in Massachusetts where she is an academic writing coach at Bay Path University, and serves as a member of the Digital Public Library of America Curation Corps.

Chad Eng is a long-time competitive intelligence professional with a "non-linear career path." After a long public library foray, he now uses his MLIS and MBA degrees to turn nuggets of information into impactful stories for business leaders. Chad has presented and trained on multiple competitive intelligence topics and has provided a non-standard set of perspectives for multiple panel discussions.

Jon Evans is chief of libraries and archives at the Museum of Fine Arts, Houston, where he has spent the past thirty-two years connecting scholars, students, and the general public with art research materials. During his tenure he has organized more than two dozen book exhibitions. He has been an active member of the Art Libraries Society of North America (ARLIS/NA) for more than two decades, serving as president of the society in 2012. He regularly presents on the topic of photobooks in the art museum context, including collection building, community engagement, as well as issues of discovery and access.

Alba Fernández-Keys is borderlands curator and assistant librarian at the University of Arizona Libraries, Special Collections, where she manages collections related to the US Mexico border region. Prior to joining the University of Arizona, she worked at the Indianapolis Museum of Art at Newfields in various roles within the library, most recently as head of libraries and archives where she led multiple grant-funded archival projects focused on digitization and archival access.

Cindy Fesemyer is the principal of Fesemyer Consulting. Her passion is helping information organizations see the big picture as they strive for equity and social justice. Community engagement, strategic planning, staff and trustee training, and coaching are her areas of expertise. Previously she was the adult and community services consultant at the Wisconsin State Library and served seven years as director of the Columbus Public Library (WI), a finalist for Library Journal's 2017 Best Small Library in America. She teaches continuing education and academic courses for the UW-Madison iSchool and is a trustee for the Madison Public Library, MLIS UW-Madison, 2012.

Maria Fesz has been working as a digital content librarian with OverDrive for five years. Prior to OverDrive, Maria earned her MLIS from the University of Pittsburgh and has worked in collection development, instruction, and reference roles in public and academic libraries. Maria is also a cellist and plays in several groups in the Northeast Ohio area. She earned bachelor's (Mount Union) and master's (Youngstown State University) degrees in music performance before going into library science. She tries to read a little bit of everything, but she'll especially talk your ear off about fantasy, romance, and science fiction titles.

Nell Fleming is teacher librarian and archivist at the Wisconsin School for the Deaf in Delavan. Her interests are local history, a variety of performing arts, and dog training. Her research in graduate school was the demographics of picture book covers from 2000–10. She currently serves on the Wisconsin Library Associations literary awards committee.

Clara S. Fowler currently serves as the director of the Research Medical Library at the University of Texas MD Anderson Cancer Center in Houston, Texas. She has held leadership roles in the Texas Library Association, ACRL, and the Medical Library Association. She is coauthor of international clinical practice guidelines and scholarly articles. Her expertise in education has been recognized through multiple awards including Educator of the Year at MD Anderson, Texas Library Association LIRT Outstanding Service in Library Instruction Award, and the MLA Research Advancement Award in Health Sciences Librarianship.

Deborah Lang Froggatt served as director of library services for Boston Public Schools for eight years. Prior to that she directed Boston Arts/Academy Fenway High School Library. Her school library career and public school advocacy span twenty-six years also serving in Danvers and Beverly, MA, and in Brookfield, Ridgefield and Woodbury, CT. She was the Sherman, CT, library director and the Calumet Public Hospital (MI) librarian. Academic credentials include: Miami University BA (History), Princeton Theological Seminary MA (Education), Southern Connecticut State University MLS, Simmons University PhD. Her research focuses include the informationally underserved and school librarian assessment.

Rebecca A. Givens (Becky) is the technical services librarian for the J. Oliver Buswell Jr. Library at Covenant Theological Seminary, where she has been since 2019. She has served in a variety of roles with Atla, ACL, and the Mobius Library Consortium. She has an MLIS from the University of Alabama, and a Theological Studies certificate from Covenant Theological Seminary. When not working, she can be found in the forest hiking, sitting under trees, or planting them. She also enjoys the study of Hebrew and theology.

Linda Marie Golian-Lui earned her EdD, EdS, and MSLS from Florida State University and holds a postdoc certificate in leadership and ethics. She has been serving as the dean of University Libraries for Florida Atlantic University since 2022. Her previous experience includes serving as associate dean of the Kennesaw State University Library System (2012–22), dean of libraries for the University of Hawaii at Hilo (2002–12), head of public services for Florida Gulf Coast University (1997–2002), serials department head for FAU Libraries (1990–7), serials librarian for the University of Miami Law Library (1987–9), and as a staff member at the University of Miami Richter Library (1981–7).

Michael Golrick is an associate state librarian at the State Library of Louisiana. In this role, he is responsible for library development, which provides support to all the public libraries in Louisiana. He is also the state data coordinator responsible for public library statistics reporting. His professional activities include service in the Connecticut Library Association including as president and American Library Association (ALA) chapter councilor. In the American Library Association, he has served on the ALA council, the ALA executive board, as president of a division (ASGCLA), and of a round table (LSSRT).

Jenifer Grady, MSLS, MBA, CAE, loves to encourage people to advocate for themselves, particularly as it pertains to salaries, and was able to do this for seven+ years as the previous director of the American Library Association-Allied Professional Association (ALA-APA) in Chicago. She came to ALA-APA after completing an MBA from Case Western Reserve University. Jenifer's MSLS is from the University of North Carolina-Chapel Hill. and her undergraduate degree is from Oberlin College. She has been the chief operating officer of an association, and executive director of a statewide library consortium. She has written extensively about the importance of diversity, salary negotiation, association work, Nashville, and Nashvillians. She, her daughter, and her shih tzu live in Nashville, Tennessee.

Susan Fulkerson Gregory joined the Bozeman Public Library team as director on November 7, 2011. She moved from Norman, Oklahoma, where she was a management member of the Pioneer Library System for twenty-two years. She has more than thirty years experience in public, corporate, and academic libraries. Susan is an active member of the American Library Association, Public Library Association, Freedom to Read Foundation. and Montana Library Association.

Lisa Grimm, executive consultant, ICP, has been directing DAM, taxonomy, and enterprise content programs in the United States and Europe since the mid-1990s, for companies including Elsevier, GSK, Amazon, and more. Recent roles include positions as global director, DAM, at Novartis and VP

DAM evangelist at Digizuite. She holds BA and MA degrees in archaeology and an MS-LIS, all of which have been extremely useful in her career in both predictable and unexpected ways. She is a regular writer and speaker in and beyond DAM, and a cohost of the Beer Ladies Podcast. Find her in Dublin, Ireland, or at lisagrimm.com.

Steven Guerrero is the media arts and digitization librarian at the University of North Texas where he serves as a subject librarian and liaises with faculty in the Media Arts department. He also digitizes obsolete magnetic tape-based formats in an effort to preserve content in danger of being lost. He has worked in academic libraries for over ten years and his scholarly contributions span a wide variety of topics including presentations on tabletop game circulation, creating captioning for streaming content, and a publication on creating a sustainable career development program for academic libraries.

Misty Harris is a former news researcher at the *San Antonio Express-News*. Currently she is working as a media researcher at Muck Rack, a software company connecting journalists and communication professionals. She earned a bachelor of journalism from the University of Texas at Austin and a masters in library science from the University of North Texas.

Dale F. Harter is the library media specialist at Albert Hill Middle School, in Richmond City (VA) Public Schools. He also has been a school librarian at a private girls boarding and day school (grades 8–12), at a public combined middle and high school, and at two other public high schools. He is the editor of *Voice*, the online quarterly professional newsletter of the Virginia Association of School Librarians. He is also a professional journalist and historian with more than 300 published articles. He earned an MA in history and an MLIS from the University of South Carolina.

Ayesha Hawkins is the manager of education and outreach for the City of Fort Worth Public Library System. Her background is in higher education, community engagement, diversity, and leadership development. She holds a doctorate in higher education administration from Texas Tech University.

Michele Hayslett has been the librarian for numeric data services and data management in the University Libraries at the University of North Carolina at Chapel Hill for fifteen years. She worked previously in similar jobs at the State Library of North Carolina and the North Carolina State University Libraries. She has served on the national steering committee of the American Community Survey Data Users Group and is coeditor of the *IASSIST Quarterly*.

April Oharah Hernandez is system consultant at Southeast Kansas Library System and a PhD student in Information Studies at Dominican University. She obtained her MLS from Emporia State University in 2015. April has held many different library positions in both academic and public libraries. She believes that libraries build relationships, connections, and community, and the best way to do this is for libraries to be out in their communities, reaching members where they are. Her research interests focus on outreach and how it can increase the utilization of library resources.

Shanna Hollich is a learning and training manager and supports all of Creative Common's (CC's) programs and projects by identifying and developing professional development and learning opportunities that are relevant to CC's mission, including (but not limited to) the CC Certificate. Prior to joining CC, Shanna worked for fifteen years as a librarian across multiple institutions: K-12 school, public, government, and academic. They have worked in public/access services, technical services and cataloging/metadata, and administration. Their research during this time primarily involved copyright reform, cultural heritage, open access, open education, and social justice.

Laura Kathryn Nicole Jones (lauraknjones@gmail.com) is the curator and archivist for the Grand County Historical Association in Grand County, Colorado. Jones graduated with a master of library and information science and graduate certificate in museum studies from the University of Wisconsin, Milwaukee, in May 2023. Outside of traditional archival and museology experience, Jones has training as an American Sign Language interpreter, bookbinder, paper conservator, papermaker, and paper marbler.

Mary Kamela is a student support and engagement librarian at the University at Buffalo. Her research interests include information literacy pedagogy, instructional technology, and academic library programming.

Lorene Kennard is the information services manager at the Rockford Public Library in Rockford, Illinois. She has achieved the grand slam of libraries having held leadership roles in public, corporate, and academic libraries, as well as owning a freelance research business. She produces and hosts The Librarian Linkover podcast where she and her guests are changing the paradigm on how we view librarians' skills. She writes the Substack newsletter "Pondering Leadership: A Deliberate and Thoughtful, Yet Informal Look at Managing and Leading." Lorene has held a variety of leadership roles in professional and service associations.

Nancy S. Kirkpatrick, JD, MS, is the dean of University Libraries at Florida International University (FIU) in Miami. She joined FIU in Fall 2023 after nearly five years as the executive director and CEO of OhioNet, a multitype library consortium representing a diverse membership throughout Ohio and the region. She practiced nonprofit law and advocacy before entering the library space. She holds an MS in library and information science from the iSchool (formerly GSLIS) at the University of Illinois at Urbana-Champaign, a JD from the School of Law at the University of Richmond, and a BA in journalism from Drake University.

Jamie Lin's library career spans fifteen years in public, academic, corporate, and nonprofit sectors of the information profession. She is currently head of community and user research at Skilltype, where she combines her interests in technology and learner-centered design to build community networks for information professionals to develop and share expertise. She has also served as education and professional development manager at Atla, a member association serving religious studies and theological librarianship, as an educational technology designer and digital technologies librarian in the higher education industry, and as a corporate researcher at Qualcomm.

Margaret Lirones is senior librarian at a state prison in California. She worked in a public library and school libraries before entering prison librarianship.

Jami Livingston is the adult services librarian at Wolfner Talking Book and Braille Library in Jefferson City, MO. She has worked in the library field since 1991. She graduated from the University of Iowa with her MLS in 2008. She has previously worked as a public library director in Missouri and in southern Iowa. Jami is married to Jeff, a hospice nurse. They have an adult daughter and two dogs. In her free time, Jami enjoys reading, exploring Missouri, and watching really bad television.

Dominique Luster is one part archivist, one part researcher, full parts natural-haired bourbon connoisseur. After working at universities, libraries, and museums across the country, she came to understand that history is not merely a listing of events in chronological order, but rather a meticulously curated phenomenon of power. All too often, the stories of marginalized communities are suppressed, oppressed, erased, or forgotten. Dominique's research seeks to help individuals and organizations uplift, honor, and tell stories that represent the lived experiences of diverse voices and the Black diaspora. Dominique started The Luster Company to rechart that path. The Luster Company is an outpour of spirit by way of helping individuals and organizations uplift, honor, and tell stories that represent the lived experiences of the Black diaspora.

Tracy Z. Maleeff, aka InfoSecSherpa, is a senior cybersecurity analyst at a Fortune 200 company. She holds degrees from Penn State, Temple, and the University of Pittsburgh. Tracy frequently writes and presents about integrating library science into information security to improve best practices. She maintains an open source intelligence blog at infosecsherpa.medium.com. Tracy, her husband, and their dogs are all fervent Philadelphia sports fans.

Susanne Markgren is the director of technical services at Manhattan College in the Bronx, where she oversees acquisitions, electronic resources, cataloging, interlibrary loan, and systems, and serves as the subject librarian for the English department. Susanne has coauthored two books: *How to Thrive as a Library Professional: Achieving Success and Satisfaction*, for Libraries Unlimited (2020), and *Career Q&A: A Librarian's Real-Life, Practical Guide to Managing a Successful Career* (2013). She holds an MLIS from the University of Texas at Austin, and an MFA in creative writing from Manhattanville College.

Jamie Markus worked at the Wyoming State Library for over eighteen years, the last seven as state librarian. Jamie is a past president of the Western Council of State Libraries and Wyoming Library Association (WLA). He was the director of the 2020 WLA Outstanding Library of the Year and was named both the 2011 WLA Librarian of the Year and a 2009 *Library Journal* Mover & Shaker. In 2014, Jamie was honored as a White House "Champion of Change" for promoting libraries as essential partners in community outreach efforts.

Laura Marlane is the executive director of the Omaha Public Library, a thirteen-branch municipal library system serving the citizens of Omaha and Douglas County. Laura has over thirty years of experience working in academic, research, and public libraries, in a variety of capacities ranging from systems administrator to executive director. She received her BA in English from Rhode Island College and her MLIS from the University of Rhode Island. Providing free and open access to information and promoting literacy have been lifelong passions.

Pam Matthews is a content and workflow strategy consultant working for ProQuest, part of Clarivate. Her long (very long) and varied career includes stints working for both public and academic libraries and for library vendors. She is passionate about librarianship and promoting equality of access to information.

Elizabeth F. McLean, MSLS, CKM, CKS, launched Knowsaic, a knowledge and information management consultancy based in Maryland, in 2018. She applies her previous experiences with corporate, legal, executive government, and international development organizations to champion knowledge exchange for collaborative learning and innovation. Liz consults with nonprofits, international development and NGO projects, and cultural heritage/GLAM clients to grow and implement human-centered knowledge and information sharing. Liz earned her MSLS from the Catholic University of America. She is an active volunteer for AIIP and participates in professional groups such as the Knowledge Management Community of DC (KMDC), KM4Dev, DEVEX, and the Society for International Development-Washington (DC).

Amanda McLeod is the social sciences and government information librarian at Clemson University Libraries. She earned a BA in psychology from Winthrop University and an MS in information studies from the University of Texas at Austin. Her research interests include collaborative approaches to librarianship and outreach, government information and open education, and the impact of onboarding practices in libraries.

Andrew McDonnell is the digital archivist for the University of Kentucky Libraries Special Collections Research Center. His research interests include virtual machine archiving and best practices in workflow documentation. His most recent book is *November 123* (2020).

Gloria Miller started with the US Air Force as a librarian intern while earning her MLS. After eighteen years in Air Force libraries, she worked for the Navy for three years before moving to the Army. She has worked in seven different states in both MWR and sci-tech libraries, all with the same employer, the Department of Defense.

Emerson M. Morris (he/they), MLIS, received his library science degree from the University of Denver. He has worked in both public and academic libraries, in all departments from shelving, to archives, to reference, and everything else in between. As a transgender librarian, he works to make libraries a safe space for all 2SLGBTQIA+ people, through education, collection development, writing, and creating a safe space for the students of his university. He is currently the research services coordinator for Tomlinson Library, at Colorado Mesa University.

Jean Myles is the middle school librarian and equity and inclusion coordinator at St. Luke's School in New Canaan, CT, a secular college-preparatory school for grades 5–12 from thirty different Connecticut and

New York towns. She received her BA in education from the Neag School of Education at UConn and her MLIS from Southern Connecticut State University.

Somer Newland is the director of library support services at Houston Community College. Earlier, she was the technical services manager for Pasadena Public Library in Pasadena, Texas. Her library experience includes public services (youth services and adult reference), web services, systems administration, and technical services management. She lives in Houston, Texas, with her husband and two cats.

Zack North is a queer adult and teen services librarian in Mitchell, South Dakota, where he builds community through developing collections and programs with a focus on the library being the center of the community. He graduated from Simmons University in 2020 and was named New Librarian of the Year by the South Dakota Library Association in 2023.

Joy Oehlers, information literacy librarian and associate professor at Kapi'olani Community College Library, contributes to research and documentation instruction as well as reference and collection management. Her publications, apart from information literacy topics, include her experiences with grant applications to provide programs and events for students. The best part of her job is when students tell her that they love coming to the library because they feel so welcome and comfortable. She received her MLIS from the University of Victoria in Wellington, New Zealand, in 1999, where she worked as a liaison librarian supporting faculty, graduate research, and undergraduate research.

Lona A. Oerther is the library director for the Mental Health Hospital in Pueblo, Colorado. She has lived in many places around the world being raised an Army brat but chose to go to college in Pennsylvania, first at Lock Haven University and then Clarion University for her MLS. Her interests are tenor sax, which she plays poorly, Victorian era literature, gaming, graphic novels/manga, and the two dogs that take up most of her free time.

Patrick Olson first joined the rare book trade in Chicago in 2003, while still in college. He later earned his library degree from the University of Illinois, then spent a decade holding a variety of positions working with rare books: as a rare book cataloger at the University of Illinois and MIT, as a curator at the University of Iowa, and then as a curator and eventually head of special collections at Michigan State University. Patrick returned to the trade in 2018, under his own name, and is a member of the Antiquarian Booksellers Association of America.

Angela O'Neal is the manager of local history and genealogy at Columbus Metropolitan Library. She previously served as director of collections at the Ohio History Connection. She has a master's of library and information science from Kent State University. She is a graduate of the History Leadership Institute and Leadership Columbus. She has also served as president of the Society of Ohio Archivists and chair of the Reference and User Services Association's History Section.

Melody D. Parker came to the Centers for Disease Control and Prevention (CDC) as a fellow in 2010 and somewhat recently moved to the National Center for Immunization and Respiratory Diseases (NCIRD) within CDC as an analyst focusing on immunization information systems in 2020. A multifaceted professional, Melody D. Parker holds degrees in music performance from the University of South Carolina and East Carolina University and MLIS from Wayne State University, which makes her a professional librarian, a professional musician, and a professional goofball.

Selma Permenter is the assistant vice president for development services and administration at the University of Texas at Arlington. She began her development career in 1992 as a part-time gift processor while attending graduate school. Since that time, she has worked in almost all areas within the development field. She is active in the Council for the Advancement and Support of Education District IV, where she has served on the conference committee numerous times. She earned a BA in English from the University of Texas at Arlington in 1991 and a master's in information science from the University of North Texas in 1993.

Chrissie Anderson Peters resides in Bristol, TN, with her husband and their three feline sons. She has been published in regional publications such as *Still: The Journal*, *Women of Appalachia Project*, *Salvation South*, *Pine Mountain Sand & Gravel*, *Clinch Mountain Review*, and *Mildred Haun Review*. She has self-published three books, *Dog Days and Dragonflies*, *Running from Crazy*, and *Blue Ridge Christmas*, and is included in *23 Tales: Appalachian Ghost Stories, Legends, and Other Mysteries*. Her passions include all things 80s and traveling. You can check out her blog and other writing on her website, CAPWrites.com.

Emily Pojman is the former media circulation manager of the Media Library at the University of North Texas, where she managed the game collection and spaces. This included supporting patron access, inventory management, and facilitating coursework and instruction in library spaces. She is currently a processing archivist with UNT Special Collections. Her degree is an MS in library science with a concentration in archival studies and graduate academic certificates in archival management and digital curation and data management. Her scholarly pursuits include presentations on game collection access and maintenance.

Amy Pulliam earned her MLIS from the iSchool at University of Illinois Urbana-Champaign. After working in education internationally for five years, she began working as an elementary school librarian in East St. Louis School District 189 in 2018 and eventually transferred to the high school before being named the district's lead librarian. She loves her job and is thrilled to be sharing a small piece of it in this publication. She lives in St. Louis, Missouri, with her wife and two dogs and is an avid cyclist and rower. She can be reached at amy.pulliam@estl189.com.

Alissa Raschke-Janchenko is the youth services manager at the New Lenox Public Library. She has been in children's services in public libraries for more than twenty-five years. Alissa sits on the Illinois Youth Services Forum, has served on the Illinois Monarch Award Nominating Committee, and has presented on the topic of using improv comedy in working with children. In her spare time, she founded and runs a nonprofit community theatre company.

Michael Rawls is serving his twenty-fourth year as an elementary school educator and the sixth year as an elementary school librarian in Atlanta Public Schools. He was named Teacher of the Year for his school in 2017–18 and the district's School Library Media Specialist of the Year in 2020–1. He shares his love of children's literature and school library advocacy with over 100K followers as @thebookwrangler on Instagram.

Ari Negovschi Regalado, technical director of the Texas Archive of the Moving Image, has over a decade of experience working with archival media in academic, commercial, museum, and nonprofit settings. She holds a master's in library and information science from the University of Illinois at Urbana-Champaign and a bachelor of fine arts in film and video from California Institute of the Arts. She can be reached @media_archivista on Instagram.

Kearin Reid is a research librarian and independent information specialist providing services in systematic reviews, guideline development, and evidence synthesis. Prior to becoming a librarian, Kearin worked for ten years as a medical technologist in clinical laboratories. Her clinical experience combined with expertise in systematic reviews make her an asset to guideline development teams and evidence synthesis projects. She has published her own research and coauthored systematic reviews and clinical guidelines. Her most recent publication is "A Comparison of an AI Screening Tool vs. Dual Human Review in Systematic Reviews Used in Guideline Development" (2024).

Ira Revels is a strategic management consultant with over two decades of experience in art, tech, and social impact. Trained at Cornell University's Johnson School of Management, she specializes in blockchain technology and AI. As a private advisor, Ira aids clients in business development, impact investing, and digital transformation. She has successfully raised millions through grant writing and project management for educational and tech-focused organizations. A thought leader in innovative technologies, Ira educates and inspires through her writing and speaking, emphasizing technology's potential for positive social and economic change.

Diane Robson is the games and education librarian for the Media Library at the University of North Texas. She oversees collection development, cataloging, and outreach related to the game collection, and liaises with faculty and students who wish to use games for scholarship, research, or instruction. Scholarly contributions include publications and presentations on game collection management, tabletop game cataloging, and outreach. Her most recent publication is *Video Game Equipment Loss and Durability in a Circulating Academic Collection* (2023).

Christina Rodrigues is a senior program manager for member relations and supports OCLC member libraries and the OCLC Global Council. Prior to OCLC, she worked for Columbus Metropolitan Library as a youth services specialist. Throughout her career, Christina has been very involved in ALA and local library associations. She currently serves on the executive board of the American Library Association and has been active in both ALA's Membership Committee and New Members Round Table. She holds a master of public administration and an MLIS from Kent State University. She is a passionate advocate for libraries and believes in fostering connections within the global library community.

Lee Schwartz is a senior library division manager, branch services, at the Marion County Public Library System in Marion County Florida. He received his MLIS from Florida State University in 2011. He enjoys a well-told story and is addicted to pickleball.

Laura Semrau currently serves as humanities librarian at Baylor University. Her previous roles include research and prospect management analyst at a hospital foundation and collection development and public services librarian at New York University Abu Dhabi. Laura and her family enjoy exploring the Waco, Texas area and spend much of their free time at little league games.

Priscilla K. Shontz (priscilla.shontz.lis@gmail.com) has written/edited several LIS career books and has more than twenty years of experience in academic, special, public, and private school libraries. She is a reference librarian at Lone Star College and has served as president of the ALA New Members Round Table. Priscilla earned an MLS from the University of North Texas and a BS in communications from the University of Texas at Arlington.

Christy Shannon Smirl, MLIS, is the founder of Foxtail Books & Library Services. She provides private library services to clients around the country and internationally from her home base in Jackson Hole, Wyoming. Her work in private libraries of the rich and famous has been covered in publications like *Oprah*, *Domino*, *Mountain Living*, and *Luxe*.

Ann Snoeyenbos is manager, international sales and special markets, for Project MUSE (a division of the Johns Hopkins University Press). She has worked for Project MUSE since 2004. Prior to joining Project MUSE Ann was librarian for West European social science at the Elmer Holmes Bobst Library, New York University, NY. Ann has an MA in West European studies and an MLS in library and information science, both from Indiana University Bloomington.

Amanda Standerfer is the founder and lead consultant for Fast Forward Libraries, a small consulting practice based in Champaign, IL. Her passion is helping libraries and nonprofit organizations advance so they can create meaningful impact in their communities. Amanda has fifteen years of experience at various positions in public libraries, most recently as the director of community engagement for the Urbana (IL) Free Library. She also has seven years of experience working in the philanthropy sector. She has a BA and MA in history from Eastern Illinois University and a MLIS from the University of Illinois at Urbana-Champaign.

Daniel Stevens is the electronic resources and cataloging librarian for Edens Library at Columbia College in Columbia, South Carolina. He received his MLS degree from North Carolina Central University. His focuses are on diversity, equity, inclusion, and mental health within library resources and its environments. He also volunteers as the librarian and book club facilitator at the Harriet Hancock Center, an LGBTQ+ center for the Midlands of South

Carolina. He is originally from Moyers, West Virginia, and earned his BA in English with a concentration on creative writing from West Virginia University.

Julia Stone (she/her) is a digital scholarship librarian at the University of Idaho and community liaison for CollectionBuilder, an open-source framework for creating digital collection and exhibit websites. Her research interests focus on digital collections, outreach to diverse communities, inclusive design, and digital pedagogy. While pursuing her graduate studies at Kent State University, she served as site designer for Project VOICE, an IMLS grant-funded project focused on creating a toolkit for library staff who want to better support young children and their families from underserved communities through outreach.

Kelly Stormking is a library specialist at St. Jude Children's Research Hospital's Biomedical Library, responsible for electronic resource maintenance, author support services, and collection assessment. Their interests include community engagement, universal design, and board game programming. Kelly recently completed their research project as part of the 2022 Medical Library Association's Research Training Institute program on library communication practices for the NIH public access policy through online guides.

Shelby Strommer is the collections care coordinator in the Preservation Services unit in University of Illinois Urbana-Champaign Library. She holds a master of science in information from the University of Michigan, where she specialized in preservation of information. She is also a member of the National Heritage Responders, a volunteer group of professionals who provide support to cultural heritage institutions during emergencies and disaster recovery.

Lara Taylor has worked in libraries for just over five years, with experience in both public and academic settings. She earned her MLIS from the University of Southern Mississippi. Lara's engagement in research and presentation initiatives began during her graduate studies. Her final project, a paper focusing on the use of AI in academic libraries, is currently undergoing peer review for potential publication in an international journal. Prior to her career in librarianship, Lara dedicated over thirty years to the world of live television sports broadcasting. She specialized in boxing and traveled globally, contributing her skills as a graphics operator and producer to renowned networks such as HBO Boxing, Showtime, ESPN, and CBS Sports.

Reagen A. Thalacker is the public library consultant at the Library of Virginia in the Library Development & Networking Division. She spends her time building programs, services, and connections to empower the library directors, trustees, friends groups, and foundations to thrive across the Commonwealth of Virginia.

Mychal Threets got his first library card at the age of five. He got his first library job at the same library and worked his way up position by position. He is in awe of every library story he encounters and shares his bookjoy on Instagram at mychal3ts.

Yesenia Villar is a librarian and certified mindfulness facilitator in Los Angeles, CA. Her research interests focus on racism and oppression in US libraries. She uses her skills as a mindfulness facilitator to bring racial trauma awareness and healing to children and adults by teaching social emotional skills to mitigate and heal trauma. She has been published on topics of racism in libraries by the American Library Association (ALA) and the radical series *Librarians with Spines*. You can find her advocating for anti-racist libraries on Instagram and TikTok as @unboundlibrarian.

Elaine Walker is the scholarly communications librarian at the University of Alabama and is dedicated to expanding the growth of institutional repository and advocating for equitable open access publishing practices. Elaine is committed to service in librarianship and serves as the leadership development director for the New Members Round Table (NMRT), a division of the American Library Association; cochair of the ASERL Scholarly Communications Interest Group; and assistant technical editor for *Scholarly Editing*. Elaine holds a master's degree in library and information science (MLIS) with a graduate certificate in archives and special collections from the University of Southern Mississippi (2019).

Emily Weak is a part-time librarian for Chattahoochee Technical College in Georgia. She is also the equity advisor coordinator for the Networking California Library Resources Grant and the founder of HiringLibrarians.com. She has previously worked in public libraries, most recently as senior librarian for programming, outreach and engagement at the Oakland Public Library. She is proud of having pedaled the bike library for Oakland, started the seed library at Mountain View, and been on the board of directors of the California Library Association (2018–21). Before becoming a librarian, she was variously: a circus student, a cheesemonger, and a grocery store manager.

Jessamyn West is a library technologist from Vermont. She is a nationally known speaker, writer, and educator on the issues facing today's libraries. Her blog focusing on libraries and politics, Librarian.net, is one of the earliest and longest-running librarian websites. She wrote a column for *Computers in Libraries* magazine for fifteen years and is the author of *Without a Net: Librarians Bridging the Digital Divide* (2011). She was on the advisory board to the Wikimedia Foundation and is currently community manager for the Flickr Foundation. She spends most of her time working with her local community as a hands-on technology educator.

Beth Filar Williams is an associate professor and user experience research librarian at Oregon State University Libraries, with more than twenty years of experience in many types of libraries and locations. She applies this experience and an evergreen curiosity to understanding users' needs, connecting people, and empowering libraries as societal strongholds. More here: bethfilarwilliams.wordpress.com.

Dee Winn earned an MLIS degree from the University of Western Ontario in 2007. She is currently the MLIS program manager in the Department of Information Studies at UCLA. Her research interests focus on social justice issues in the LIS field and her most recent publication is a book chapter, published in September 2022, in *Dismantling Constructs of Whiteness in Higher Education: Narratives of Resistance From the Academy* (edited by Teresa Y. Neely and Margie Montanez). If you're thinking of applying to an MLIS program and you'd like to chat, please email Dee at winn@gseis.ucla.edu.

Emily Wros is a systems and discovery librarian at Western Carolina University. Their research interests include information history and the history of science communication. Their favorite things are going for walks and eating grilled cheese sandwiches.

K. Zdepski is the resource sharing librarian at the University of Massachusetts, Amherst Libraries. K. received an MS in library and information science from Simmons College (now Simmons University) in 2015. Their work focuses on improving interlibrary loan technology and workflows, enhancing accessibility of shared materials, and supporting affordability in higher education. They were a cochair on the Boston Library Consortium Controlled Digital Lending Steering Committee (2021–3), and currently serve on the ALA RUSA STARS Codes, Guidelines, and Technical Standards Committee.

Alicia Zuniga is the public health and science librarian at California State University, Sacramento, where she supports students, faculty, and staff with research and instruction in public health, nutrition, physical therapy, and health sciences. Her previous role, and the one described here, was media library specialist for the California Tobacco Control Program within the California Department of Public Health. She has held previous roles in government, public libraries, and open access publishing.

Index

advocacy 24, 139
   community 9, 140, 184
   employees 127, 185
   resources 123, 143, 156, 167
   roles 140
   self 15, 198, 246
   services 24, 185, 226, 317
autonomy 68, 206, 245, 255, 308

change, adapting 6, 11, 33, 42, 45, 102, 127, 128, 137, 157, 158, 173, 176, 180, 184, 189, 227, 239, 246, 253
   career paths 2, 40, 78, 92, 114, 128, 131, 148, 168, 177, 199, 200, 212, 254, 262, 280, 292, 307
   openness 1, 25, 40, 71, 97, 110, 163, 178, 209, 216, 254, 262, 269, 279, 286, 315, 318, 333, 342
   technology 40, 113, 116, 119, 123, 133, 136, 169, 174, 192, 193, 224, 233, 254, 293, 295, 299
challenges, materials 10, 36, 39, 46, 48, 49, 72, 80, 102, 189, 207, 215, 253
   patrons 9, 27, 29, 30, 31, 79, 128, 146, 184, 215
   spaces 187, 193
communication 11, 33, 48, 67, 83, 87, 95, 104, 106, 107, 113, 116, 117, 124, 137, 155, 169, 172, 173, 179, 184, 198, 209, 210, 212, 213, 225, 229, 245, 269, 271, 273, 275, 290, 307, 331
   improvisation 50
   styles 248
compensation 3, 46, 56, 58, 67, 95, 125, 143, 147, 157, 203, 247, 272, 278, 249, 255, 258, 259, 263, 278, 281, 298, 302, 328, 336

benefits 56, 147, 203, 303
conflicts of interest 25, 33, 88, 159, 175, 179, 180, 244
creativity 9, 14, 49, 69, 94, 202, 219, 328
curiosity 32, 94, 136, 174, 179, 181, 201, 275, 295, 313, 329, 339, 340
customer service skills 31, 47, 77, 79, 89, 92, 141, 147, 233, 267, 272, 286, 308, 331

diversity 5, 16, 28, 32, 35, 38, 49, 54, 55, 56, 58, 64, 66, 109, 116, 125, 134, 135, 153, 171, 184, 203, 245, 259, 263, 283, 288, 275, 315, 325;
   equity 22, 72, 119, 147, 248
   inclusion 15, 54

flexibility 17, 32, 38, 43, 48, 60, 68, 74, 78, 91, 94, 98, 101, 105, 128, 130, 138, 180, 198, 224, 244, 286, 290, 296, 320, 337

humor 28, 30, 49, 146, 241

internships 26, 34, 86, 91, 107, 120, 149, 159, 163, 168, 171, 195, 198, 205, 220, 249, 256, 325, 333
   practicums 7, 120, 134, 168, 198, 311
interviewing 10, 29, 34, 40, 58, 99, 148, 168, 170, 198, 249, 275, 281, 286, 307, 323, 344
   informational interviews 114, 153, 260, 324

job security 117, 196 342
   downsizing 274, 307
   layoffs 74, 254, 310
   outsourcing 201

joy 11, 14, 35, 36, 65, 70, 92,
    109, 219

language skills 55, 58, 61, 62, 95, 137, 157,
    188, 204, 222, 307, 341
    computer languages 98, 160, 170, 313
leadership skills 21, 25, 43, 48, 78, 89, 104,
    177, 230, 248, 282, 325

mental health 36, 301
    balance 15, 38, 41, 68, 94, 109, 144, 334
    burnout 21, 145, 164, 286
    stress 7, 14, 18, 32, 42, 50, 78, 85, 112,
        122, 128, 163, 210, 213, 216, 218,
        229, 232, 235, 244, 248, 256, 261,
        268, 286, 302
    patrons 214
misperceptions, roles 14, 49, 53, 53, 62,
    152, 162, 175, 295
    services 26, 126, 159, 200, 207, 238, 274,
        302, 307
mistakes 9, 44, 103, 164, 256, 334

networking 1, 17, 40, 48, 93, 95, 103, 110,
    247, 254, 259, 269, 275, 287, 291,
    308, 327, 332, 333
    associations 7, 92, 103, 131, 140, 151,
        157, 194, 195, 233, 236, 250, 255,
        263, 289, 291, 293, 300, 308, 311,
        331, 324, 328, 334
    organizations 34, 51, 54, 89, 99, 113,
        124, 166, 172, 229, 230, 235, 237,
        250, 287, 289, 294, 320, 331;
    social 260

organizational culture 10, 32, 44, 63, 101, 137,
    141, 176, 178, 195, 196, 201, 227, 231,
    248, 258, 272, 311, 316, 330, 345
    environment 3, 28, 55, 62, 70, 92, 95,
        96, 115, 122, 131, 133, 167, 168, 174,
        180, 185, 203, 210, 228, 230, 252,
        254, 261, 272, 275, 334, 337
    user interaction 55, 86, 90, 119, 121,
        122, 137, 173, 179, 326
    welcoming spaces 70, 102, 215, 227

passion 7, 11, 14, 48, 52, 80, 86, 110, 124,
    134, 145, 146, 166, 178, 188, 205,
    243, 279, 292, 311, 314, 321, 331
patience 72, 79, 100, 198, 187, 212, 244,
    257, 288, 299
politics 15, 20, 21, 23, 29, 48, 65, 148, 232,
    239, 260, 334
    bureaucracy 115, 207, 241, 244,
        254
problem solving 9, 60, 68, 92, 109, 115,
    128, 136, 225, 243, 245, 267, 273,
    285, 308, 314, 345
professional development 3, 54, 56, 65, 73,
    77, 79, 87, 89, 91, 130, 141, 154, 161,
    164, 165, 168, 172, 210, 223, 237,
    255, 291, 317, 323, 334
    conferences 34, 40, 48, 75, 80, 93, 99,
        105, 108, 111, 114, 130, 169, 183,
        204, 257, 274, 285, 300, 306, 317,
        320, 323, 337, 345

remote work 112, 117, 146, 171, 251, 253,
    255, 262, 268, 288, 294, 301, 306

schedules 3, 21, 32, 38, 56, 78, 91, 94, 100,
    102, 109, 146, 168, 218, 244, 264,
    291, 308, 320, 345

tenure 80, 105, 111, 119, 127, 143, 164, 166,
    171, 177, 288, 306, 319, 324, 338
time management 11, 21, 99, 130, 132,
    150, 226, 336
    prioritization 11, 32, 52, 99, 149,
        203, 278
    project management skills 41, 42,
        89, 109, 117, 157, 228, 265, 272,
        288, 290
transferable skills 2, 27, 87, 113, 140,
    160, 174, 198, 213, 252, 260,
    262, 275

volunteering, work experience 12, 49, 124,
    131, 162, 168, 187, 195, 204, 255
    professional associations 33, 79, 86,
        120, 131, 135, 230, 300, 308